CW01510459

The Slingshot Formula

How Angry Birds *launched its way from indie game to global icon*

PASCAL CLARYSSE

First published in Great Britain by John Murray Business in 2025
An imprint of John Murray Press

2

Copyright © Pascal Clarysse 2025

Illustrations © Adsilium

A CIP catalogue record for this title is available from the British Library
Library of Congress Control Number is on record

Hardback ISBN 978 1 399 81991 6
Trade Paperback ISBN 978 1 399 81992 3
ebook ISBN 978 1 399 81994 7

Typeset by KnowledgeWorks Global Ltd.

Printed and bound in Great Britain by Clays Ltd, Elcograf S.p.A.

John Murray Press policy is to use papers that are natural, renewable and recyclable products
and made from wood grown in sustainable forests. The logging and manufacturing processes
are expected to conform to the environmental regulations of the country of origin.

John Murray Press
Carmelite House
50 Victoria Embankment
London EC4Y 0DZ

John Murray Business
Hachette Book Group
123 South Broad Street
Ste 2750
Philadelphia, PA 19109, USA

www.johnmurraybusiness.com

John Murray Press, part of Hodder & Stoughton Limited
An Hachette UK company

The authorised representative in the EEA is Hachette Ireland, 8 Castlecourt Centre,
Dublin 15, D15 XTP3, Ireland (email: info@hbgi.ie)

Contents

"As someone who has been close to the action through many startups I have advised and/or invested in, I particularly enjoyed the attention to detailed stories in this book, as well as the depiction of the human side of our industry. This is a must-read for any entertainment executive, entrepreneur, wannabe expert or even the next generation of students."

Michael Vorhaus, CEO Vorhaus Advisors

"Thrilling, insightful and at times hilarious, this book is a layered case study breaking down the practice and activities of many entertainment industries with detailed accuracy and clarity."

Ludovic Bodin, co-Founder Kalibrio, Author *Atomic Scaling*, President, La French Tech, China

"An amazing knowledge bible for any modern businessperson or aspiring entrepreneur anywhere in the world!"

Paul Chen, ex-General Manager, Rovio, China

"Drawing on exclusive interviews and his own career in gaming, Clarysse breaks down pivotal strategies into actionable insights on navigating failure, building resilient teams, and scaling IP across media, making it essential reading for anyone in the games industry."

Nitish Mittersain, CEO and Founder, Nazara Technologies

"This is more than just a behind-the-scenes look at the creation of the birth of a mega-hit game. It's a guidebook to the challenges that many start-ups face and the strategies that helped them to grow and succeed in the global market."

Tomo Hisanaga, Country Manager, The Sandbox, Japan

"A unique testimony of how a new industry, that of mobile games, was born, and how the first successful pioneers went about it."

Cédric Littardi, President and Founder, KaZé (Crunchyroll, Europe)

"A captivating insight into the still largely undocumented world of mobile gaming and the global phenomena that have shaped it, paving the way for the rise of new worlds and iconic brands that have defined entire generations."

Martial Valéry, CEO and co-Founder, Oh BiBi

"Pascal Clarysse is one of the most creative and insightful minds I've worked with in the games industry. In *The Slingshot Formula*, he masterfully distils the magic behind *Angry Birds*' rise from indie gamble to global phenomenon, blending sharp marketing acumen with a deep understanding of what makes games resonate."

Georg Broxtermann, Founder and CEO, GameInfluencer

Praise for *The Slingshot Formula*

"There was always a lot of friendly rivalry between Rovio and Halfbrick and our respective games, *Angry Birds* and *Fruit Ninja*. Both were synonymous with the top of the App Store charts. This book helped me to see how Rovio relegated Fruit Ninja into the number 2 position. I take my hat off to the team. Well played!"

Shainiel Deo, CEO and Founder, Halfbrick

"The *Angry Birds* franchise is a masterclass in transmedia storytelling, brand expansion, and emotional design. From a simple mobile game to a global cultural icon, Rovio has demonstrated how deep character work, playful irreverence, and relentless creativity can power a brand for over a decade. *Angry Birds* didn't just entertain, it redefined what a game brand could be."

Reinout te Brake, Founder, RTB Consultancies

"*Angry Birds* spearheaded the era of Mobile blockbusters. *The Slingshot Formula* is an amazingly thorough, honest and brilliant analysis of how it all came to be. Through this exhilarating and sometimes hilarious story, a vast amount of learning treasures are unlocked about the last two decades in the mobile-first entertainment industry."

Phil Hickey, CMO, SYBO (Subway Surfers), ex-VP Marketing, Rovio

"In my forty years developing and shepherding intellectual properties like *Teenage Mutant Ninja Turtles*, Tamagotchi, Nano, and *Power Rangers*, I've learned that lightning in a bottle rarely strikes by accident—it's a mix of instinct, grit, timing, and the courage to ignore the rulebook. *The Slingshot Formula* captures the improbable flight path of *Angry Birds* and is more than a post-mortem of a hit game; it's the anatomy of a cross-media phenomenon that soared across industries. A masterclass in how to build wings as you fly."

John Schulte, Founder and CEO, Pangea Corp.

"A rare inside look at how *Angry Birds* became a global phenomenon—not by chance, but through relentless iteration, data-driven decisions, and a bold focus on brand-building beyond the game itself."

**Shayan Sanyal, Global Games Industry Business Development Leader,
Amazon Web Services**

"Pascal offers a compelling look back at the early era of mobile gaming through the lens of Rovio's beginnings. His accessible and well-researched narrative makes this book a valuable read for both industry veterans and newcomers."

Mickael Bougis, Business Development Europe, Epic Games

"*The Slingshot Formula* captures the wild energy behind *Angry Birds*' rise, with all the heart, hustle, and weird luck that came with it. It's honest, funny, and full of moments I still can't believe actually happened. A must-read for anyone curious how a small Nordic team built a global phenomenon that launched all the way to space."

Marja Konttinen, ex-Marketing Director, Rovio

About the Author

Pascal Clarysse is a games industry Samurai, serving for 27 years as an entrepreneur, CMO or marketing consultant across 4 continents. After starting an online business at the beginning of the internet, he moved to Hong Kong at a young age to work in hardware productions and ecommerce as the Partner CMO at once iconic Lik-Sang.com.

Clarysse then became a gaming industry globe-trotter, working across more than 30 countries, for a multitude of video games companies such as Seriously, Miniclip, Ubisoft, Space Ape, Lightneer, Nazara, Eden Games, Garena Free Fire, Super Evil Megacorp and many more. Among the pioneers of influencer marketing, Clarysse also connected the top hit games with the most popular YouTube creators and many top athletes.

Clarysse has regularly contributed insider reports about his industry for publications such as EDGE, JeuxVideo.com, CMO.com, Inc.com, Pocketgamer.biz, and Gamesindustry.biz.

Father by heart of Sofia and Ariana, a little girl born with disabilities, Clarysse is the Founder and CEO of Big Karma, a startup producing video games starring champions who leverage their disability to win.

Preface

From Indie Game to Entertainment Icon in a Few Slingshots

In 2009, a small independent video game studio in Finland called Rovio was on the brink of bankruptcy. It employed 18 young people, none of whom had any previous corporate experience. By the time its 52nd mobile game, *Angry Birds*, came around, it was make-or-break time for the company.

Over the following four months, *Angry Birds* was downloaded 1 million times on the Apple App Store and became the next mobile hit. One of those downloads was mine. Like many, I experienced that feeling of having to complete "just one more level," becoming temporarily addicted to the game and growing a bond with the quirky little characters. With a couple of decades of experience in marketing and startup entrepreneurship under my belt, I couldn't resist looking into the background of the Finnish studio, with a keen eye on the marketing tricks it used to break away from the rest of the pack. The co-branding deal that Rovio made with Fox Interactive for *Angry Birds Rio* maintained my intrigue. In the meantime, I had joined in on the "mobile gold rush," and it had become part of my job to stay abreast of the latest developments in the market. *Angry Birds* and Rovio constantly kept popping up on the radar. However, I must admit I was also one of those who initially doubted its capacity to sustain the momentum. Like many industry insiders at the time, I wondered: What's its next step? How do you top the initial success of *Angry Birds*? The small team was making hugely ambitious statements in the press, and you had to ask: Can it deliver? Hit video games come and go. They peak, they drop, and then they vanish. Sometimes, a rare few become franchises, but that is usually achieved by investing in advertising campaigns on a scale that Rovio couldn't afford.

Then came 2012 and *Angry Birds Space*, the first video game to be launched from outer space, made in partnership with NASA. How could a small company perform such a stunt with such a credible partner? Well, it all started with a tweet. What happened next is entertainment history as *Angry Birds* took a slingshot trajectory that's in a class of its own.

Fast-forward to the present day, and *Angry Birds* is nothing short of a phenomenon. The mobile games have several billions of downloads and hold a place in the *Guinness World Records. Angry Birds* has evolved from a mobile game into a globally recognized entertainment brand and a pop culture icon. According to surveys, 90 percent of Americans are familiar with it, 94 percent of the urban population in China know about it, and 60 million (out of a total of 65 million) inhabitants have played it at least once in South Korea. Merchandise, consumer products of all kinds, books, comics, animation series, and motion pictures have expanded the *Angry Birds* universe.

During this transition, Rovio has been the subject of countless celebrity endorsements and the birds have made a number of cameo appearances in show business. Red, the iconic leader of the flock, has toured the world, showing up in iconic landmarks such as Times Square, Red Square, Shanghai's Oriental Pearl Tower, the Space Needle Tower, Rio de Janeiro's Maracanã Stadium, Cannes Film Festival, and the White House, to name but a few. *Angry Birds* has also enjoyed a tie-in with George Lucas's iconic *Star Wars* series. Even high-profile government officials from around the world have referenced it numerous times.

How did Rovio do it? How did such a small and young outfit from a country of just 5 million inhabitants break through the glass ceiling and maintain its momentum for so long?

There is always a bit of luck involved in the process of making a genuine hit—that is true in any entertainment industry. However, it's what you do with that luck that is important—what you do to sustain it over time and how prepared and informed your next steps turn out to be. *The Slingshot Formula* is an in-depth analysis of the decisions Rovio made which have led it to unparalleled success and changed the face of multiple industries forever.

This investigation is filled with interviews from many of the key figures who participated in this highly collective effort. It guides you through what happened inside and outside the walls of Rovio during its four years of hyper-growth. By retracing Rovio's footsteps, we will understand how a small startup leveraged modern communication methods and combined them with great storytelling, creative marketing, and disruptive strategies that all helped to rapidly transform *Angry Birds* into a 360-degree cross-media universe.

Looking at the success of *Angry Birds* allows us to better understand the way successful business is conducted in these times of globalization, social media, and mobile communications. We can observe the practices of multiple industries, including gaming, television, cinema, merchandise, books, animation, music, and advertising. Analyzing the establishment of an iconic brand allows us to glimpse into the mobile revolution, the emergence of novel business models, and the paradigm shift that the mobile gaming industry has subsequently experienced, evolving from a niche product area into a mainstream service with billions of consumers.

We will also hear about the valuable, sometimes difficult, lessons Rovio has learned along the way, which will be useful for companies of all sizes, regarding digital marketing, business development, and social media in today's world. With its fan-centric approach to communication, Rovio has been touted by many as the poster child of "content marketing," a trend that has emerged as the new way of conducting communication in the globalized era. We will connect the dots and establish how this direct relationship with fans was paramount when launching one of the fastest and, more notably, most affordably built brands of all time.

Many of Rovio's achievements in the last decade are unprecedented, and, looking ahead, the potential of Rovio as a company, and *Angry Birds* as a brand, may still be widely underestimated. In fact, I was guilty of underestimating it back when I set out to write this book.

The Slingshot Formula tells the astonishing rollercoaster story of how *Angry Birds* became a new kind of franchise for the digital millennium—possibly a Mickey Mouse or Hello Kitty of the 21st century. Rovio is nowhere near Disney's sheer size. But reading the coming pages will make you realize that the *Angry Birds* brand is here to stay, while giving you access to a vast amount of insights and knowledge about modern-day marketing and growth.

CHAPTER ONE

Learning Success through Failure

Our story begins three years after the Y2K bug nonevent. At this time, Google was still an infant company trying to figure out how to generate income with its nascent search engine business. Facebook and Twitter didn't yet exist. Nokia from Espoo, Finland, was dominating the cell phone industry, anecdotally releasing the first mobile game in history, *Snake*. Gamers were playing on Sony PlayStation 2, Microsoft Xbox, and Nintendo GameCube. Some of them were still using SEGA Dreamcast, but that was because they were hardcore rebels, and proud to be. In the handheld market, it was all about Nintendo's Gameboy Advance. An "app" wasn't a thing yet; nobody used that word. In fact, full-on digital distribution was nothing more than a concept based on a few practical experiments—the best experts forecasted that it could take up to a decade before household penetration rates of broadband internet in the Western world would reach levels that would enable such a breakthrough in software distribution.

Rovio is Born

In the capital city of Finland, three ambitious youngsters, Niklas Hed, Jarno Väkeväinen, and Kim Dikert, were studying computer science at Helsinki University of Technology (since renamed Aalto University School of Science). In 2003, they teamed up to submit a game creation called *King of the Cabbage World* to a mobile development competition sponsored by Nokia and HP— the Assembly Demo Party. At the time, it was the first commercial game to run on a mobile phone and support real-time multiplayer (RTM) gaming. It went on to win first prize.

The sweet taste of victory boosted the trio's self-confidence so much that they decided to go pro. Mikael Hed, Niklas's older cousin, joined the bunch as CEO, and in 2004 they founded a little startup called Relude. Four years older than Niklas, Mikael had attended business schools in France and New Orleans and was more of an entrepreneur whereas Niklas was a developer at heart. Their skillsets were complementary, and they viewed the world through different prisms.

Relude became Rovio (or "Rovio Mobile" back then) in 2005, after securing its first round of funding. *Rovio* is a Finnish word that translates to "bonfire" in English, chosen as the symbol for the fire that burned in the founders' bellies—that irrepressible fire that means they always want to improve, always want to learn more, and always question conventions. Note that the company logo resembles the silhouette of a question mark. The initial capital came from within the family circle. Mikael invested a few thousand euros from his savings and landed a development outsourcing contract from publisher Digital Chocolate, which would help pay rent and staff for a few months. Mikael's father, Kaj Hed, also backed the company with money from his own savings. Kaj Hed had been an entrepreneur for much of his career—some efforts successful, others less so—and from 2005, Kaj funneled a total of €1 million into Rovio's coffers, becoming its majority stakeholder in the process. The company hired and grew.

The year 2004 saw plenty of conflict between father and son in the Hed family. As an experienced and seasoned businessman,

Kaj was pretty hands-on with his startups, and in this instance his vision differed from that of his son. With the world still licking its wounds from the bursting of the dotcom bubble a couple of years earlier, Mikael wanted to build for the long term. Kaj, on the other hand, was focused on the bottom line. He wanted to make cash as quickly as possible and without too many overheads. He didn't want to spend too much time dreaming about the future. Differences of strategy between two partners can often lead to bitterness. When the two partners are father and son, "it can only get personal" as Mikael reminisced to *Wired* reporter Tom Cheshire a few years later.[1] The generational clash resulted in Mikael leaving the company. Kaj and Niklas Hed subsequently positioned Rovio as an outsourcing contractor for top-tier publishers.

Rovio Mobile carried out multiple contracts before catapulting *Angry Birds* into our hands. In total, Rovio produced, developed, and delivered no fewer than 51 full games for various platforms in the first decade of the 21st century. Most of these were on so-called "work-for-hire" terms, where Rovio performed the development work for publishers who funded the entire production. Some of these publishers were top-tier giants such as Real Time Networks, Electronic Arts, Digital Chocolate, or Bandai Namco. Some of the games even sold millions of units. But while the "work-for-hire" model holds little risk, since the development is fully paid for by the publisher in advance, it also offers little opportunity for financial independence, business growth, or, put plainly, getting rich.

On a "work-for-hire" agreement, the share of the revenue generated through the sales of the game tends to be skewed heavily in favor of the publisher, since it owns the intellectual property rights. Furthermore, once the game is released, the copyrights and trademarks stay with the publisher. After a few years of chasing after the next gig, Rovio Mobile's finances began to suffer.

By 2007, the company employed 50 people, and there were salaries and bills to pay. Yet, the nature of the deals it signed, whether successful or not, meant that each and every game it made led to more constrained cash flow. Another reason behind this bleak state of affairs was the fact that they sometimes cared too much. According to Niklas Hed, "We always tried to keep the bar as high as possible. It was kind of tough to face a limited budget, because we were always going overboard. We just couldn't let go of quality."[2] Rovio, in short, would avoid the risk of releasing a bad game by self-financing a bit of extra development out of the company's coffers.

As cash reserves dwindled, the workforce simultaneously declined, falling to 16 employees by 2009. Niklas Hed had to personally, and painfully, lay off 20 of his friends. Rovio Mobile was in dire financial straits. Its business model was unsustainable. But the Heds didn't want to give up. They could make great games, but they didn't have the distribution or marketing.

Facing a crisis with bankruptcy looming, the Heds decided to reinvent Rovio: It was back to the drawing board. It was clear to the Heds that they needed to create their own hit game if they were to break out of the rat race and truly thrive. Like most sectors in the entertainment industry, the video game sector is driven by hits: A small minority of titles provides the vast majority of gross income year in, year out. They did, however, quickly spot the target platform of the project. A couple of years prior, Steve Jobs had taken the stage in jeans and turtleneck to announce one of his notorious "one last things"—the iPhone—and the product subsequently hit American store shelves on June 29, 2007. Over the next year and a half, the adoption rate of this sleek device was extremely fast and, more importantly, the App Store tackled a critical problem from Rovio's strategic standpoint: digital distribution was now a reality. This enabled the Rovio team to cut out the middleman and self-publish its products directly to consumers in a way that was commercially viable. When analyzing the demographics of iPhone usage, the Hed cousins realized that it included just about everyone, across all ages and genders. Rather than picking a niche, they decided they would make a true "E for Everyone" and target their game at the broadest population possible, ages 3 to 103, just as Disney and Nintendo had before them.

Rovio first tried the easiest route by converting two games from its existing portfolio for older-generation feature phones to iPhone. User review scores, however, were low, and there were a lot of complaints about the controls, so both apps quickly vanished. The lesson wasn't lost on Niklas and Mikael: Games had to be designed for the target platform from the ground up and had to challenge traditional gaming conventions in order to adapt perfectly to the iPhone's key features. Niklas asserted: "Let's get rid of conventions and use our six years' experience to try and make the best smartphone game ever."[3]

Mikael added one key requirement to Niklas's list of checkboxes: It had to be "brandable." During his hiatus away from Rovio, Mikael had dipped his feet into the world of comic book publishing. This really opened his mind to how great characters and great stories can be presented across many media. Deep down, all forms of entertainment have one aim in common: to give emotion to the audience.

After tweaking and refining their plan, the Heds' faith began to grow. This was the tipping point for Mikael to rejoin the company. Niklas Hed convinced his uncle that they would definitely need Mikael. Kaj Hed reached out to his son, and they resolved their issues. Kaj agreed to step down from day-to-day management and became more of a chairperson, looking at things from the sidelines and providing advice about the bigger picture.

Birds and Blocks

First, though, they needed to come up with the right game idea. The task was handed to Jaakko Iisalo, Rovio's principal games designer since 2006. Iisalo had grown up with a Nintendo Entertainment System (NES) at home and played Commodore 64 games at his neighbor's house. The Nintendo Gameboy was the first game machine he had bought with his own savings. He was so in love with Mario games that his teenage friends nicknamed him "Nintendo-Jaska," Jaska being the nickname version of Jaakko. Iisalo was something of a one-man band. He had been a musician for over a decade, had studied and practiced programming for 18 years, and had been a graphic artist for eight. In his youth, the homebrew demo scene had taught him that he needed to be versatile if he was to get things done. (For those unfamiliar with it, the homebrew demo scene is to the gaming industry what high school rock bands are to the music business.) "I was so excited about our demos that I was annoyed when the others were lazy," says Iisalo. "So I had to do it on my own. I learned programming because I couldn't get anyone to do the programming for me. I always was coming up with too many ideas and the others couldn't keep up. I always had a burning passion for creation that made me pursue new things."[4]

At Rovio, Iisalo started pitching concepts by the dozen, presenting each of them in the form of a screenshot. In March 2009 the Rovio team started talking around an image that would eventually become the *Angry Birds* we know today. The image showed stylized sketches of birds on one side and colorful blocks on the other. In his spare time, Iisalo created the charismatic, cartoonish, heavy-browed red birds that have one quirky flaw: They don't have wings. Iisalo has commented:

I've been drawing animal characters since childhood. At that time, we had been working on another project that was eventually canceled, and it involved some birds. So I guess it kind of stuck with me. When I came up with the idea though, the whole core of the concept was the attitude, and the energy of that angry flock. I added the aggression aspect, especially through the eyebrows, which is a very important part of the design, but also by opting for red, the color associated with anger. How the bird is structured graphically is very important to me. I always try to do the minimal design, reducing everything so that there's nothing unnecessary in the character. It's something that just came naturally out of me.[5]

Iisalo insists that his idea wasn't inspired by the cardinal bird, as has sometimes been erroneously reported.

"People saw this picture and the response was just magical," remembers Niklas Hed.[6] The wingless bird screenshot got the internal green light as the next development project. The decision to make it a physics-based game was a somewhat natural one for Niklas who had been into physics-based games since his early childhood days learning to code in Pascal and Turbo Pascal programming languages. Niklas remembers, "I really liked the idea of making a physics-game because if you use physics, you don't have to explain the rules."[7] The fact that physics-based games were in the gaming zeitgeist made it easier for him to convince his cousin that this was the right bet. What's more, there was an open-source engine called Box2D, created by Erin Catto, which would be of considerable help in keeping the costs down.[8] Mikael Hed assigned an initial budget line of €25,000 (approx. $35,000) for the development of the game. However, in order to make ends meet and keep the studio financially afloat, the company continued to accept work-for-hire gigs and worked on its own title only when the schedule allowed. This went on for six months.

Gradually, through the course of iterative design, everybody inside Rovio realized that they were on to something. "Whenever you had to shoot the bird once to test a feature, you accidentally started playing the game for 15 minutes, and there would be five guys watching you," recalls Iisalo.[9] The team kept refining the game throughout the cold and dark Finnish winter, applying thousands of tiny changes to variables calculated in pixels or milliseconds. This ended up blowing the allocated development budget and multiplying it by four—the eventual cost of making the original version of *Angry Birds* turned out to be approximately €100,000 (approx. $140,000).

After eight months of iterative development, Niklas Hed watched his mother almost burn a Christmas turkey when she was distracted playing an almost final version of *Angry Birds*: "She doesn't play any games. I realized: this is it."[10] While heading to a family dinner in Turku, western Finland, Matthew Wilson, the young marketing and PR manager of the company at the time, faced a similar situation. Wilson recalls:

> I gave my iPhone to my dad in the back of my car, "Dad, this is what we are working on." He had no interest in games. But then he sat there and played throughout the whole drive ... And the whole drive back. When he gave me the phone back, he was like, "I think that's actually pretty good." Coming from my dad, who at the time couldn't care less for games or the industry I live in, I thought yeah, this must be pretty good.[11]

Mikael Hed agrees, adding, "We felt we had done our best game so far."[12]

It takes 52 weeks to make a year. It took Rovio 52 games to make a gem. *Angry Birds* was an "overnight" success that took seven to eight years to get to. To learn poker, you have to sit at the table and lose a lot of hands, or, to put it bluntly, burn money.

The same holds true if you get into baseball; don't expect to hit a home run the first time. It takes a lot of practice to hit a home run. In sports, they call that training. In gaming jargon, you could say it's a bit of a mix between grinding and navigating the learning curve. There's a well-known "4P" principle in creative fields that was developed by David Trottier in *The Screenwriting Bible*: Passion, Patience, Perseverance, and Practice.[13] Good things take time; great things require even more.

CHAPTER TWO

What Makes *Angry Birds*

In abstract, *Angry Birds* was not a completely new or never-seen-before concept. That's not where the magic comes from. Iterative design is the norm in the gaming industry. Borrowing from others and incrementally improving on formulae is just the way things are.

In terms of gameplay mechanics, the first edition of *Angry Birds* closely resembled other contemporary browser games in which you also use slingshot movements to catapult objects at constructions in an attempt to destroy them. In any entertainment medium, it's not about the One Big Great Idea; it's about execution. Motion picture screenwriters and novelists will all tell you that there are only a handful of good plots worth using and that both Homer and Shakespeare pretty much covered them all, while the likes of Hitchcock and Chaplin laid the groundwork for cinema. We're narrating variants of the Hero's Journey, *Romeo and Juliet*, or *Hamlet* over and over, and the template doesn't actually matter all that much. Form, style, characterization, era, location, twists—these are the elements that help paint an interesting and original take on an existing formula. That's how you surprise, entertain, and engage an audience.

In the gaming field, creators don't quite reinvent the wheel to design a new car either—much is owed to a few pioneers. These could be iconic board games or toys like *Scrabble, Monopoly, Risk,* or the Rubik's Cube, or classic interactive masterpieces from the early days such as *Pong, Space Invaders, Pac-Man, Tetris,* and *Mario Bros,* along with more contemporary efforts. A lot of inspiration is also drawn from sport, and not just sports video games but sports in the general sense of the term.

The original 20th-century game which enables you to destroy things with cute creatures using slingshot mechanics happens to be Team17's *Worms* from 1991. Many games have iterated on that formula since. *Angry Birds* didn't invent the genre.

The magic of *Angry Birds* didn't come from the basic concept but rather from the level of polish and, more importantly, the elaborate and fun universe Rovio created for and around the basic product. *Angry Birds* essentially ticked all the boxes needed to make a great video game: astute and diverse level design, outstanding cartoonish visual art, gameplay mechanics immediately accessible to even a toddler, and yet enough depth and nuance to retain the more demanding gamer. There's also a great variety of combos and tactics and a tightly balanced reward system (essentially revolving around the awarding of three "stars" per level).

Don't Reinvent the Wheel, Make an Awesome Car

Rovio didn't reinvent the wheel with *Angry Birds,* but it made an awesome car that looked and felt like no other. And that's the first thing you need at the beginning of any race. The idea that marketing can turn substandard products into big brands is a misconception. Marketing can find ways to make quick profits out of poor products but it cannot build a framework for a business to grow in the long term based on mediocrity. Customers may be fooled once, but not repeatedly. A good marketer will always explain to clients upfront that without a fantastic product that truly stands out, momentum can't be sustained. You need a spark to make a fire. The knowledge divulged in this book won't lead to your own success *unless you have a fantastic product.* Feel free to continue reading anyway—it makes for a great story. But if you're reading this with dreams of total success, first ask yourself this: Is my product polished and exciting enough that people will love it when I put it in their hands? If not, go back and polish it some more. Marketing only puts the product in front of people's eyeballs, and then into their hands. Capturing their hearts, however, is up to the product itself.

It was this diligent fine-tuning that saved Rovio from the prospect of mediocrity that we all face. In the summer of 2009, the team was heading in the wrong direction, and *Angry Birds* was almost canceled. The magic was gone. Jaakko Iisalo, the creator of the original screenshot, was put in front of the game, in his own bubble, without interruption or interference. He kept playing and tweaking, modifying the physical parameters, changing the block materials attributes to adjust their "bounciness," adding the yellow and blue birds, and basically fine-tuning everything until it felt right to him. Eventually, he found the sweet spot. Iisalo adds, "I trust myself in that I can find the fun if I can just iterate and if I keep working on it until the magic happens in front of my eyes."[1]

Game design can be explained through a metaphor. A video game is like an onion. The most important part is the core. In *Angry Birds*, it's the friction, the way birds and pigs collide—until you get the core right, you have to keep working on it. And then you start layering. A casual game (i.e. one aimed at a mass audience) like *Angry Birds* is essentially an exercise in simplicity, much like a successful pop song; the hard work, subtleties,

13

depth, and technique should remain hidden in favor of the player experience. Acclaimed French product designer Ora Ito calls this product philosophy "simplexity," a portmanteau combining "simplicity" and "complexity"—a complex design that delivers an experience that feels simple to the user. Later, when Rovio put *Angry Birds* onto other platforms and outsourced it to other development studios, external teams would really struggle to find that magic. That simplexity was very hard to replicate.

Angry Birds also nailed another critical point in game design: Fit it to your targeted platform. That was what Niklas Hed was getting at when he set out to make "the best smartphone game ever." We have already established that you don't need to reinvent the wheel to design an awesome car. What you do need to keep in mind, though, is that the car must be able to be driven on actual roads. In other words, the product has to fit the environment, the context, and the conditions it will inhabit. Designing a commercial product is a balanced exercise of creativity within constraints. With *Angry Birds*, Rovio walked that tightrope impeccably.

First released on iPhone, the original *Angry Birds* perfectly met the list of natural requirements for a portable pocket device featuring a tactile screen. Playing on a handheld system is a different experience than playing on a home entertainment system or computer. People can potentially pop out their gadget while commuting, sitting on the toilet, or standing in line at the coffee shop. A mobile game has to be designed so that the so-called "core loop" experience it offers can be enjoyed in quick, short bursts and still feel compelling and entertaining. By its nature, mobile gameplay can be interrupted at any moment, so you have to get your player "in the zone" within seconds. You can't afford long expository scenes or cumbersome user interface layouts with too many options and long loading times.

When navigating the *Angry Birds* user interface, you're never more than one tap away from what you were thinking of doing next, and that tap is always clearly visible. The intro screen, for instance, features a big fat PLAY button that will take you to the first level in a single tap. From there, you get to play the game immediately, without wasting time looking at a whole bunch of passive tutorials trying to teach you all the game's rules and controls. In fact, if you look at it closely, excluding advertising and incentives, the original *Angry Birds* contained only a handful of words. Instead of explaining its game experience, Rovio delivered it seamlessly through clever level design and a tightly controlled difficulty curve. In a panel that revered game designer Don Daglow delivered at GDC Europe in August 2012, it was rightly pointed out that, "Users are 'turbo-browsing' the internet and their attention span is tiny. Commercials on TV used to be 60 seconds long, then they were reduced to 30 seconds, and now when clicking on a YouTube video you'll be faced with a five-second advert. With such an extremely tiny window to grab eyeball attention, anything frustrating will cause the player to switch off."[2]

Another thing that *Angry Birds* is full of is "sticky frictions." This expression has been coined by Tim Rogers, a flamboyant game designer and author from Action Button Entertainment, to describe that feeling you experience when an onscreen action is triggered at the exact moment you press a button or slide your finger. There's a positive feeling of power that results from creating "friction" on the screen with your own hands. The better that illusion is timed, the more compelling, engaging, and immersive the gameplay will feel. On iPhone, *Angry Birds* delivers sticky frictions with the impression that the bird launches at the exact moment your finger is released, with a variation of trajectory determined by the level of pressure your finger imparts and its inclination. This is where a lot of play-test and balancing to the millisecond was necessary, as this is precisely why the destruction caused on the other side of the level feels empowering to you. *You did this.* The fact that your finger touches the left-hand side of the screen is also a smart choice on mobile devices: Your finger never covers the area where you need to watch the action to understand the cause-and-effect logic behind it. What's also important, from Mikael Hed's brand-building perspective, is that the sticky frictions of *Angry Birds* are easy to translate to other control interfaces, such as a computer mouse. The plan was to find success on iPhone first, then surf that momentum to successfully bring the game to as many platforms as possible, starting with the browser, in the form of a click-based game.

Finally, you never experience "game over" in *Angry Birds*, eradicating the very concept of "lives." Instead, you get to try a level as many times as you see fit. This atmosphere of constant gratification is especially important for younger people, according to the GDC Europe 2012 panelist Don Daglow. Daglow says, "[...] Users see failure in a game or app as a problem with that game, not a user error. The solution for game designers is to break down the experience simply, minimize text, and show the audience things rather than tell them. They reward success constantly, even in tutorials where there is only one button to press."[3]

First-Play Experience

You never get a second chance to make a first impression. This is especially true when talking about a mobile game priced under a dollar and which is supposed to be played on-the-go, between other activities. After loading *Angry Birds* v1.0 and pressing the PLAY button for the first time, you are immediately taken to the first level of the game. That first level is as simple as can be: only one type of bird ("Red" bird), available in sufficient quantity to ensure that you will win, and only one bad piggy to kill, located in an obvious position right in the middle of a simple construction. A quick interstitial screen shows you how to slingshot the birds with your finger. The aim of that first level, as well as the following second one, is not to pose a challenge; it's essentially a hands-on training session, disguised as a level. The first level teaches you a lot about the game: It lets you get familiar with the game objective, controls, trajectory of the slingshot curve, and the physics system hidden behind the destruction mechanics. A whole lot of information is delivered to your brain in just a few seconds.

The increase in difficulty between the first and second levels is so slight that you are still highly likely to succeed at the first attempt. However, the probability that you'll reach three stars out of three with your score is much lower. This is an opportunity for your brain to register that there is replay value in those levels. You'll get back to this in a latter phase, whether you've already realized that or not. "There's the one key shot you have to do in every level. But I tried to get the team to build the game so that there are two layers. The one-star, finish-the-level layer, which is casual, and also the three-star level—hardcore. So that my mother can enjoy the game, and I can enjoy the game," explains Iisalo.

Then comes the third level. You are still playing exclusively with Red Birds, though this is probably the first time you may experience losing. There's a reason why this scenario is prevented in the first two levels: The experience must initially feel rewarding. Winning makes you feel good about yourself, and therefore about the game you are playing. But there comes a point where winning too easily would make the game boring, hence the need to introduce a challenge. It's time for you to think and become more precise with your movements. You won't get stuck for long, because the game designer wouldn't want you to become frustrated and close the app. But that little tension before winning again will only make that victory sweeter. No guts, no glory. By the time you finish that third level, the ground rules are established and it is assumed that you are familiar with the game's core principles.

The next two levels serve the purpose of introducing the other birds: first the blue one that can be split into three separate birds midair with one extra tap, and then the yellow bird that can be launched at full velocity, again with one single, well-timed tap. Those birds are introduced one at a time, in abundant quantity, to let you "try again" after learning from your first failed launch.

The first time you get to play with a combination of different birds is level 6, which is when the game begins for real. Until that juncture, everything has been put in place to make you feel good about yourself while covertly teaching you the game. Everything is done to get you hooked through that short loop. Then starts the "just one more" feeling that many users feel as they hone their skills through the dozens and dozens of levels that follow.

That addictive nature is not accidental, according to Mark Griffiths, Professor of Psychology heading the International Gaming Research at Nottingham Trent University, UK. "It's very similar to the research I do on gambling," he explained to *Wired*.

"When you can pinpoint where you went wrong, this is called a near miss. It's used all the time in terms of how scratch cards and slot machines are designed. When we fail to win, we create a reason in our mind why we didn't. The losses effectively become near-wins and feel "cognitively frustrating." And the only way you can get rid of that frustration is to go back to the start and play again.

> It's also incredibly simple. If it were too complicated,
> people wouldn't persist. Addictions in the true sense are
> about constant rewards. I've never met anyone addicted
> to a bi-weekly national lottery, because there are only two
> chances a week. On a slot machine, when you can gamble
> 30 times a minute, that's very rewarding. On a game like
> *Angry Birds*, it's every few seconds."

Planting the Seeds of Commercial Success within the Game

Besides the ingredients that made for a great video game, and those that made it suitable for the mobile landscape, the first version of *Angry Birds* also contained the necessary elements for future branding. At a time when many fellow indie developers had little or no interest in marketing and sales considerations, Rovio refused to rest its fate on word of mouth alone. It knew full well that such organic success happens about as rarely as winning the lottery. However, when the *Ice Age* video game tie-in was released on the App Store at the same time as *Ice Age: Dawn of the Dinosaurs* (2009) hit cinemas and went straight to number one, that was a revealing moment for Mikael. He asked Niklas: 'Wouldn't it be great to get the chance to work with such a powerful license?' And a few seconds later it hit them: "Wait a minute. How great would it be to actually own a brand like this." They then started studying what it takes to build a franchise, deeply analyzing the history of iconic brands like Hello Kitty, SpongeBob, or Pokémon, and taking some lessons and ideas from them.

A lot of care and attention went into crafting an actual universe with relatable characters and a background story. As a marketing professional who has advised many developers over the last few years, I can't stress enough how important this can be. In Mikael's opinion, that depth in the story is precisely what makes the difference between a "flash in a pan" success and an evergreen with staying power.

Little things that may sound trivial to an outsider, such as the title or the little app icon shown on the App Store and iTunes virtual shelves, are given a lot of thought and go through a lot of A/B testing surveys (where two or more versions of an app are compared). These seemingly inconsequential small decisions do have an impact. The app icon is the first thing that millions of prospective customers will see while browsing for the next app to download. It has to stand out, just as a magazine on a shelf has to or a retail product at the supermarket. No matter how great the game is, people won't uncover that greatness unless they tap on the icon. It is important to make it appealing. And the best way to know whether it is appealing is not to go with the whimsical gut feeling of an artist or a producer, or even a team: You have to poll a sizeable population that is diverse enough to form a representative sample. Rovio showed as many variants as possible to as many people as it could, looking at statistics like click-through rate (a percentage obtained by dividing the number of people who click on the icon by the number of people who have been shown an icon) and running comparative benchmarks between them. And it also gathered the advice of seasoned businesspeople within its network, such as HP business developer Peter Vesterbacka, who helped choose a color code for its app that would make it stand out. According to Vesterbacka, "No high-profile app had a red icon when *Angry Birds* launched."[4]

The app's name was also carefully chosen. "Birds" conveys the theme and characterization while being a very strong keyword for search engines. People might type it in for a multitude of distinct reasons, be it in Google or in the App Store search field, and then run into the game accidentally. "Angry" gives the birds quirk and personality. Furthermore, it hints at action and induces a subliminal question about context: "Why are those birds angry?—Let's find out!" Click.

From a visual standpoint, the Red Bird character is unquestionably potent and a highly recognizable face, right from the first time you glance at it.

And if you think about the longest-lasting video games or cartoon franchises of all time, you'll find that having a standout character is a tremendous asset. You'll also realize that all these famous characters of past and present have a story. Initially, the birds were flying at colorful blocks, triggering "match-3" puzzle mechanics similar to the ones you can find in games such as *Bejeweled* or *Candy Crush Saga*. In the early assessment sessions with a bunch of civilian testers who were asked about their impressions, there was in fact some confusion about why the heck these birds were angry. To answer this, Jaakko Iisalo created the green pigs. Interestingly, he doesn't see the pigs as evil villains. "They just can't help themselves!"[5]

Reports of the global swine flu epidemic were all over the news at the time of the game's release, and articles speculated that these stories might have influenced Iisalo's design of the porcine nemesis. The reality is somewhat different and comes from the same origins as the design for Red Bird: Iisalo was used to drawing animals, and it was not the first time he found himself toying with pigs; it just came to him naturally and he can't quite pinpoint how and why. Despite being green, the pigs were never ill in his mind.

The theme song also ticks off all the appropriate boxes with regard to branding. It is very identifiable, but, more importantly, it's a simple, upbeat, and repetitive tune that sticks in your brain and is easy to hum, like the theme songs for *Looney Tunes* or *The Simpsons*. Ari Pulkkinen, a talented and acclaimed Finnish composer responsible for the soundtracks and sound design of titles such as *Super Stardust HD*, *Trine*, and *Dead Nation*, composed the track. Pulkkinen acknowledges the roots of the composition lie in Balkan folk music, although his primary intention was to make it the sonic signature for *Angry Birds*.

In fact, Pulkkinen's main inspiration for the *Angry Birds* theme was birdsong—short bouts of cheerful melody. The theme captures the game's whole storyline, starting off with light-hearted tones, then building tension and conflict as things progress. "It was definitely one of the most enjoyable pieces I've been commissioned for," Pulkkinen says. "It had just the right mixture of uplifting melodies, with a taste of complete mayhem and chaos bubbling under the surface, like many of the levels in the game."[6] Amusingly, the pig and bird sound effects came from unlikely sources: Pulkkinen visited the Rovio offices to record them with the development team. He remembers: "I briefed the development team to make the quirkiest, craziest, and just plain weirdest bird sounds they could imagine. After a couple of practice rounds, everybody was relaxed and we had a great recording session going on. Somehow, they had more of a knack for the pig sounds!"[7]

From the core loop to the user interface, through the music, the sound effects, the characters, their backstory, the polished mechanics, and the reward system, all the way down to the subtle marketing considerations, everything in the *Angry Birds* universe was set up to warmly welcome you and to make sure that you'd stay put with the game firmly planted in your mind.

CHAPTER THREE

Launching the Birds

In December 2009, the first version of *Angry Birds* hit Apple App Stores worldwide (which at the time meant 77 countries) and was available for players to discover and enjoy on iPhone and iPod Touch (no, there was no such thing as an iPad at this time).

Many observers today believe that *Angry Birds* was an overnight bestseller. From a bird's-eye perspective, this may appear to be the case. Although the game was certainly sticky and had a viral aspect, the reality is that a lot of work was needed just to get the title on the radar. Every morning, Rovio anxiously checked its daily analytics, as all app developers do. One metric was very encouraging: They were looking at an amazingly high retention rate, with a high percentage of players sticking to the game till absolute completion. But much like other non-famous studios breaking out a completely new and unknown game on the App Store, they struggled with "discoverability." Mikael Hed had expected this, though. He knew it would take time and effort.

Small, underfunded, and unknown, Rovio faced the same problems on the App Store that the vast majority of developers face: It's live—now what? How do you get players to try out the new game? How do you go about raising awareness without the millions of dollars that a top-tier publisher would blast in online advertising, billboards, media buying, TV commercials, and so on? How can you even get the enthusiastic gaming press to talk about the new game without any track record of previous hits? And, finally, how could Rovio get on Apple's sweet side, with a chance to obtain one of those glorious "featured spots" on its hugely trafficked App Stores?[1]

Raising Awareness

Initially, *Angry Birds* didn't get featured by Apple anywhere. Not even in Finland. After a couple of weeks, the game was nowhere to be seen in the Top 25 sales charts, which is where real organic growth tends to kick in. At the time, the discovery process already supported a principle that is still valid today: Most download spikes come from the most valuable real estate of all, the App Store Top 10 chart. The App Store charts are dynamically calculated based on the sales statistics from the latest 24 hours. Furthermore, each country has its own variant of the chart, which is based on the trends within that territory. What a typical iPhone user does when they want to get a new game is to open the App Store or iTunes, go straight to the Top 10, see what's entered the chart since the last time they visited, and tap on the big fat "purchase" button (if the app is cheap enough). Nowadays, to trigger an impulse buy, you generally have to replace the words "cheap enough" with "free to play." Back in 2009, the $0.99 price tag for *Angry Birds* was still considered cheap enough.

Canadian Matthew Wilson, the PR and marketing manager at the time, went on an online mission to raise awareness about the game. *Angry Birds* sat in 600th position in the U.S. App Store chart, but he decided not to focus immediately on the biggest country. Wilson is well aware that the bigger a market gets, the harder it is to penetrate and attract attention. Gaming news giants like IGN, Destructoid, or GameSpot receive a torrent of press releases, event invitations, and exclusive scoops about current and upcoming games every hour and they're just not the right targets to email when you're looking for 15 minutes of attention for an unheard-of game. Similarly, there's little point in contacting the editorial team at Apple's Cupertino headquarters unless you have sacksful of media praise to bring with you. Furthermore, Wilson refused to engage in paid user acquisition (a practice that consists of placing ads in other apps on a pay-per-install fee that is very common among well-funded companies). Rovio couldn't really afford to be a big player in this arena at such an early stage, and the practice seemed a waste of time unless big money was invested. It would be like playing poker short-stacked at a table of whales. At the Casual Connect 2012 trade fair in Kiev, Ukraine, Wilson stated during his presentation panel: "The amount of money that we spent on launching the original title was my time and my really bad pay. But we had a lot of motivation; the company would have gone under if we hadn't busted our asses. I tried to do creative things. I noticed little trends."[2]

During these long sleep-deprived months of elbow grease, Wilson figured out that the smaller a country's market, the lower the number of necessary purchases required to climb the local chart. By leveraging patriotic goodwill among the local press and friends, he got the momentum needed to push *Angry Birds* to the top spot of the Finnish App Store chart. It took only a few hundred sales to do so, thereby confirming his theory. Quickly, he turned his attention to other small markets. Two countries caught his attention: Denmark and Greece. Each had only a couple of key native-language websites reporting on gaming apps. A review of the game published on each website simultaneously would be enough, he believed, to reach every gamer in both countries. Wilson sent an email in English, accompanied by a Google-translated version in Greek and Danish, pitching the game to the editors of the identified websites and convincing them to try out the game for a few minutes. They liked it and all posted highly positive reviews on the same day. And it worked: *Angry Birds* shot up to a top five spot in those nations, too. Wilson replicated the tactic in Sweden and in the Czech Republic. Wilson was totally convinced that "it's much better to be a big fish in lots of small ponds rather than 500-something in the US."[3]

Wilson then observed a very encouraging fact: Once established in the top five in a given country, *Angry Birds* tended to stay in this position for weeks in a row, without the need for further sustained effort. This was highly unusual. And Wilson was aware of that fact: "Our market analytics at the time basically consisted of me going through the top 100 positions and manually copying and pasting them into Excel. So I had a pretty good idea of how everything was doing."[4] This proved that *Angry Birds* was indeed going viral.

Virality

An object, be it a video, a game app, a picture, or anything else that might be a topic of interest among human beings, is "viral" if it automatically spreads around the online community without any advertising or promotion, much like a virus. Commonly called "word of mouth," the *virality* of said social object (= *n*) can be measured by taking the number of contacts an average user circulates the object to and subtracting from that number the average number of immune targets (e.g. owing to tastes, technical limitations, or simply because they don't see the tweet in that time window). The higher the *n* of the object, the higher its chances of continued growth. For example, if a viewer of the video clip for Korean pop singer Psy's global hit "Gangnam Style" spreads it to an average of ten friends, out of which two can't connect to YouTube and one just hates K-Pop with a passion, then the n of "Gangnam Style" is (10 − 3 =) 7.

Viral Spread

With Wilson's methods showing outstanding results, Rovio decided it was time to poke the English-speaking territories and take the game to Apple. "We went up the charts and never dropped in any of those places," says Wilson. "So we kind of built a proof of concept that we can get this game charted, and it stays there."[5]

The problem was that Rovio had no direct connection with influential people inside Apple. What's more, it would seem a bit out-of-the-blue if the studio reached out to Apple directly. It was, however, aware of Clickgamer, a mobile U.K. publisher that had established a nice track record for itself and served as a relatively effective distribution system. The downside of using a publisher is that the developer must agree to share the backend revenue. For every 99 cents collected from selling a copy of *Angry Birds* in the App Store, 30 percent immediately goes to Apple, the platform-holder. The balance is funneled into the developer's bank account once a month. When signing with a publisher, you let them collect a double-digit percentage of that revenue balance in exchange for their services. Sometimes, it can be more than half of the revenue stream.

Clickgamer's host of services encompassed public relations in Western countries, free cross-promotion between your game and its slate of already launched games (by late 2009, Clickgamer had 80 published games on the App Store), and a strong relationship with Apple. The deal with a publisher sometimes included a guaranteed spend in advertising and marketing dollars (if it had great expectations of return on investment for a particular title) and even, sometimes, a so-called minimum guarantee sum paid up-front, recouped from future royalty earnings. If you have an app that's hot, putting multiple suitors in competition with each other will naturally help you leverage those terms and get closer to the higher end of the spectrum.

After Clickgamer presented the game at Apple's London office, Apple agreed to give the game a shot by featuring it as the "Game of the Week" in U.K.'s App Store in February 2010, the most prominent spot available.

A Mobile Gaming Innovation: The Trailer

In such happy times, many would start pouring champagne and raising their glasses before the occasion, while sitting back and enjoying the download analytics skyrocket for the week. Rovio, on the other hand, decided to go the extra mile. Anyone who can run 26.2 miles deserves to be called a marathoner. The greatest of marathoners can sprint in the final stretch. If Rovio was going to get featured, it might as well create a buzz around it. The decision was made to unveil two additional pieces of the *Angry Birds* nascent universe: a free "trial version" of the game and a short animated film on YouTube to publicly introduce the story of the birds and their swinish foes.

The cinematic trailer idea may sound unremarkable nowadays, but at the time it was novel. Matthew Wilson remembers: "We were looking online at the iPhone market and nobody had made a trailer. The only good trailer that we saw was from RedLynx for *Monster Truck Madness*, which had roughly 130,000 views. The best I had seen besides that was about 6,000 views."[6] Most YouTube videos at the time were just a handheld camera filming over the shoulder of someone playing the game. Mikael and Niklas saw an opportunity. "I think we were the first people in mobile to take advantage of that,"[7] said Wilson on stage at Casual Connect 2012 in Kiev. If one looks at what is spent on that trailer versus the results that it yields, it ends up making a world of difference.

This extra step illustrates a key principle in the theory developed by W. Chan Kim and Renée Mauborgne in their 2004 book *Blue Ocean Strategy*: The pioneers of a sector grow above the average of the sector, with a "blue ocean" to sail in front of them. "Migrators" who are quick to act on others' recent improvements still perform well, while "settlers" are left struggling to turn a profit. An innovator in a field is extremely likely to generate immensely superior income than the late imitators who will flock in after an idea is already proven. Those imitators will compete for a tiny bit of space in a "red ocean," filled with the blood of the fierce ongoing battle.[8]

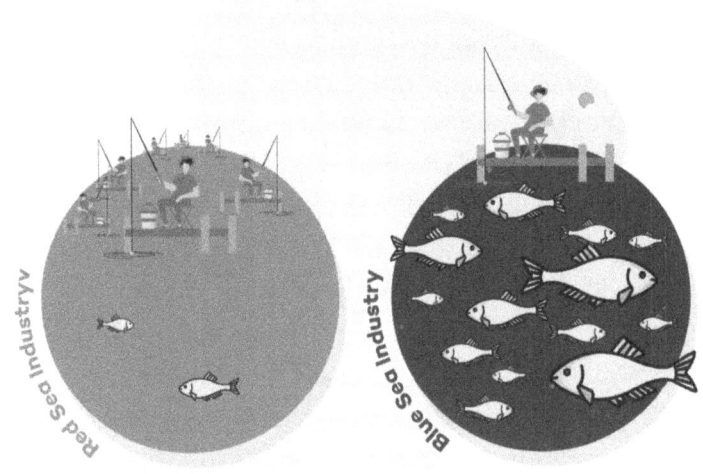

Blue Ocean vs Red Ocean

When first faced with this theory, you might think it takes a big leap to innovate. This isn't always the case. Sometimes, all it takes is a small twist on a common everyday activity. In the case of Rovio, all it took was an understanding that cinematic trailers are popular marketing tools for AAA console games and that they could work with mobile game apps in the same way. No other app developer had done this before, as far as they could tell.

In truth, there were a few other video game apps available on the iPhone which delivered their backstory through animated cartoons in the weeks preceding *Angry Birds*. This debunks another popular myth that paralyzes way too many young entrepreneurs: You don't necessarily need to be the absolute first in the world doing something in order to still qualify as a pioneer, and you can still reap the rewards of your effort. As long as you are in the early pack, you stand a chance of getting noticed. I believe deep down that the precise tipping point between innovator status and the "hot-stepper" label would be this: An innovator may be working on the same thing as other contemporary pioneers, but they're not necessarily aware of it and work on their own attempt in parallel, in a race with the other pioneers (whether they're aware of the fact that it's a race or not). The hot-stepper waits for the first results of the pioneer and quickly copies them once the results prove to be positive, maybe iterating a bit on the formula while they're at it. The hot-stepper clearly knows they are not the first. The innovator is not necessarily the first, but they firmly believe they will be while they are working on their thing.

And so, it's not systematically the *chronologic first* who wins out, it's the best one out of the first ones. And out of the handful of cinematic trailers that came out in that era, *Angry Birds* was clearly the better one.

The *Monster Truck Madness* trailer had been the best-quality video footage Matthew Wilson and Mikael Hed had found for all the mobile games they were researching. RedLynx, the game developer behind that game, also happened to be Finnish. It turned out that a small animation studio called Studio Kombo was behind it. Kombo was an animation startup cofounded by former Relude/Rovio employees Lauri Konttori, who had been a friend of Niklas since their teenage years, and Ilmari Hakkola, who actually drew the original Rovio logo, as well as Ilmari's sister Salla Hakkola and his roommate from art school, Jussi Kemppainen. The world may be global, but it's still a small village. Kombo agreed to perform the work for just €8,000 and the chance to further build their reputation and portfolio in the gaming industry. Given a deadline of two short weeks, Konttori and his small team worked around the clock, including nights and weekends. In the end, due to the quality of the work delivered, as well as the outcome, Rovio increased Kombo's pay to €13,000 for the gig.

The trailer proves that constraints can drive creativity. Short and to the point, it lasts just 90 seconds, in line with the quickfire nature of online media. Every shot delivers a plot point and a comedic pun. "The shortest path between two persons is through humor,"[9] said French cartoonist Georges Wolinski. The director of the trailer, Lauri Konttori, concurs. According to Konttori, "We were crying tears of laughter while working on the material."[10] The clip borrowed a lot in terms of attitude and facial traits from comedy cartoon classics such as *Looney Tunes*. It included a bit of gameplay footage near the end to ensure that viewers understood it was a mobile game that could be downloaded. The catchy theme music was well presented for branding purposes, as were the game's wacky sound effects. This was important: To appeal to the widest possible audience, Rovio decided to exclude all spoken dialogue throughout the entire segment, thus bypassing the need for localization in foreign languages. This astute decision immediately positioned the trailer as a truly universal short film. It broke down linguistic barriers and saved a lot of money in overhead costs. In fact, the low budget remained the first natural constraint; Rovio, after all, was not a rich company at this point.

To ensure that the video would get seen, Rovio linked the YouTube film directly to the game's menu screen. Where it broke from convention was that it wasn't forced upon users at the beginning of the game, as is common with the introductory cinematic videos on console games. Since players would be playing on the go, there still needed to be minimal fuss between their impulsive download and their first play.

The extra effort paid off big time. Within the first month, the trailer attracted 200,000 views. More importantly, it put Rovio on the map of the gaming industry. "That gave us an embryonic brand,"[11] says Wilson.

At the time of writing, the original animation cinematic has exceeded 110 million views on YouTube (since that first trailer, Rovio has gone on to produce an enormous number of other animations, as we'll get to cover in detail in later chapters). The trailer was a defining moment for the company. Lauri Konttori says, "When making *Back to the Future*, Robert Zemeckis told the music composer to make the music deliberately grandiose so that it would increase the impact of their low-budget movie. The animated trailer was the trick that helped our game look bigger than it was."[12]

Hugh McLeod, cartoonist, author, and founder of brand image consulting agency Gapingvoid, would tell you that the animated trailer served as the "social object" for *Angry Birds*.[13] According to McLeod, "The hard currency of the internet is Social Objects. The Social Object, in a nutshell, is the reason two people are talking to each other, as opposed to talking to somebody else. Human beings are social animals. We like to socialize. But if you think about it, there needs to be a reason for it to happen in the first place. That reason, that node in the social network, is what we call the Social Object."[14] The trailer was the node in the social network that most people linked to when recommending *Angry Birds* to their friends, and it gave them all something with emotional value to talk around.

Pricing and Add-ons

There are many areas in which one can boldly innovate without ever looking at what competitors are doing. Pricing is not one such area. This is an economic decision, which means that it has to be in line with the preexisting reality of the market. After all, the capitalist system means that everything is interconnected and tied together. The value of a product is determined through comparative benchmarking across products of the same kind. Put simply, to be competitive a company needs to offer perceived value. So, unless you have a product that is objectively more desirable than the rest of the pack (such as an exceptionally famous and established brand, or an objectively superior offering, or an exclusive stock of a finite resource), or you have sufficient finances to build that brand from scratch, you need to price your product in accordance with the market.

At this point, Rovio was far too small to change consumers' habits on a wide scale, so it got itself in check. The dominating trend at the time was for casual games to be priced at $0.99 with a so-called "lite" version available as a free download that served as a demo of the full game. The main difference between lite and the premium versions was that the former contained far fewer levels and was traditionally filled with ads, to both compensate for the loss of revenue and to encourage users to purchase the full game. Rovio decided to produce a free "lite" version of the app in time for the promo feature by Apple in the U.K. The company was so wary of pricing conventions that it created an artificial price drop just before the game was featured and just after Mikael and Niklas read case studies that proved a discount during the time of featuring on the App Store had a positive effect. Since the Apple App Store didn't offer pricing sub-options between $0.99 and $0.00, Rovio temporarily increased the price to $1.99 for the sole purpose of dropping it again to $0.99 one week later.

To further differentiate the free lite version from the premium product, Rovio added 42 levels to the initial 63 in the paid version of the game. These 42 levels stretched the original formula a bit and undoubtedly delved deeper into the mechanics and layers of complexities available. Meanwhile, the Heds had conducted a thorough analysis of all previous App Store number ones. One steady-seller they wanted to emulate was *Doodle Jump*. Lima Sky, the game's developer, regularly added free levels to its endless jumping game and, every time it did, virality stepped up a notch. Many observers pinpointed this as one of the key factors that propelled *Doodle Jump* into becoming a proper hit. The Heds were convinced that this was the right way to meet demand. Matt

Wilson pinpoints, "I was looking at the 4-star reviews. Those who had not given a perfect score were basically saying 'great game but needs more levels.' There was a clear pattern there."[15]

The team was put to work on an update, and many of the developers expressed surprise. "An update?! What do you mean, an update? We [should] make another game!"[16] Jaakko Iisalo vividly remembers hearing from many members of the development team. After all, despite the *Doodle Jump* exception, it was still the general convention in development circles at the time that once you finished and published a game, you moved on to the next one. Jaakko Iisalo, however, was extremely satisfied with the decision. "I was really happy. I had done a lot of work-for-hire projects before, but this was the first time that my own idea became a game. When we made the original game, we were just experimenting and we didn't know what we were doing. The game really improved a lot through the updates."[17]

For early-adopting customers, the add-on was delivered free and triggered quite a bit of excitement. Rovio fully grasped there and then the potential of digital distribution, and this went further than just cutting out the middleman. Digital distribution enabled a shift in paradigm compared to the old console model. A game is no longer a product—it's a service. If applied correctly, this could considerably expand a hit's life cycle. We'll get plenty of opportunities to revisit this point in later chapters.

Angry Birds' time as "Game of the Week" turned out to be a major success. The sales curve took on the shape of a hockey stick. *Angry Birds* rose to number one in the U.K. and stayed there. Wilson's prophecy turned out to be right: Once the game reached the top five in any given market, it didn't go down after that. Apple took the ball and rolled with it on a global scale, featuring *Angry Birds* in all territories, including the crucial U.S.

In April 2010, *Angry Birds* became number one in the U.S. App Store chart. At the time, the iPhone team was looking for a game that reacted very accurately to the touch of your fingertip in order to demonstrate that the touch mechanics of its latest screen were better than the competition's. After proving its staying power with the benefit of the editorial promotions on the App Store, *Angry Birds* was picked as a highlight by Apple, which ended up showing the game for a couple of seconds in all its TV commercials during the last few months of 2010. This propelled the popularity of *Angry Birds* even further.

Today, it's amusing to find a news release in the Rovio press archives announcing that *Angry Birds* had been downloaded 500,000 times. Matt Wilson candidly confesses, "We were not sure it would ever pass the million mark. We released the press release announcing the 500,000 downloads because we thought that if we waited and didn't make it, we might get stuck on 750,000 downloads, which is not such a round number and would look strange."[18] All in all, it took Rovio four months to achieve the first million downloads of *Angry Birds*. It hasn't been a quick overnight sprint, as legend would have you believe, but instead a marathon—the first in a long series of fast-paced marathons.

CHAPTER FOUR

Spreading Wings

Even if *Angry Birds'* download figures were going from strength to strength in the Apple App Stores and the game remained at number one, Rovio didn't rest on its laurels. It finally had its hit. Knowing the games industry as intimately as they did, the Heds were aware just how rare it is to score a hit. But they were equally aware of the dominant trend: "Peaks. Drops. Vanishes." That was true even for a big license like *Ice Age*. How were they to avoid that seemingly inevitable fate?

Rather than commencing work on the next game project, Rovio chose to embrace and ride its success by doing everything in its power to fuel it. The plan for the next phase initially focused on what had been the most effective factors in terms of impact.

The Art of the Update

The 42 extra levels delivered in the *Angry Birds* update, titled *Mighty Hoax*, proved one thing: The fans' reception of content updates had been extremely positive. The practice prolonged the title's period of popularity, activating what game analysts call the "long tail" effect. People felt that here was a gaming company that actually cared, rather than just saying that it cared.

Rovio put its design team and one programmer to work on regular extra content updates with the intent of continuing to feed players' appetites. Rovio kept adding new levels at least once a month. In his 1997 book *The Laws of Online World Design*, Raph Koster argued that "It's a SERVICE. Not a game. It's a WORLD. Not a game. It's a COMMUNITY. Not a game. Anyone who says it's just a game is missing the point."[1] Long familiar with this theory, the guys now fully understood that this was where the true revolution of digital distribution lay. Bypassing the middleman is more than a mere financial blessing—the direct connection with consumers is the game-changer. Video games had once been products that you packaged and put on a store shelf, with no technical means of ever modifying them. Once published, the product was final. Now a game was like an online store, or a blog, or a live show—you had the technical means to change and augment it over time.

Iisalo recognized that it was through the updates that the team would be able to develop *Angry Birds* into a fully fleshed-out game. "With the first release, the recurrent complaints in the reviews were pointing at the fact that it was a very dry game, with no extra features," he says. "It was only the levels and nothing else. That's when I came up with the Golden Eggs concept, which was inspired by the idea of breaking the game and adding to the overall mystery, like you can also find in *Super Mario Bros.*, for example."[2] The Golden Eggs are hidden in hard-to-reach areas of the levels. When hitting the egg with a bird, a player unlocks a special hidden level. Over time, Iisalo's team also came up with a formulated structure for the updates: They would always systematically include 30 levels and a few key mandatory elements.

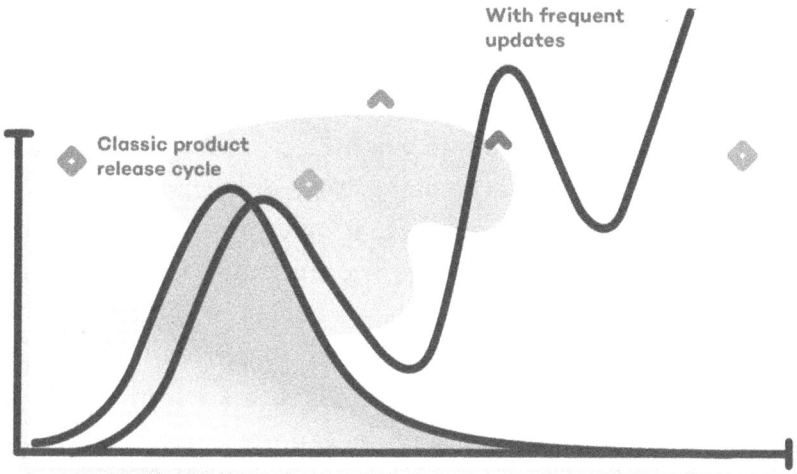

Growth Curve with Updates

One of these updates came out as a Halloween celebration, which we'll return to shortly. Another update introduced a new bird named the Mighty Eagle. This new character served several purposes. From a player's perspective, it introduced the well-known "Smart Bomb" concept into the game. The Smart Bomb is an item or action that can be triggered in a game that wipes out every enemy, hurdle, or problem in a level in just one move. It helps beginners advance through levels they might otherwise get stuck in. It is conventionally available in a limited quantity so as not to break the challenge of the game entirely. In *Angry Birds*, users could only use the Mighty Eagle once every third level.

From a monetization perspective, it offered Rovio a way to extract more revenue from its existing user-base. Because the Mighty Eagle could be earned only every now and then, the impulsive player who wanted to progress immediately had the option of purchasing more Mighty Eagles through in-app purchases (also known as "micro-transactions"). The item could be purchased multiple times during the game, making it what is called a "commodity" in virtual goods classification. This presented the opportunity to generate more revenue from existing players, in both the paid and free versions of the app, and, in turn, to finance the workload on the content updates.

Since this had worked well for Rovio in the past and because it served the "branding" efforts that were so important to Mikael Hed, the Mighty Eagle update was announced through a cinematic trailer, introducing a new chapter in the story of the birds. Studio Kombo was once again tasked with this aspect of the mission. The introductory video for the Mighty Eagle is an enhanced and slightly prolonged revision of the original animation cinematic. This time around, Lauri Konttori and his team were given one month and a slightly increased budget to direct the clip, which explains the improved quality and the art style evolution compared to the original material. Furthermore, Konttori acknowledges that Kombo consciously went over budget, knowing the Mighty Eagle short would probably generate millions of views, just as the previous cinematic had done. "Kombo was getting hot at the time, and we went the extra mile for signature reasons. We did much more than they expected,"[3] he says.

To bring the art style of animations closer to that of the games, lead character designer Miguel Francisco, who had been among the layoffs during the hardships of 2009, was rehired and assigned to the project and temporarily embedded into Kombo. Originally from Barcelona, Spain, Miguel Francisco admits the influence of 1970s Belgian comics, such as *Gaston Lagaffe*, and had already had a long career before joining Rovio, spanning video games, animation films, comic books, and even creative concepts for the famous 1990s advertising agency McCann Erickson. He initially moved to Helsinki for a woman, of all reasons. Francisco recalls ironic details of his hiatus:

When I packed my things and left the office in 2009, I went to Jaakko Iisalo's desk to say farewell. He was drawing very tiny birds attacking very tiny pigs on a sheet of paper. He explained to me the concept of the game and how great it was going to be. I quipped "Jaakko, you should see a shrink." But then with my stuff in my hands going down the elevator, I thought to myself, "Hey, this is actually pretty funny." When I came back later, Jaakko greeted me with "Remember those birds I was drawing? It worked!"[4]

Interestingly, the animation only hinted at the new gameplay feature and put a much greater emphasis on story and character presentation. The Mighty Eagle is introduced as the isolated grandfather figure in the flock, in a very sneak-peek fashion. To raise fans' anticipation, the video was published four months before the software update itself. As in console games and movies, Rovio gradually but naturally started favoring storytelling communication over the bullet-point-style USP marketing commonly used in the mobile apps commercials of the time.[5]

Vesterbacka: The Mighty Eagle

"Mighty Eagle" was also the official job title given to Peter Vesterbacka when he quit his job at HP in the summer of 2010 to take care of business development for Rovio full time. Niklas Hed had encountered Vesterbacka as early as 2003, when the mobile game developer happened to organize and preside over the jury at the HP coding competition that Hed and his buddies ultimately won. During the first semester of 2010, Vesterbacka has already been moonlighting for the company as a freelance. The initial deal was struck with the mindset of a small startup: Rovio needed somebody to represent it in the U.S. every now and then, and Vesterbacka was already stateside most of the time anyway. So it was agreed that he would simply give Rovio two days a month in his schedule, where he would meet American companies that could be suitable business partners.

Through his monthly interactions with outsiders, Vesterbacka had already become aware that *Angry Birds* was a runaway hit. During a trade fair in July 2010, Vesterbacka experienced a moment that made him realize that the game maybe amounted to more than an ordinary success—it could be a once-in-a-lifetime chance to build a franchise. As he finished talking at a seminar, two people walked up to him and asked if they could take a selfie with him. "I was only wearing a simple badge with Rovio on it. I didn't even wear a Red Hoodie that day. This had never happened to me in my entire life. This was just not normal. Why would you want to take a picture with me?"[6]

Vesterbacka has been close to many hit products early on in their life cycle in one way or another, but the little app now resonated with users like nothing he had worked with before. He recognized that there was a huge opportunity in front of Rovio and that the window was wide open. The right time to seize it was "immediately."

From this moment on, he embraced every opportunity to sport the Rovio trademark Red Hoodie, with its logo of heavy eyebrows and beak (Vesterbacka has never been seen doing business without one during his Rovio years). He went back to Helsinki to convince Mikael, Niklas, and Kaj Hed that they had to go out and conquer the world, and that they would need him full-time from then on. Vesterbacka gave a bold, ambitious condition for his joining the team: "Big is not good enough, we must go huge. And we don't sell to the first company who offers to buy us out; we wait and build for a crazy high valuation instead."[7]

Vesterbacka's "Think Huge" mentality is similar to that of the "Get Big Fast" philosophy of Amazon's Jeff Bezos and contrasted with the humility of the Hed cousins, who at that point were playing it very safe. The team still consisted of just 20 people. Niklas and Mikael had not given themselves salary increases. "They had slightly increased my pay, but that's only because it was really bad prior,"[8] remembers Matthew Wilson. Despite the rise of *Angry Birds*, Rovio even continued to deliver work-for-hire obligations to which they had contractually agreed, until June 2010.

Nonetheless, hiring Vesterbacka was aligned with the founders' plans. Mikael had been obsessed with the idea of building a brand and was willing to go all in on *Angry Birds*. Rovio finally decided to withdraw from the work-for-hire business entirely and to focus all its resources on the fledgling brand. It was also keen to hire a few more people. Last but not least, after conquering the Apple App Store, the Heds were eager to get to work on the second phase of their initial roadmap by bringing the game to other platforms.

Having worked on mobile games for the previous six years, Rovio had built proprietary tools for *Angry Birds* that allowed for smooth port jobs to Java and other mobile-based platforms. If it wanted to deploy on computers, in Flash, HTML5, or MAC OSX, it knew plenty of fellow indie development studios looking for the next work-for-hire gig, just as Rovio had been. However, they had learned from the iOS experience that growth accelerated exponentially after getting featured and advertised by the platform-holder. Becoming Apple's darling had shot their download pace into another league. Yet they didn't want to rely on the Clickgamers of the world to break the ice with big telecom corporations and internet giants that owned the other channels. So they needed Vesterbacka to go out and knock on doors.

Vesterbacka's first meeting with the team was still remembered by those in attendance years later. He had barely got going when he made a bold, borderline-crazy prediction. Rovio was already approaching the 5 million download mark on the Apple App Store, but Vesterbacka told them that the new objective was to surpass 100 million downloads one year later. Matthew Wilson remembers: "There were literally people coughing around the table: 'Bullshit!'"[9]

Vesterbacka, though, had reason enough to believe that this previously unachieved goal was within reach. This far, by staying at number one in the Apple App Store, *Angry Birds* had captured a good chunk of the existing app market and had garnered quite a bit of attention from the current user-base. So long as they could stay at number one, they would grow with the market. And all the analysts' reports that Vesterbacka was looking at predicted huge growth for Apple in the crucial fourth quarter of the year and even more impressive numbers for 2011. All they had to do was to stay at number one.

As the development team was preparing for a multi-platform release anyway, Vesterbacka made it his mission to evangelize the game to all platform-holders with high traffic or the potential to give huge exposure. Combine his ambition with Mikael Hed's constant analysis of benchmarking role models and the team's aptitude for versatile multi-platform porting and what emerged was what they called the "*Tetris* treatment." As the Tetris Company and EA Mobile has done with *Tetris*, Rovio vowed to port *Angry Birds* onto every possible platform that sported the minimum specs required to run the core of the code. Interestingly, it was announced in January 2010 that *Tetris* had become the first game ever to surpass 100 million downloads across all mobile platforms during the previous five years.

With this goal burning in his back pocket, Vesterbacka visited every possible trade fair and contacted everybody in his network to garner as much exposure as possible. He was accompanied in his mission by Juhana Kotilainen, Matthew Wilson, and Ville

Heijari, who joined at the same time to help shape a proper marketing strategy and to structure work within the department. For Wilson, this represented a pivotal period. "I was told that Peter would be my boss from now on," remembers Wilson.

> I thought I had been doing a good job. I wanted to be the boss. So I was a bit hurt, I'm not going to lie. I've forgiven him by now; he taught me a lot of things. I was a little risk averse and didn't travel much. Peter Vesterbacka went to Silicon Valley and kicked in doors all over the place and got everybody to promote us. Peter was absolutely kicking ass, knocking down doors left, right, and center and then introducing us.[10]

Vesterbacka puts a lot of hard work into making contacts, but he is not a doer per se. Vesterbacka is a thinker, a dreamer, a negotiator, a "convincer," and a connector. He always ended his meetings by saying: "Here's Matt Wilson, he'll make it happen." Or "Here's Juhana Kotilainen, he'll take it from here." While Vesterbacka's strengths lay in business development and big-picture thinking, Heijari orchestrated and synchronized the team back at company headquarters. Wilson increasingly specialized in marketing, both within the App Store and inside the game. Later, as more marketing staff joined the crew, they would all pitch in to help realize Vesterbacka's big ideas with the big partners he was seducing into working with the company. Wilson comments:

> I think that's what really got us into explosive growth. Peter turned out to be a great mentor figure to me. I still remember the first conference I went to with him. I'm a pretty social person myself so I thought I was doing well. And then we got to the airport in the evening and he asked me, "Matt, how many cards did

you get?" I pulled out my little deck like this [Wilson indicates a ¾-inch pile with his thumbs]. He pulled out like this massive wad [the space between Wilson's thumbs increases fivefold]. And he said, "Next time, try to match me." I never did. But I got pretty close."

Eventually, Wilson would give the speech about networking to new people who were on business trips with him: "Make sure you talk to everyone, and make sure they're all your friends."12

Vesterbacka also kept pushing the message in the press, arranging key sit-down interviews about the early success of *Angry Birds* with major American business-centric media such as *TechCrunch*, *VentureBeat*, and *BusinessWeek*. This ensured his targets had heard of the title before he reached out to them. It was a bit of a self-fulfilling prophecy game. Peter was shouting everywhere that *Angry Birds* was successful, which meant it became even more successful.

Good Neighbors

The first concrete deal quite naturally came from Rovio's neighbor in Espoo—Nokia. Without garnering nearly as much visibility as the iPhone original, *Angry Birds* had in fact already been available for months through the Nokia Ovi Store, for the latest, and ultimately last, device on its Symbian mobile platform: the high-end N900. As decade-long global leaders in the cellphone industry, Nokia had a strong foothold in many countries, with the ability to advertise its products through so called P.O.S. (Point Of Sale) material in thousands of brick-and-mortar stores around the globe. P.O.S. material refers to the posters, cardboard ads, banners, stickers, and flyers that surround you when you visit a phone store. The cellphone companies pay commercial fees to the store chains for the extra exposure with a view to boosting sell-through rates. To get *Angry Birds* featured on all those valuable ads—something normally completely out of reach for a small indie game developer largely focused on digital distribution—Rovio agreed to help organize an online competition with Nokia, a campaign that would remain exclusive to N900 users.

As the downloads numbers rose acceptably on the N900, Rovio drew further confirmation from the user reviews about the intrinsic qualities of the game and the fact that it truly was for everyone. Niklas Hed points out that Rovio checks every user rating, comment, and review, wherever it may be, and frets when the overall average rating of the game drops from 4.82 to 4.81 out of 5. The N900 was targeted at tech geeks and hardcore gamers, whereas the iPhone had a broader following. Therefore, many members of the development team, as hardcore gamers themselves who are very proud of their creation, were interested to see how things would pan out on the N900. To their delight, the average user rating and the number of five-star ratings were higher on this niche platform than they had been on the Apple App Store. What's more, the references to how "robust and precise the physics engine is," or how "impressive the graphics look at 30 frames per second on a mobile device" came in droves from these gaming connoisseurs.

Aside from the N900's user-base itself, which was significantly smaller than on the iPhone, the P.O.S. joint efforts had a broader scope and a larger impact: If you walked into one of the stores with posters showing N900 devices with *Angry Birds* art filling the screens, this was something that caught your eye and stuck in your mind, whether you owned a N900, an iPhone, or something else entirely. It helped raise awareness of the brand in the real world, a real world that hadn't quite disappeared with the digital era.

Two other deals quickly followed: one with Palm that included a port to its high-end Tre model in exchange for further P.O.S. ad placements, and another with Google for the unveiling of the app store for its Chrome web browser. This particular store didn't quite reach the heights Google had anticipated, and the user-base acquired on the platform was not significant compared to the success of the title on other platforms. However, it was well aligned with the original strategy outlined by Niklas and Mikael, which included moving to browser-based platforms once the iPhone had been conquered. After all, the rise of mobile app usage didn't mean that the internet was disappearing any time soon. Furthermore, Google was by now a giant that owned many channels, plus multiple means of advertising Rovio's products: the 100 million Gmail accounts in use every day, the fact that its search engine was still the most visited website on the planet, the fact that it also owned YouTube—all these were good reasons to make friends with Google. However, the one Google activity most closely related to Rovio's at the time was undoubtedly its burgeoning mobile platform: Android.

As the smartphone and tablet market rose, multiple other companies entered the space. Google had unveiled the semi-open Android operating system, licensed the software to multiple partners, and successfully activated its first million devices. It was still a pretty small platform, but the iPhone's platform dominance was for the first time facing a viable challenge. As a platform agnostic, Rovio wanted to get on board from the start. By July 2010, it already had a conversion of the game running smoothly on a DroidX phone. Vesterbacka's mentality said, "That's another million customers we can get to play our game." Rovio wanted them all.

The nascent Android ecosystem went through a few teething problems, the main and most famous ones at the time being poor monetization and fragmentation. The Android OS, opposite to iOS, lets users side-load apps of all origins, without even having to "jailbreak" the device. Even now, installing a pirated app found on the internet is so easy that some people may be pirating without being aware of it. As a result, sales of premium games on the platform were disastrous. There were also some technical issues on the IAP (In-App Purchases) side of things in the early days, so that free-to-play games didn't bring in much cash either.

Rather than bemoaning the platform's shortcomings, Rovio decided to view Android as a formidable advertising vehicle. Since revenue streams were flawed anyhow, it gave away the full game for free. The theory was that by maximizing the number of people playing the game on Android, the number of people discussing the game would increase in parallel. The Android users would help fuel word-of-mouth, which was likely to also generate an uptake of the paid app on the more favorable Apple App Store. After all, Android users and iPhone users did talk to each other! In an attempt to generate at least some revenue from the Android version itself, Rovio opted to go with the ad-supported model that exemplar *Tetris* had also adopted on Android a couple of weeks prior. After all, the television industry had steadily relied on this system to make money for half a century.

Google's strategy with the Android OS was similar to that of Microsoft's licensing of the Windows OS on personal computers. The license-based model allowed the operating system to be installed by many manufacturers on different devices that aimed for different market segments in different countries. The practice resulted in wide variations in the technical specifications of the diverse hardware systems. To accommodate the entire spectrum of models, from low-end to high-end, Google produced different versions of its Android software. Many developers faced headaches when it came to porting their app to this fragmented ecosystem. Many adjustments were needed for the code to run on phones and tablets from Samsung, Google, LG, HTC, Vivo,

Sony, Huawei, Lenovo, and many more. The whole thing made beta-testing a nightmare. At least, this was something Rovio had had *some* experience of from its six years' working on Nokia's Symbian phones (a product line that also offered a wide range of specifications).

One thing that made life easier with Nokia was that, on the Symbian platform at least, you only had to speak to one contact person over at Nokia for marketing considerations on the Ovi Store across all territories. Once you had the software running, the relationship was pretty much the same as with Apple. On Android in the early years, it was a completely different ball game.

Although Google was already running its own store—at the time called Android Marketplace (later renamed Google Play)—it also allowed others to run their third-party stores on the platform. It's worth noting that Apple had been collecting massive revenue from its 30 per cent cut on all sales from the App Store. Other electronic giants were keen to add a similar stream of income to their bottom line, too, as were legacy service carriers. In many countries, telecom corporations tried to run their own Android store, with varying levels of success, and, as a result, the number of digital stores carrying Android apps exploded.

In October 2010, Rovio launched the free Android version of *Angry Birds* on a single Android store, GetJar, to test the waters. The game was downloaded 1 million times in the first 24 hours. Another day saw another million. On the third day, the GetJar servers crashed. GetJar tended to run server capacity at seven times the expected demand. *Angry Birds* broke the forecast made by GetJar 20 times over. It was immediately clear to Rovio that it was time to multiply the number of stores offering the game for download.

At the time, many executives from other companies in the gaming field were puzzled by Rovio's unconventional approach: "These guys are going to so many small platforms. What are they doing? It doesn't make any sense," might sum up the typical response. And from a game development standpoint, it *didn't* make any sense. As a small startup, the common wisdom was that you were supposed to identify the channels that give you the best return and focus on them. But where it made sense to Rovio was that it was a cheap way to proliferate the brand. To Ville Heijari, Vesterbacka, Wilson and Kotilainen, all these companies represented extra opportunities to score additional P.O.S. advertising in many stores across the world.

In every big market, there's a national leader with millions of subscribers and access to retail outlets. Many of these companies are keen on adding value to their customers, in order to differentiate their offer. At that time, so-called pre-load deals had already become quite common. A pre-load deal consists of installing an app or a game directly onto a device, during production or over the counter, before selling it through to consumers. To obtain the rights to pre-load content, device manufacturers entered into a licensing agreement with the copyright holder. Under this agreement, the device manufacturer paid a percentage per software unit, purchasing multiple licenses in bulk, which it paid for up-front: fresh cash for the developer in one clean swoop. For the manufacturer, if you entered such deals with a bunch of hot apps, you gave the consumer the impression that you were offering a vast free content bundle worth over $100, while in fact the software package cost only a fraction of the recommended retail price.

There was a big snag, however. Because so many manufacturers were competing with one another, the ever-growing number of developers and available apps was weakening the practice of pre-loading significantly. Supply was slowly but surely exceeding demand. The unit licensing rate offered kept dropping lower and lower, and scoring a deal became increasingly difficult, as did the lengthy negotiation process.

Rovio cut through all the red tape and went straight for the jugular by designing an aggressive strategy that had one ultimate objective: to get the game pre-loaded on every possible device that got produced, no matter who produced it. To achieve this goal, it simplified things for the decision makers: since the game was a free download on the Android store anyway, Rovio renounced any potential royalties and basically granted them all a free license to pre-load, with no limitation in terms of quantity. Since a pre-loaded app on a phone is likely to be tried out by the phone buyer, the thought process behind this action was that this would rapidly provide *Angry Birds* with a massive reach.

To improve its chances of being picked for ad campaigns, Rovio took steps to simplify the process even further. It prepared what Matthew Wilson terms an "asset dump" containing a multitude of visual files for *Angry Birds*, in every size, resolution, format, and dimension imaginable. This huge folder was shareable with anybody in a couple of quick clicks. The contract regarding licensing rights fitted on one page. The pitch to developers relations managers at the various Android stakeholders was pretty straightforward: Do whatever kind of advertisement you want with our material, send us a brief email presentation with a screenshot, and we'll reply with a one-line comment. Most of the time, a reply would return within minutes simply saying "Approved."

Often in marketing, timing is everything. There are so many parts of this story that are a testament to this golden principle and here was one of them. Rovio's aggressive campaign came at the precise time that all these giants wanted to get a piece of the Android market and find a way to position their device as either better or cheaper than the iPhone and iPad. Major advertising campaigns were put out to show off the new devices, and they needed one quick image that promoted the gaming possibilities on offer.

The Yellow Jersey Effect

What better symbol than the current number one in the global Apple App Store charts? *Angry Birds* had now held the top position in the charts for so many months that every industry insider could not help but be aware of it. You could call it "the yellow jersey effect." Everybody wants to use the leader of the Tour de France for their promotional campaigns—few remember the name of the runner-up, after all. This "yellow jersey effect" was already making *Angry Birds* the most desirable target possible, and with Rovio's tactic of obtaining goodwill by offering it free, it became pretty much a no-brainer. Why would you, as a platform-holder, even consider any other option?

Most of the big corporations took a bite. Ferociously, it should be added. In fact, the outcome of Rovio's campaign far exceeded the team's expectations, to the point that it almost missed out on the biggest opportunity of all.

While Rovio succeeded in appearing on P.O.S. material everywhere, and fully benefited from its easygoing approach to preload deals, it also started receiving offers for placement in TV commercial campaigns for the holiday season. Many big companies selling phone subscriptions in big countries, or distributing devices on a global scale, wanted to use the *Angry Birds* brand. The only problem was that Rovio didn't expect to receive the offer from so many different angles, and it committed to a timed exclusive on one early deal. It temporarily absolved its right to advertise on TV with any other company in the field until January 2011 in order to feature in a multimillion media-buy campaign planned and signed the previous summer. "We banned the word 'exclusive' from our vocabulary after that,"[13] Wilson states.

Although the marketing team remembers the fourth quarter of 2010 as a frustrating period, because they missed out on so many

TV commercial opportunities, the Android operation remained a massive success. The free Android version of *Angry Birds* had amassed 10 million active players by December just on that platform. Furthermore, with hindsight, it can be argued that the error that led to the lack of TV advertising may have unintentionally strengthened Rovio's position come January 2011.

CHAPTER FIVE

Eggs in Different Baskets

At this stage, Rovio was putting out *Angry Birds* updates about once or twice a month. However, one update had received special care and was being set up as a big event. New levels were being prepped to be released for the Halloween season, all of them fully themed around the celebration's traditions: Pigs were surrounded by pumpkins and the color code was notably darker and scarier, with a lot of orange and black (though still in a cartoonish, family-friendly manner). The theme song, too, was revisited, with sounds added reminiscent of horror cartoons to add to the atmosphere. "With the Halloween Theme, I wanted to create something that would capture the essence of the festival without being too scary," Ari Pulkkinen says. "Something quirky like *The Simpsons Halloween Special*, with influences from classical sources like *Tales from the Crypt*."[1]

As Peter Vesterbacka was attending yet another trade fair in San Francisco with Matthew Wilson, running from successful meeting to successful meeting, swamped with praise from all corners, he had yet another premonition: *"Angry Birds* is bigger than we thought." Something bothered him, though. Some of the people he encountered were more aware of Clickgamer being the publisher of *Angry Birds* than of Rovio being the actual developer behind it. That was because the seller's name appeared under the game title in the App Store rather than the developer's. Wilson vividly recalls: "Suddenly, as we were heading out to the café right next to the Moscone Center, Peter flipped off his phone and told the guys in Helsinki, 'We're not going to release the Halloween levels as an update. We are helping *them* more than we are helping ourselves. We need to self-publish it as a standalone game, as Rovio.' I just couldn't believe it."[2]

The team back at HQ faced a tight schedule. As Jaakko Iisalo remembers, "It was roughly two weeks before Halloween. The levels and the graphics were ready. But they told the development team that they now had to make a full game out of it."[3] That would need to include a user interface, a virtual shop, a menu screen, and all the other bits and pieces required to make an app. "And they just ran with it, working day and night to get it done,"[4] Iisalo says. Sure, spur-of-the-moment decisions from Vesterbacka increased the pressure on the team every now and then. But if the company founders hired a business-savvy guide to tell them what the market needed from them, then they might as well listen to him and put their heads down when he was truly convinced of something.

When October 20, 2010 came, *Angry Birds Halloween* was released as a standalone game on the Apple App Store and racked in 1 million paid downloads in six days. The fans of the initial episode weren't forgotten, either. Although Rovio would self-publish all its future titles, it would continue to update the original *Angry Birds* game once a month even though it was distributed on the App Store through a different seller. It wouldn't have been fair to the fans to discontinue them. They were still playing and loving the game.

Around the same time, calls from the film industry were starting to come in following an interview given by Mikael Hed to *Variety* magazine in August 2010. In the interview, Hed explained,

"There will be a huge concentration of games coming to smart phones. We hope we can be the first major franchise to come from mobile."[5]

At first, Rovio was quite seduced by the idea of making a full motion picture based around *Angry Birds*. But the money wasn't right. Maybe a property coming from the mobile gaming industry didn't seem sexy enough to the Hollywood moguls. Maybe they thought this small Finnish company knew nothing about the film business and would be easy to sign. Vesterbacka and Kaj Hed discussed the matter and advised Mikael Hed to wait it out. Their logic was that when you first receive such a call, the second one can't be far behind and, pretty soon, they would come in droves. This would, in time, prove to be sound advice.

As for *Angry Birds Halloween*, it was renamed *Angry Birds Seasons* in December 2010, with the addition of 25 Christmas-themed levels delivered at the pace of one per day in the style of an advent calendar. A few months later, a second update added levels themed on Saint Patrick's Day. This positioning of *Angry Birds Seasons* around a calendar of festive dates from different cultures would serve to further connect the *Angry Birds* virtual world with the real one, wowing the populations that followed the traditions while at the same time globalizing awareness of diverse cultures. In a way, it was a bit as if *Angry Birds* was touring the world, stopping by your town and recognizing your beautiful differences.

Keep Doing Your Homework

Too often during times of success, startups lose track of their core daily duties. It's easy to get carried away chasing the biggest deals, and to begin neglecting the smaller routine tasks. It's easy to lose yourself in the euphoria of the moment. The gaming industry has its history of giants that have fallen by the wayside just as they started thinking they had made it. Perhaps it was the presence of a falling empire in Nokia less than a kilometer down the road that helped Rovio not to forget this principle, but its people were careful not to get too complacent because of their hyper-growth. Some recurring practices strikingly revealed their determination to stay focused.

Niklas Hed dedicated much of his time to reading all the reports published by mobile data and analytics platforms App Annie, Distimo, Flurry, and others. Forecasts, big data about mobile usage, activations stats—he devoured them all. He cross-checked everything with his own analytics, which were starting to become quite robust, given the size of the population that now played *Angry Birds*. He wanted to be aware of where the market was heading next. Says Matthew Wilson:

> We saw our early success on iPhone as an advertising vehicle to create our cross-platform brand, but then the continuous adoption of the iPhone by new users kept us at number one for months and it became profitable on its own. We became paranoid about staying there. We wanted to do everything to keep it up there for as long as possible. In a way, we maintained the momentum thanks to that paranoia. But the downside of it is that you cannot fully enjoy the ride.[6]

The upside is that you stay two steps ahead of the competition and remain aware of any little detail that could prove useful. One of the founding pillars of the capitalist economy happens to be asymmetry of information: The ones who know more tend to make more money than those who know less.

The other recurring, and revealing, practice was the way Rovio handled customer support emails and fan engagement on social media. On top of the frequent content updates, this was another page that Mikael Hed readily admits to having borrowed from the *Doodle Jump* playbook. According to advertising agency Ayzenberg's white-paper case study of *Doodle Jump*, "A top-down look at the current and ongoing media mix of *Doodle Jump* is rooted in owned media. *Doodle Jump* embraced its core audience, built a relationship, and established core credibility with their fans. Those fans amplified their enthusiasm for the game to anyone with an iPhone or iPad."[7]

From the beginning, Wilson had tried to answer every email from every fan to the best of his ability. On Facebook, Rovio interacted with commenters as much as possible and encouraged fan art posts. In July 2010, Peter Vesterbacka asked Wilson to create the company's Twitter feed. The Mighty Eagle then made it his own job to reply to every single tweet, day in, day out, no matter where he was. Wilson shared: "We were at the South by Southwest festival in Texas. It was Peter's birthday, so we had a few drinks. Later I just found Peter asleep in front of his iPad and he had typed up, 'That's coo—,' no L. Just, 'That's coo' written. That was fantastic. He was tweeting in his sleep."[8]

Social media is the best way for a startup in the entertainment field to stay in touch with fans. It helps amplify the PR message you already want to push. Since the ultimate target of getting covered by the institutional media and blogs is to enter consumers' consciousness, you might as well cut out the middleman and build your own audience with whom you can interact directly. Furthermore, in this day and age, journalists use content curating tools that take social media activity into consideration to measure the buzz around a topic. The more you build engagement from followers and fans on Facebook and Twitter, the more you increase your chances of getting covered by the press. It's all about creating a spiral of activity that keeps growing exponentially, day by day.

By engaging fans on a personal level, rapidly and daily, you create a proper relationship with them, one on one, one by one. It makes you seem easygoing and approachable. You're just a tweet away. Whenever there's a technical problem, you help out with a fix or a troubleshooting tip. When they joke with you, you show your sense of humor. You are, in essence, humanizing your brand.

People are now one step beyond playing a virtual game. They are talking to the makers of the game, which allows them to relate when they see the company in the public sphere. This direct bond greatly increases the chances these player-followers-now-turned-fans will download your next update instantly when you tweet about it, or that they will retweet your next announcement or YouTube video to their own following. If you're in the business of making fun games, think of social media as your stage to show you're playful, fun people to boot.

It's scary how many entertainment brands and sometimes even smaller "indie" gaming outfits still approach social media the wrong way. By behaving as if they are above the crowds and that engaging with the fan base is somewhat beneath them, many companies use Twitter or Facebook only when they need or want something from their fans. By focusing monolithically on promoting their services or products, they turn the whole thing into a one-way relationship rather than a reciprocal one. This approach risks being perceived as self-centered and fails to display any real personality. If you think of social media as a metaphorical house party, this type of behavior is worse than being the shy guy who's afraid of talking to anybody; you end up coming across as the selfish, pretentious ass who has an agenda and can talk only about himself. Open up and establish a genuine dialogue instead. The motto above the Rovio Marketing-Communication department's door is: "Surprise & Delight." It's all about "wowing" the fans. They don't see the fans as beneath them. If anything, they look up to fans as the ones who dictate the fate of the company.

According to Saara Bergström, who joined the Rovio team from Nokia in the summer of 2011:

> Many gaming companies are too technical with regards to community management. There's a huge difference between saying, "Hey, we have 16 new levels and this new feature in update 1.1 coming out this date on that store," and instead saying, "Red Bird continues his quest to save the eggs." We consciously use storytelling in our marketing. Furthermore, we are conversing with the fans both proactively and reactively. We always collect ideas from them and the fans really fuel our inspiration, which completes the engagement cycle.[9]

Around 2012, some theories surfaced to describe this emerging model under the buzzword "content marketing." "Hasn't marketing always been about content?" Bergström pertinently wonders, with a smile. "The adoption of this model came to us gradually and organically. Long before all these theories came out,"[10] she says.

In the beginning, nurturing your social media presence can feel like a grind. When you only have a dozen fans, you might feel lonely and start questioning why you're doing this. But don't drag your feet, even when it does feel like a repetitive chore—and there certainly are days that it will.

Good social media communication is all about rhythm. If you stick to it and maintain the rhythm, your following will grow proportionally with your sales, as your accessibility attracts more and more of your customers and turns them into a fan base. In the long run, the rewards of building such an audience can be immense. "Things change because of people interacting with other people, rather than technology or design really doing things to people," Mark Earls writes in his book *The Hidden Truth about*

Who We Are.[11] Therein lies the key difference between catering to an audience and building a community.

Philip Hickey, who joined the team a year later, elaborates on the culture he found and the healthy obsession he, too, developed for fan reactions: "Facebook brought a bunch of casual internet users into the joy of commenting and participating, where in the past only tech-savvy hardcore internet bros would post on user boards and forums. With the invention of the like button, you didn't even need to use words anymore, to feel like you participated. So this kind of democratized the opinion-leaving joys on the web."[12] And, according to Phil Hickey, "This accelerated the pace and scale at which we could read the pulse of fans. And I was healthily obsessed with this. Saara Bergström, Robin Squire, and myself all couldn't wait for the next post to come up so we could read the comments and monitor the reactions. To a point, you could say we were insider fans sitting among the other fans. We were one of them. When we would make a decision or a comment in a meeting, we would make it as 1 million fans living inside of us."[13]

A direct connection with a significant fan base is mandatory when you pull a quick stunt like the surprise release of *Angry Birds Halloween* as a standalone app. How else could Rovio manage 1 million downloads in three days? No amount of press coverage could ensure such a sharp uptake. It came from direct communication with the fan base through the likes of Twitter and Facebook. If you have access to your followers on a daily basis, they will know immediately when you have important news. Failing to do this means that you have to rebuild user acquisition from scratch every time you release a new app. Those free-to-use assets would prove to be the most crucial communication vehicles with the best conversion, be it as a ratio or overall numbers, not only when launching *Angry Birds Halloween*, but with any subsequent version of *Angry Birds* as well.

The more you respond to fans, the more you encourage them to provide further feedback, which can lead to unexpected surprises. In the last months of 2010, Rovio started witnessing a lot of fan art popping up online, from people making their own Red Bird costumes for Halloween to parents baking interactive and playable *Angry Birds* cakes for their children's birthdays. Since then, there has been nail art, pixel art in *Minecraft*, crocheting, origami, paper-crafts, cupcakes, "mashups," weird cover versions of the theme song, real-life re-enactments, and even *Angry Birds*-themed weddings! The community was so vibrant and its foundations so solid that, in October 2010, a few hardcore fans gathered together to create an unofficial, independently run community site on AngryBirdsNest. com, which at the time of writing still thrives.

As astonishing as it may sound to us now, the encouragement of fan-made material was unusual among big brands at the time. Often, having fun with somebody else's intellectual property on YouTube could get you landed with a copyright infringement claim and a takedown notice. You would be surprised how many entertainment corporations were squashing the viral creations made about their products or characters as soon as they spotted them. Rovio retweeted the best of them, shared them on Facebook, and even sometimes republished the most popular videos on its YouTube channel.

Angry Birds Addicts

As you grow your download numbers in the high millions and your followers become a significant audience, soon enough you'll bump into a top celebrity who happens to own one of these sleek and hip smartphone devices. Such are the laws of large population statistics. And if you have a lot of action going on in your social media networks, these stars will start to reach out. By doing so, they raise awareness among their loyal audience members about your product. For *Angry Birds*, it all started with six-time Olympic medalist Swedish skier Anja Pärson giving an interview to Stockholm-based daily *Aftonbladet* after a slalom, in which she admitted to playing *Angry Birds* as part of her pre-competition relaxation routine.[14] Tweets then followed from pop music idol Justin Bieber about how he couldn't stop playing it, and from Academy Award-nominated actress Anna Kendrick: "I have three stars on every level. It's sort of disgusting how much I play the game. It's not, Oh, what level am I on? It's, Do I need therapy to break myself from playing *Angry Birds*?"[15]

Things soon snowballed to the point where comedians referenced the game in sketches on mainstream television. In late November 2010, one of Israel's most popular TV shows, *Eretz Nehederet*, aired a "U.N. Peace Treaty" satire between birds and pigs. Recorded by a viewer, it went viral as soon as it hit YouTube, attracting 13 million views and being featured on hip blogs and traditional media such as *hotair.com*, *The Guardian*, and the MSNBC news channel. It also got mentioned on the next day's edition of Israel's leading national newspaper, *Haaretz*. Then, on December 12, 2010, Americans' favorite comedy show, *Saturday Night Live*, mentioned the game in a sketch parodying WikiLeaks founder Julian Assange. This skit kicked off a month of unprecedented TV exposure with further references from Daniel Tosh in *Tosh.0*, Jon Stewart on *The Daily Show*, and Conan O'Brien who, in his plea to Finland to air his talk show, *Conan*, on Finnish national television, thanked the country for making *Angry Birds*. A true fan of the game, Conan would regularly mention it on the air and on his social media accounts, where the late-night talk-show host is very active.

In March 2011, "Plan B," the 98th episode of Emmy Award-winning *30 Rock* showed Oscar-winning screenwriter Aaron Sorkin (*The Social Network, West Wing, The Newsroom*) complaining to main character Liz Lemon that, "Our craft is dying while people are playing *Angry Birds* and poking each other on Facebook," followed by him providing a tip on how to improve her high score.

Meanwhile, the craze spread into political circles, with American journalist Jake Tapper mockingly introducing U.S. Senator Chris Coons as the "*Angry Birds* champion of the Senate," during the National Press Club annual dinner. U.S. Vice President Dick Cheney, Australian Prime Minister Julia Gillard, and U.K. Prime Minister David Cameron also admitted to playing the game, as did author Salman Rushdie. Sports superstars were not immune either, with basketball professional Kevin Durant admitting he often competed with other NBA stars and thought some of them were cheating. In August 2011, the Milwaukee Brewers played the *Angry Birds* theme song during their pre-game introduction of their arch-rivals, the St. Louis Cardinals, in reference to former Cardinals' manager Tony La Russa and his habit of instructing players to bean opposing players. As for the Sergey Brin who regularly appeared in the top ten of the global leaderboards, it's not an imposter—it really is Google's cofounder; Sergey Brin is known to be an *Angry Birds* expert. Over the years, many more stars, celebrities, and heads of state would join the *Angry Birds* family, and references appeared in many Hollywood films.

For a game as successful as *Angry Birds*, coverage at the celebrity level was neither unprecedented nor unexpected. By replicating *Doodle Jump*'s idea of running the "game as a service," complete with free updates and active fan engagement on social media, Rovio achieved the same kinds of results as its benchmark reference had garnered the year before. As a matter of fact, after some 30 content updates, months at the top of the charts, and thousands of tweets, *Doodle Jump*, too, had racked up nods from pop stars and TV icons, most notably Jimmy Fallon, Rainn Wilson (*The Office*), and a mention on *The Big Bang Theory*. The whole trend climaxed when the Doodle character appeared on stage during

Lady Gaga's *Monster Ball* tour. As it happens, Lady Gaga, a year later, would join in the *Angry Birds* party on Twitter. Although not unheard of, this kind of mass-market attention was less common in the console era as pure gaming systems were regarded as more niche. By 2010, times had changed with the mobile revolution, which was putting gaming-enabled machines in everyone's pockets (including those who would never have considered purchasing a games console), concurrently with the booming adoption of social media. After 40 years in existence, gaming had become ubiquitous and was finally getting recognized as an intrinsic part of pop culture, alongside music, film, and cartoons.

It was in the last quarter of 2010 that Rovio truly started envisaging itself as a fan-centric company, a concept that originates from the music industry. Amazon had been the trailblazer of that model on the internet since its launch in 1997 and was generating record-breaking annual revenues. It's a pity, and kind of crazy, to think that, almost 15 years later, Rovio was still a rare example of a company that was following Amazon's lead. So many companies were still missing the point. The fan-centric model implies that whenever a decision needs to be made, the question "What would the fans think?" is entertained. It also implies that if you don't know the answer with certainty, you go out and ask them. Fan-centric means taking the lead on organizing cool community-centric events for your followers.

The maxim says that money can't buy you love, but in the entertainment business a lot of love can lead to wealth. It is important to monetize, but you shouldn't focus on this aspect alone. If you concentrate on the fun factor and the quality of your product, and build a sizeable audience on top of that, business will become much easier.

CHAPTER SIX

More Than a Game

While the sales forces were busy taking over the digital space bit by bit, Mikael Hed pursued his dream of building a true brand by branching out into physical merchandising.

Technically, the Red Hoodie, with heavy eyebrows and beak on the front side, was the first physical *Angry Birds* item ever produced, though it was restricted to Rovio employees representing the company at trade fairs and conferences around the world. The first consumer product made available to the public was a line of T-shirts produced through the American company Fifth Sun in March 2010. These were available only online and through a relatively low-traffic website, so quantities sold remained quite low during 2010.

Mikael wanted to do something more meaningful, and Niklas was totally on board with the idea. Convinced that the birds would make for great-looking plush toys, Mikael Hed asked their cousin to make a prototype. On seeing her work, Niklas immediately fell in love with it and took it with him to show everyone else around the offices.

In mid-2010, Niklas and Mikael took the prototype on a trip to San Francisco, where a casual encounter reinforced their faith in the power of the character in and of itself, outside the game universe. Matt Wilson recounts:

> We decided to make a journal of *Angry Birds* touring the U.S. We took this tourist bus: "Deluxe Sightseeing." It was awful. It was so bad! It was perfect for what we were after. As Niklas was sitting on the bus, a mom walked in with three or four kids and spotted the plush toy on his lap. They all stopped and she spontaneously asked, "What is that?" He replied, "It's *Angry Birds*." And she said, "Of course!" because it looked angry. That small moment captured something special, "If that's the gut reaction, from somebody who doesn't know the game, we should definitely give it a try."[1]

Unfortunately, toy manufacturers and licensing houses don't often base their decisions on gut feelings, but instead base them on projections of numbers. That's their compass. And compared to motion pictures, music, or iconic comic books that have been around for decades, a one-year-old mobile game didn't look all that enticing. "A mobile game? I don't think so," was a line that the Heds kept hearing. Multiple companies turned down the proposals from Rovio, one after the other ... until it heard from Commonwealth Toys.

Commonwealth was at a critical juncture itself, the sort that Rovio remembered well. The little toy manufacturer hadn't struck a commercial hit in quite some time and was struggling financially. It needed to take a risk. The download numbers for the *Angry Birds* games were high. More intriguingly, the retention rate and the amount of time users were playing every day were remarkable. Commonwealth rolled the dice. It made a bunch of prototypes, and the quality convinced the Heds it was the right partner. An initial production run of a few thousand units was ordered from China in October 2010.

When looking at the proposed operation, Kaj Hed was skeptical, to say the least. Besides the logistical implications—would there even be demand?—as much as he doubted the whole venture, Kaj Hed had promised to take a step back and let Mikael take the lead, so he didn't interfere.

If demand for the merchandise was high and *Angry Birds* could sustain its number-one spot in the U.S. App Store into 2011, Commonwealth Toys would offer the plush toys to retailers across the U.S. That was the second phase of the plan. First, Rovio exclusively offered the goods directly to its global audience, shipping worldwide and taking care of order fulfillment in-house. "I set up our online store in a week and a half. I had never made a website before,"[2] Matthew Wilson remembers.

The amount of traffic directed to the animation trailer on YouTube, as well as the time spent by fans playing the game on a daily basis, had planted a permanent question at Rovio. He pondered: "We have so much volume. How can we utilize this commercially? Because compared to the time that players are spending in the game, we were only taking a very little piece [financially]."[3]

While the digital story of *Angry Birds* so far had been a long streak of making the right decisions at the right time, the boys entered the world of physical merchandise and its complex logistics with the naivete that comes with inexperience and initially delivered a masterclass in what not to do when launching a product into the real world. Rather than opening the webstore first, looking at the numbers to gauge demand for a few days, and seeing how workers coped with dispatching from the warehouse—"soft-launching" in a sense—Rovio instead came out full-steam, not only unveiling the webstore with a press release and a flurry of actions in social media but also adding a link to the store directly from the main menu of the game, across all apps. This exposed the new line of plush toys to millions of daily active users at once, in over 100 countries.

Boom! In a moment, they discovered that success can exceed one's expectations to the extent that it becomes a nightmare.

Overnight, customers ordered over $200,000 worth of goods from every corner of the globe. Time to bring out the champagne? Not quite. It was more like a crisis.

According to Matt's recollection, PayPal, the gateway processing all payments for the new plush toys, called in the early morning and quizzed Niklas Hed: "'Who are you guys? Yesterday you had zero sales and today you have over $200,000.' They thought it was money laundering."[4] And as PayPal usually does in such dubious circumstances, it preemptively froze the money on the account. This meant that Rovio had no access to the cash until it could explain the situation and prove who it was. That was just the start of it, however. Much worse was to follow.

In the digital world, there is no such thing as a shortage of supply. Once an app is available on the App Store, it doesn't matter how many millions of customers order at the same time, the Apple system reproduces the code for them and delivers a copy of the game smoothly within seconds. The developer has nothing to do with it. Everybody is served instantly. There's no queue. Rovio hadn't quite anticipated the overhead that comes with real-life logistics. Having previously shipped only a few T-shirts, the warehouse was not prepared for such a storm. Demand had been widely underestimated. In logistics, such mistakes are like time bombs. If you under-produce in October, you'll lack inventory in November and December, and by January you'll still be running around playing catchup to try to clear the backlog of orders. Overall, customers ordered $2 million worth of *Angry Birds* plush toys during the Christmas 2010 season. The last parcel was delivered only in February 2011—a notable, and disastrous, delay by all online retail standards.

While launching a new physical product near Christmas is ideal from a commercial point of view, it couldn't be worse timing when it comes to shortages and logistical failures. There is a surge of purchases for entertainment products and merchandising goods in the last quarter of the year. Everybody knows that. Internet traffic shoots up, too. This stems from what the holiday season has come to represent: People are buying gifts to put under the Christmas tree. There's a fixed deadline on these orders. More importantly, there's an emotional value tied to them. If a company receives orders toward Christmas, it takes on an extra responsibility: To let consumers down during such a sentimental time of the year risks triggering explosive reactions. As their patience wore thin, customers emailed Rovio constantly, and in a tone that grew angrier by the day (and not funny-angry like the birds in the game). Although Rovio hasn't shared with me any specific correspondence, out of respect for customers' privacy, Niklas confirms that some of these emails contained insults and empty threats of lawsuits. Things can quickly turn ugly in such circumstances.

From the minute they unveiled the store, until that day in February when they finally delivered the last batch of backlogged orders, Niklas and his packing team did not get much sleep. And yes, it turned out to be stressful, even stormy times for the little company (by the end of 2010, Rovio was still playing it safe, employing only 46 people). In a way, Kaj's foresight about this was on point. But, by vowing to prove him wrong, the young Heds persevered with their initial plan and built themselves a shipping center, a solid tool that would prove essential for the future. A month later, as they added the line of T-shirts from Fifth Sun into the system, sales of clothing skyrocketed, too. Niklas subsequently became COO, with his analytical skills well suited to the efficient streamlining of operations and processes.

In this chapter, we've seen the key turning point in the *Angry Birds* story where the game transcended its reputation as "the next *Doodle Jump*" and entered a higher trajectory, growing from a hit game into a legitimate brand and, later, a bona fide phe-nomenon. If they hadn't done this crazy stunt during this key period, my story here might have consisted of a dozen PDF pages rather than an actual book. As David Helgason, CEO and founder of the successful engine middleware startup Unity Technologies, once said, "Ignorance lets you start on things that are considered impossible. If you were wise about it, you wouldn't try."[5]

CHAPTER SEVEN

Land Grab

As we celebrated New Year 2011, Niklas Hed and his team were buried under piles of orders. Meanwhile, the business development and marketing teams at Rovio were increasing their efforts to conquer more of the market share on the Android platform.

During the last months of 2010, *Angry Birds* remained number one on just about every app chart around. Moreover, both on the App Store and the various Android channels, the download numbers reached unprecedented levels. This in part was due to the fact that the platforms themselves were beating all sales forecasts. The monthly activation rates of Android devices were growing at a record pace and slowly catching up with Apple, which itself was surpassing all expectations. By the end of the year, *Angry Birds* had already been downloaded a staggering 42 million times across all platforms. Even better, where the free Android version was designed to mainly be a promotional vehicle, expected to bring in only incremental revenue, it turned out that the ad-supported model was very profitable when applied to volumes as large as the ones that Rovio was enjoying. For the month of December 2010 alone, it brought in $1 million. Matthew Wilson became a vocal supporter of the model at trade events: "I believe that anybody who has a paid app on iOS should bring it across as a free app on Android with advertisements for two reasons," he commented. "One, the advertisers will pay you more money than you would make from the downloads as a paid app and two, you want visibility. You want to be able to promote your next product and that gives you a great opportunity to do so."[1]

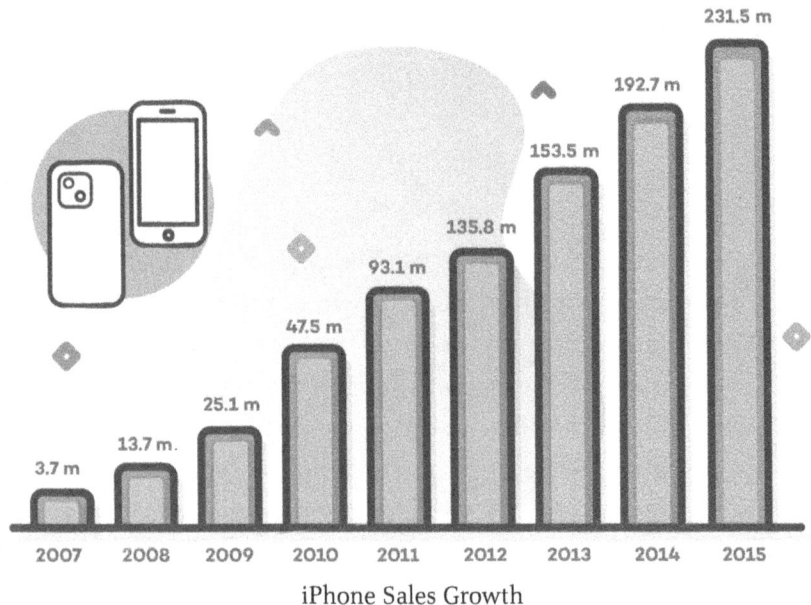

iPhone Sales Growth

Free Rein

January 1, 2011 marked the end of the timed-exclusivity clause for TV commercials, leaving Rovio free to approve anything that came into the content licensing pipeline. As bitter as the team may have been about not being able to do that in previous months, this is an example when time turned out to be on its side. One reason for this is that, from the platform-holders' perspective, being initially turned down made the brand all the more desirable. It's a bit like when one plays hard-to-get in seduction, except that

Rovio hadn't been playacting. *Angry Birds* had clearly replaced *Doodle Jump* as the figurehead of mobile gaming, and although some other games like *Cut the Rope* and *Fruit Ninja* were showing impressive sales numbers around this time, none of them had such an immediate brand impact when used in TV commercials, as advertisers realized after using different titles during *Angry Birds'* exclusivity period. *Angry Birds* was the clear system-seller of this generation of hardware, just as *Pac-Man* had been for the Atari VCS 2600 or *Gran Turismo* for PlayStation, for example.

Furthermore, the team itself had been able to fully prepare and was now ready for action. The previous months had served as a great training ground to fine-tune its system, and it was collecting and contacting new channels on a regular basis, while mapping the whole sector. At the very minute it was released from its contractual obligations, it went into overdrive.

"As soon as the exclusivity ended, we had free rein to go crazy," Wilson recalls:

> We did 30 TV commercials with different carriers and device manufacturers in multiple countries, in the space of six months. We brought in a new team member, Bijay Gurung, and we said, "Bijay, here's that list with all these contacts [of all Android channels]. Get it preloaded on as many as you can. It's free. It's got ad-support. We don't even care if it ends up on The Pirate Bay. We want the game out there everywhere with our ads."[2]

When saying this, Wilson makes decisive downward hand gestures, as if ticking tasks off a to-do list (he shares this signature gesture with Peter Vesterbacka). Wilson further explains: "The objective was pretty clear: We wanted to be everywhere and we wanted to make it so that you couldn't sell a phone without *Angry Birds* pre-loaded on it. I think we were the first to really take full advantage of that. Making sure we were just visible at every level of this new smartphone environment."[3]

Once again, all the companies that had a horse in the mobile race responded to the surge. Deals were made with T-Mobile and Verizon in the U.S., SFR and Samsung in France, Vodafone in the U.K. and all other territories covered by the service provider. Over 30 different TV commercials featuring *Angry Birds* aired around the world during the first semester of 2011. Through the flow of ideas that kept being pitched to them, Lauri Konttori noticed one recurring issue: "Because they could sometimes throw Red Bird more than one time within the same level, people were thinking that there were many different Red Birds," he says. "We once heard a pitch ending with 'And then ten Red Birds are swarming at the same time.' I realized we had to make it clear that there is only one Red and that he is the leader, like *Super Mario*, and that it's not just a generic bird, like the *Stormtrooper*."[4]

Besides TV commercials, the big telecom firms also began to try to outdo one another in coming up with real-life stunts that would garner media exposure for their respective product lines, and for *Angry Birds*, too.

Former professional basketball player Philip Hickey worked in marketing for Nokia. He had access to a massive house in Austin, Texas, where the South by Southwest (SXSW) festival takes place each year. For the 2011 edition of the festival, he wanted to create an eye-catching stunt. He reached out to Marja Konttinen at Isobar, a global digital marketing agency. Speed was of the essence. Konttinen suggested to project 3D imagery through the windows of the adjacent building. 3D projections were becoming more and more popular in the advertising business, and she knew that the stunt alone would turn a few heads. According to Konttinen,

"*Angry Birds* was drawing a lot of headlines and we knew it was just out on Nokia phones. Nobody had really used *Angry Birds* in real-life advertising yet. So, if we could get ahold of the Rovio guys, we could make the pigs steal the phone, and the birds would then attack the house to get it back and they would leave a hole in the wall behind them."[5] Hickey loved the concept and commissioned Konttinen to get it done. "I called the best agency that could do the projection and told them I had a project that normally would take six months, and we had three weeks. They laughed," says Konttinen, "When I said it's for Nokia and *Angry Birds*, they stopped laughing immediately. 'What? *Angry Birds*? Are you able to do that? We are massive fans! We know the sounds and characters. We don't need to be briefed on the assets. Let's just go for it.'"[6]

Konttinen got in touch with Wilson and Vesterbacka and pitched them the idea. She was expecting to pay some license fee, but they told her she could do it for free and that they would add a bunch of free plush toys to the mix so that Konttinen could get them thrown at people as part of the stunt. "When I asked if we shouldn't sign an agreement, Wilson told me, 'Oh yeah, here you go,' and he instantly handed me this one-page agreement," Konttinen remembers. "It was so easy. And it was really fun! I thought, 'These guys are so much fun to work with.'"[7] When she rushed to get the operation validated by her global headquarters, someone objected: "How do we make sure no one in the U.S. thinks it's a real attack on a building? People could think it's a terrorist assault."[8] The stunt ended up working wonderfully, with witnesses going nuts both on the street and on Twitter. Nobody, of course, took it for a terrorist attack. In fact, the operation worked so well that, later on, Nokia used *Angry Birds* again for multiple promotions in different countries.

Birds, Birds ... Everywhere

Even companies that had nothing to do with mobile or gaming began using the bird characters in their commercials, just as they would do with rock stars or bankable actors. This ranged from Microsoft for its Bing search engine, to Google for Chrome, Wonderful Pistachios, and Telepizza, to name a few. T-Mobile would top them all in terms of imagination in June 2011. On the streets of Barcelona, they reproduced all the elements of an *Angry Birds* level on the human scale, using plastic and wood models. A few Bad Piggies plush toys were placed around the setup and a secret treasure box front and center. Nearby, they placed an iPhone on which passers-by could play *Angry Birds*. A local brass band played the *Angry Birds* theme song to attract the crowds. For a few hours, the crowd's reactions were filmed, as the T-Mobile crew flung stuffed birds at the Bad Piggy toys. After a bit of editing magic in the postproduction room, the final video on YouTube came out with added explosions and a well-timed montage that gave the impression that the special effects were triggered by the people using the iPhone. It may all have been staged and enhanced, but the people present had a fun day and the final video montage went viral.

Numerous organic, user-generated reenactments of *Angry Birds* had already taken place prior to the T-Mobile mega event, thanks to the plush toys that were getting into more and more people's hands, giving the fans the wherewithal to explore their ideas. Many clips featured on the renowned YouTube channel *Funny or Die*. A professional Finnish soccer goalkeeper, Lassi Hurskainen, made videos of himself shooting footballs at Bad Piggies plush toys sited at progressively more distant spots. At the time of writing, that video has generated 4.5 million views! That's what you reap when you sow the seeds for creativity through social media and merchandising. When you give them the means and the freedom, fans can create unique videos that go viral.

Basically, *Angry Birds* was everywhere you looked during that first quarter of 2011. "It got to the point where, by March, we were experiencing hyper-growth,"[9] states Wilson. Eventually, interest from network carriers started to subside after the summer of 2011. They weren't investing as much in their TV campaigns to support their emerging Android products. The losers of the war were retreating and counting their losses, while the winners were cutting marketing costs to maximize profit margins. Wilson is right about the fact that Rovio was the first to fully take advantage of this platform war—but it was also the last. This "unicorn" of opportunity, as it is called in advertising jargon, vanished as soon as Rovio had finished riding it. Nowadays, getting published in the hundreds of Android stores requires as much overhead as before for indie developers, and yet they tend to obtain far less exposure from the gatekeepers in return for their sacrifices. As established above, in every race, only one contestant gets to wear the yellow jersey.

For Rovio, the first half of 2011 was highly energetic. According to Wilson, "It was a strategy somehow, but I think it was more us thinking, 'Let's get it done.' We just went out there, boom, boom, boom. Except for Peter, none of us had worked for big corporations, so we hadn't picked up any of their slow bad habits. We just went out and did."[10] The time delay between drawing the internal plan and delivering its execution was indeed always insanely short for Rovio. The Rovio marketing squad was extremely reactive during this gold-rush era, which is vital when punching above your weight. To get involved in so many marketing operations and TV commercials within one single semester would be a lot of work even for a gigantic multinational. At the time, there were still fewer than a hundred employees at Rovio.

From Eyeball to Mindshare

On seeing a brand name, a title, a logo, or a character for the first time, we are usually not paying a lot of attention. For this reason, conversion rates on paid advertising as well as click-throughs on headlines are lower on something completely new than on something well known. It's the familiarity effect. This human trait is what makes the task of a marketer so hard when promoting a new brand. One stunt or one featuring spot just won't cut it and will have only a marginal effect. You need to multiply your efforts to get seen multiple times by as many potential customers as possible. It's only the third or fourth time someone sees your message or brand name that their brain will be able to unconsciously recognize it, that their curiosity will be piqued, and that they will eventually click on it. Until that point, you'll be invisible, no matter how much or what you are waving at them.

This is why public relations aren't enough if you are trying to break out, unless you can generate repeated news coverage rounds, very close to one another. This is where the Rovio system in the early days proved to be so effective: The big commercials everywhere connected the game with a device customers desired; the customer went to buy the device at the store and saw the same game plastered all around on the walls; they connected to the digital store for the first time and the same game was featured (if it wasn't preinstalled on their device); and by the time they checked the charts, that same game was at the number one position. By then, they had been shown the game at least four times, even without their entering the ecosystem, even if they hadn't checked any game news or app reviews, and even if they hadn't received any message from their friends about it.

The perfect system is in place for maximum conversion.

CHAPTER EIGHT

Rovio Goes to Hollywood

Rovio had reached a point where *Angry Birds* was everywhere—in commercials, in point-of-sale advertisements, in movie dialogue, comedy sketches, talk shows ... and, of course, in people's hands. You couldn't take public transportation or stand in line at a coffee shop without noticing somebody playing it. Hollywood kept calling, and after almost a year at the top of the charts, the level of respect for Rovio from major studios had grown. Eventually, Rovio received an offer it couldn't refuse.

Over at Fox Interactive, Andrew Stalbow had been put in charge of finding ways to use the company's portfolio of big, successful franchises to leverage the booming mobile economy. The holding group, Twentieth Century Fox, owned the rights to many household brands born either in cinema or on television. Stalbow's video game track record included many achievements such as *The Simpsons: Tapped Out* (in collaboration with EA mobile) or the tie-in game deal for *Ice Age* with Gameloft (the game that had influenced Mikael Hed's thinking during the planning stages of *Angry Birds*). Briefly put, he was a big shot who knew the mobile landscape very well.

A Match Made in the Skies

There was a movie titled *Rio* that had been in preparation at the award-winning Blue Sky Studios (also behind the *Ice Age* movie franchise). *Rio* is an animated picture about birds, and it was poised for a release during the 2011 Easter holiday. It contained completely new characters and wasn't necessarily positioned to be a blockbuster. Stalbow was therefore searching for innovative and creative ways to market it. According to him, "It was all about birds. So it was a really nice fit."[1]

Internally at Fox, he pitched *Angry Birds* as the ideal, four-quadrant demographic fit for a family-oriented animated film. It was the one game that Stalbow's five-year-old son played with his grandfather. The term "four-quadrant demographic" means that marketers see a product or brand as appealing to both genders, male and female, and to the entire age spectrum, young and old. If your product appeals to a four-quadrant demographic, your target audience is essentially everyone.

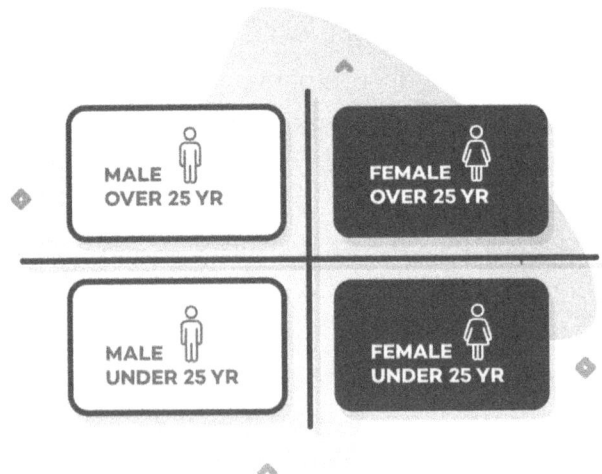

Four Quadrants

Stalbow remembers his initial call to Rovio in Danny Graydon's book *Angry Birds: Hatching a Universe:* "[T]here were only a few dozen people working there at the time—and [we] offered them the opportunity to have some Hollywood-level marketing for their brand."[2] The way in which Stalbow's offer was presented was compelling, and the guy handing it out was smart, understood the mobile space, and made a lot of sense to the Heds and their team. They jumped at the offer.

In a co-branding venture, one big point of discussion is which brand will come first in the title. Is it *Rio Angry Birds* or *Angry Birds Rio*? When two companies discuss such topics, they tend to flex their big marketing muscles to show they are the ones bringing in the most fans. The multimillion-dollar marketing budget Fox was prepared to spend was certainly impressive. Peter Vesterbacka's bold stance was that *Angry Birds* was massively popular on mobile devices and gave them a level of exposure that was both unmatchable and priceless in that ecosystem. As is the wont of Hollywood executives in that situation, Peter Levinson came back at Vesterbacka with a direct and uncompromising question, formulated in Vesterbacka's account as "How many downloads do you think we can get for *Angry Birds Rio*?"[3] The Mighty Eagle answered without hesitation: "50 million downloads."[4] That was close to the number of downloads that the first *Angry Birds* had amassed over the course of a full year. According to Vesterbacka's recollection of the call, his prediction was received with a lot of doubt and disbelief.

That call took place in late December, 2010. On January 27, 2011, the inked deal was announced to the media with another animated trailer. Although Blue Sky shared a lot of visual and sound assets from the movie, Studio Kombo was still in charge of the piece and pretty much had free rein with it. "It was our third attempt at the intro, and we also had to hook *Rio* into the story.

I still feel to this day that it's the most accomplished video we did during that era"[5] is Lauri Konttori's proud assessment. The level of polish was such that Fox approved the very first file without requesting any changes, so as not to waste any time. "Rovio were actually the ones who requested a few changes, like removing our Kombo logo from the end-screens," recalls Konttori. "The video was published almost immediately after Kombo delivered it."[6]

But forget the fast turnaround of the deal negotiations for a minute. For those familiar with video game history, the expectation is for companies to deliver a good game on time for a movie tie-in, with the tight timescale traditionally allowed between contract signature and the film's release date. In these types of ventures, the deadline for the game is nonnegotiable. I once wrote an editorial piece for *EDGE* magazine about the relationship between movies and video games, explaining why movie tie-ins constantly end up spawning under-par, and sometimes plain terrible, games that suffer lukewarm commercial reception at best.[7] The only four exceptions I had found to this rule (*Robocop*, *Die Hard Trilogy*, *Golden Eye*, and *Star Wars*) had all been released long after the theatrical release (for various reasons). This is a curse because, over time, huge numbers of motion pictures are licensed for video game iterations. Unfortunately, no matter how good the movie, and even when the premise fits perfectly, most games based on films tend to underwhelm. It stems from the fact that making a great game takes time, something that such deals generally lack. In the article, I discussed games that had typically been given six to twelve months to get made. *Angry Birds Rio* launched in the App Store by the end of March, not only on time for the U.S. theatrical release, but actually a few weeks ahead of it! Even more incredibly, the game was a great evolution on the formula, both graphically and in terms of gameplay mechanics evolution, as proven by the high review scores from customers and critics. How did Rovio manage to pull this off in just three short months?

Preparation Meets Opportunity

It is often said that "Luck is what happens when preparation meets opportunity." This moment in our story drives the point home. Over the previous 12 months, some of the team at Rovio had been secretly working on a sequel to *Angry Birds*. They overhauled the graphic engine completely, allowing for much more detailed and vibrant visuals, while still running at 30 frames per second. They were toying with mechanics, adding in new gameplay elements, and designed a flurry of new levels assimilating these new features. By the time Fox called, the work for the sequel was pretty much all in place. So much so that, to deliver *Angry Birds Rio*, they just needed to focus on replacing the Bad Piggies with the caged bird characters from the movie (the goal of *Angry Birds Rio* is to free them), change the backdrop images, and integrate a few mischievous monkeys here and there. Rovio beat the curse of movie-based games by avoiding both the need to start development from scratch and the temptation of simply recycling an existing game, which could have seemed boring. By taking a game that was already far along in the development process and associating the partner's brand with it, they almost entirely cut out the brainstorming, incubation, and alpha phases. The real work was mostly focused on the visual assets, which is never too difficult when dealing with a Hollywood studio.

This deal popped two piggies with one bird, so to speak. Although he was one of those pressing for the development of an improved version that would help keep things fresh for the fans, Mikael Hed was at the same time very reluctant about releasing *Angry Birds 2*. The games industry is plagued with "sequelitis," even more so than the movie industry. Whenever something resonates with the public, a second game follows, then a third, and so on. Beyond risk management and commercial considerations, this makes even more sense in this trade than in others given that it is a technology-driven space. But there was a trend on the App Store that Mikael Hed had observed and was wary about. Usually, when *Game Title 2* comes out, a good chunk of the fans of *Game Title 1* buy into the sequel. Not all of them, though. And the new fans flocking in are often fewer in numbers than the ones lost. And some people wonder whether they should play the sequel if they haven't played the first one. But the worst part is that the sales of the first episode systematically plummet, because the title is suddenly perceived as old fashioned and outdated. That was something that didn't sit well with Mikael.

Audiences want a sequel until they get a sequel, as the Hollywood maxim goes. A sequel can dilute the brand, lead to confusion, and cannibalize sales when releasing back-to-back on the same platform. And when you're on a surge like *Angry Birds* was, you sure don't want to jinx it by interrupting the rise. *Angry Birds Rio* helped Rovio avoid the sequel pitfall. *Angry Birds Rio* was in fact positioned and perceived more as an event than a sequel—much like *Angry Birds Seasons* had been.

Andrew Stalbow had promised some Hollywood-level marketing for the *Angry Birds* brand, and in February 2011 Fox gave Rovio its first taste. Two weeks before Super Bowl XLV, which would see the Pittsburgh Steelers face the Green Bay Packers, Twentieth Century Fox purchased a last-minute commercial spot of 30 seconds during the fourth quarter for its upcoming movie *Rio*.

A Super Bowl commercial is pretty much the Holy Grail of advertising. Every year, the annual championship final for the NFL (National Football League), known as the Super Bowl, is watched by over 100 million viewers across the U.S. It regularly breaks national audience records. Some of the most jaw-dropping (and most expensive) commercials are created by the biggest brands especially for this limelight airtime, each competing to grab the best spot at that year's event. As a result, there is a statistical spike in traffic during halftime, as some people tune in only to watch the commercials. In 2011, a 30-second spot was reportedly changing hands for around $3 million. While there are some events that gather more viewers than the Super Bowl on a global scale, such as the soccer World Cup Finals or the Olympics 100-meter finals (both surpassing the billions-of-viewers mark on a worldwide basis), the rights to the broadcast of these events are sold to different networks for each and every country, making it virtually impossible to show ads to the total audience all at once. For one single country, reachable through one television network, the Super Bowl is the biggest opportunity an advertiser can find.

When asked how the game could be featured in that spot, Peter Vesterbacka convinced Fox to do something really special with it, something that would get people's attention and stay in the collective memory for a long time. He says, "When you do something like that, stand out. Every market is crowded. What you have to figure out is how to stand out from the crowd."[8]

The trailer for *Rio* the movie featured a small visual clue about *Angry Birds* added onto a virtual crate in the backdrop of a short scene excerpt. Red Bird appeared, with the hint "13-12" written next to him. This referred to level 13-12 in the *Angry Birds* game. When players went to this level, a golden egg in the shape of a football appeared. Hit the golden football, then the second one that subsequently appeared, and you were entered into a competition. First prize was a trip to the *Rio* movie premiere in Rio de Janeiro, Brazil, on March 22, 2011.

The global media was alerted about the presence of the code during the week leading up to the Sunday event. After the event, they all reported on the clue, deciphering it for those who hadn't understood it. Sharon Stone now had a new challenger for the "most paused scene" title she holds since her *Basic Instinct* days. "Fox Makes Super Bowl Ad History with *Rio* Promo," read the *Hollywood Reporter* headline.[9] The only movie ad that people talked about after the 2011 edition of the Super Bowl was the *Rio Angry Birds* commercial. Because it was different. This was the first time ever that an in-game cheat was unveiled to the public in this fashion.

As the international movie premiere date drew near, Fox took things up a notch. Billboards and posters appeared all around the world. Wilson recalls, "I was coming out of Mobile World Conference in Barcelona and heading for lunch. The bus stop was plastered with advertising, not for *Rio* the movie but for the *Angry Birds Rio* app. I was amazed by that."[10] A trailer highlighting both the upcoming motion picture and the gaming app started showing up on TV in many countries, as well as on the big screen in movie theatres everywhere. In between glimpses of George Clooney, Leonardo DiCaprio, or Scarlett Johansson, Red popped up on the silver screen just as you were munching your way through your popcorn. It gave the game prestige by association. In addition to how many people see the ad, another parameter that affects the overall impact is the qualitative perception of the ad that people remember. To be mentioned in the columns of iconic publications like *Variety*, *The Hollywood Reporter*, *BusinessWeek*, *Forbes*, or *The Times* puts you in a different light than getting your app reviewed by *TouchArcade*, *148apps*, or *Pocketgamer.co.uk* (not that the latter publications should be disregarded). In the same way, cinema is a grander venue than YouTube. Your eyes are wide open, and your brain is more receptive. The instant is more memorable.

There was also a bit of friendly competition going on between the equally ambitious spirits of Vesterbacka and Stalbow. "The Fox guys also did stuff that they had never done before,"[11] claims Vesterbacka. The teams at Rovio and Fox both kept obsessively thinking about what more they could do and how they could stand out from the crowd. According to Andrew Hampp, writing for *AdAge*, "Fox partners with 82 brands worldwide to help get the word out. The $100 million marketing blitz features everything from *Rio*-branded blue Oreos in Latin America to a promotion at the Gap in the U.K. to adult-targeted U.S. promotions with Overstock.com and Benjamin Moore paints."[12]

The Big Launch

The *Angry Birds Rio* app launched on Apple's App Stores, Google's Android Market, and Amazon's App Store on March 22, 2011, at the same time as the movie was released in international markets. Rovio put its social media machine behind it at full throttle. The game and movie were both instant hits. *Angry Birds Rio* got downloaded 1 million times within the first 24 hours (even faster than *Angry Birds Halloween*), 10 million times in 10 days, and 20 million in 15 days (across paid and ad-supported free versions on all digital stores). The movie also opened very strongly in international markets, earning over $55 million before even launching in North America. Just before Easter, the headline "Rio plus *Angry Birds* Equals a Hit"[13] appeared in *Forbes*, where it was observed: "Fox is taking every opportunity possible to tie the movie in with the popular app. Now players can buy tickets for *Rio* through the *Angry Birds* game. Starting today the app will be linked to the ticket-seller Fandango." The magazine anticipated that "The tie-ins should help launch *Rio* to numberer 1 at the box office."[14]

Not only was Fox giving a massive boost to the *Angry Birds* brand, it was actually *Angry Birds* that got credited for boosting *Rio*'s popularity, rather than the other way around. This quotation alone, from such a reputable news outlet, put *Angry Birds* in every conversation among bigwigs and entertainment moguls in the Hollywood microcosm. The new brand on the block, and its massive audience of loyal players, was breaking new ground for both the entertainment and mobile gaming industries, and was finally earning the respect it had been seeking from the major production companies.

Rio entered the U.S. box office at number one in its opening week, grossing over $40 million and beating the fourth outing of the established franchise *Scream*. Far surpassing initial expectations, it turned into a blockbuster. As for the *Angry Birds Rio* app, it took less than a month to rack up the 50 million downloads Vesterbacka had predicted, reaching almost 300 million downloads (as of January 1, 2014). "We set outrageous goals for this collaboration and we beat all of them," Vesterbacka proudly states.[15]

According to some survey polls at the exit, of all the people who went to see the movie, almost half of them had heard of it through the game. Stalbow acknowledged at the Web 2.0 Summit, "*Angry Birds* gave Fox a way to speak organically to our fans."[16]

Speaking on stage at the MIPCOM conference later in 2012, Stalbow elaborated:

> It served as a fantastic marketing platform for Fox to reach a brand-new audience on connected devices and tell them about the new movie. To Rovio, it kind of gave a taste of Hollywood and an ability to see the amazing power of the Hollywood marketing machine. That's where it has taken Rovio: Hollywood has seen the success that *Angry Birds* has had, and Hollywood is hot for the *Angry Birds* brand.[17]

Coincidentally, another prediction from Peter Vesterbacka became a reality during the *Rio* launch month: *Angry Birds* reached the 100-million-downloads benchmark across all versions, with no sign of slowing down. The Android strategy was paying dividends, contributing a whopping 30 million to that total, having been available for just under four months. The game was also still topping the Apple App Store charts worldwide. It had been sitting on the throne for over a year at this point, surfing on a gigantic wave that nobody could have predicted, and leaving the *Tetris* download numbers in its dust.

To everyone's surprise, another very positive side effect of *Angry Birds Rio* was the unexpected boom in a new market: Brazil, a nation that counts almost 200 million inhabitants. The fact that its main city, Rio de Janeiro, had been depicted both in a Hollywood movie and in a superb hit game touched their hearts and made the Cariocas very proud. The download numbers in Brazil for *Angry Birds Rio* were astonishing. And soon enough, the newly acquired fan base picked up the other *Angry Birds* titles as well.

New Alliances

During this massive operation, a few valuable alliances for the long term were formed. Barnes & Noble, today the last-standing nationwide chain of bookstores in the U.S, also carried toys, DVDs, gifts, graphic novels, and music. Video games had once been sold at Barnes & Noble, until the division spun off into GameStop. At the time, Barnes & Noble was trying to push the gaming capacity of its Nook e-reader and wanted *Angry Birds* aboard. In exchange for porting the game to its system and its limited user-base, Vesterbacka came up with a madcap suggestion. "As always with Peter, it was a crazy idea involving crazy timelines and crazy work hours,"[18] recalls Marja Konttinen with a laugh—she had joined Rovio shortly before this operation, having pulled off the SXSW stunt.

Vesterbacka had been eyeing the trend for augmented reality for some time and was toying with how it could be incorporated into *Angry Birds* gaming when entering marked real-life locations and when approaching certain spots. He was calling the concept "Angry Birds Magic." The high number of Barnes & Noble stores, combined with the relatively small installed base of the Nook device, gave Rovio the chance to give it a try on a small scale (so any damage would be contained if something technical went wrong). The gimmick was that if you played *Angry Birds* on a Nook device inside a Barnes & Noble store, you could use the Mighty Eagle unlimited times (instead of once every third level). The ability ended as soon as you left the Barnes & Noble store premises. Giving free infinite power-ups for players meant Rovio received free nationwide exposure in return. Nooks on display in every Barnes & Noble store showed *Angry Birds* from then on, as a way of demonstrating the device to visitors. What's more, the retailer agreed to display the animated trailer of *Angry Birds Rio* on the giant TV screens in all its shop windows during launch week. This had an impact beyond the walls of Barnes & Noble, given the large full-length front windows of the outlets and their prime locations in every major city. Barnes & Noble would repeat this stunt for every game released by Rovio after that, as well as for every major update when accompanied by an animated trailer—for as long as Rovio kept providing the Nook with content.

Amazon was the second partner to be seduced on this occasion. The top e-tailer had recently entered the mobile space with its Anid-powered Amazon Kindle Fire tablet and had its own digital app shop to support it. The tablet's initial start over Christmas had been very strong, and analysts predicted it would gain a sizeable Northern American share of the mobile market, albeit still in the shadow of top dogs Apple, Google, and Samsung. Amazon had been collecting data on millions of users and building trust with its customers since the late 1990s. It was the one to watch, especially in the U.S. market, where its domination was most established. Rovio let Amazon list *Angry Birds Rio* for free, 24 hours before anyone else, and without any ads. In exchange, Amazon gave it premium exposure across all its channels.

The hugely successful collaboration with Fox reassured the Heds that they had a proper brand, and, having witnessed what over-the-top marketing stunts and broad partnerships could do, the "Rovians" realized they had not yet been thinking big enough. They wanted more of that same "Hollywood marketing machine" juice. They wanted to keep playing in the big leagues. Niklas and Mikael finally embraced and adopted the "nothing is impossible" attitude and the "Think huge" mentality that Vesterbacka had been advocating. Until this juncture, during board meetings Vesterbacka had been constantly telling Kaj Hed, the company chairman, that, in his opinion, "We are not growing fast enough."[19] Mikael had been providing the balance in the company so far, by keeping Vesterbacka in check when he wanted to dance faster than the music, sometimes overlooking the time it takes to build great products for the team. But now, with the prediction of 100 million downloads accomplished, they were all on the same page. The time to think big was indeed immediately.

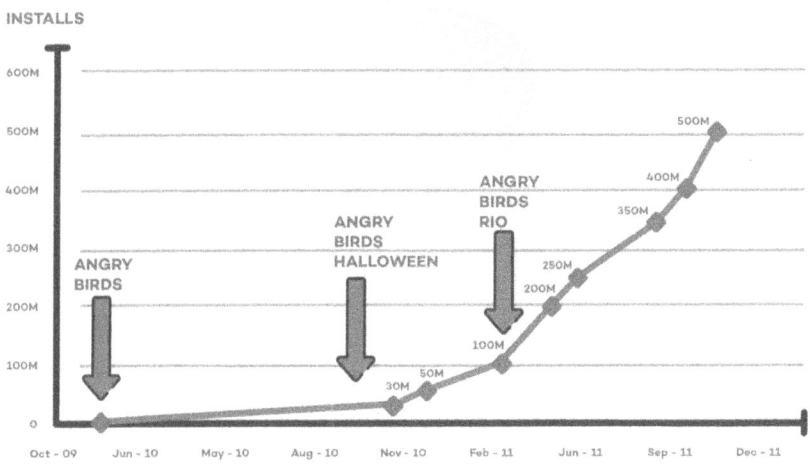

Angry Birds Downloads Curve

In August 2011, *Angry Birds* was plastered on the cover of *Mad* magazine, one of the ultimate symbols of having become part of U.S. pop culture.

During the same summer, *Angry Birds* passed the 200-million mark and entered uncharted territories that even *Tetris* hadn't had the chance to tread. The franchise had yielded a rate of 1 million downloads per day since June 2011. Yet, as they broke records and standards, the Rovians remained hungrier than ever. "Our eyes were already big before. They were way bigger after *Angry Birds Rio.*"[20]

CHAPTER NINE

Recruiting a Flock

When you dream bigger and decide to up your ambitions, the natural course of things is to grow the workforce. People's workload is not infinitely extendable, and time is a finite resource. If you want to do more, you need more staff. You can't possibly say yes to all opportunities unless you have the bandwidth to deliver quality work on time and on all fronts.

Being exceptionally profitable, and with revenue numbers consistently on the up, Rovio certainly could afford it. It had been playing it safe long enough to allow itself a calculated risk in terms of salary caps.

A Tricky Transition

If you think money can buy you everything and that going out and hiring a hundred people is easy, think again. Between the various growth phases a company could face, often the toughest transition for a startup is when going from small- to medium-sized, or, to put it in numbers, when going from a few dozen employees to the hundreds. In the first phase, everything is centered around top management, who, if they are thorough and responsible, keep an eye on everything and everybody. The size of the business and of the team makes it possible to keep up with daily activities, to remember everybody's first name, and to monitor productivity levels. Furthermore, there is often a symbiotic and organic osmosis among team members who all know each other, especially if the company happens to be successful. Winning increases team cohesion. That's as true in business as it is in sports.

Once you're moving from 1,000 to 5,000 or 10,000 employees, I won't say it's easy, but the burden on the top pyramidal layer is usually lighter. It so happens that among the first thousand employees, you have divisional directors, middle managers, and bright individuals who have already been trained and who know best practices, corporate values, and hierarchical procedures. These senior employees can train the newbies without intervention from company founders or top-level executives.

It's making the jump from 25–40 employees to 100–200 that's the big challenge. A lot of time is taken up selecting and appointing the recruits, making sure they are the right choices. Mikael and Niklas Hed vetted the first hundred employees personally, meeting all candidates themselves. This alone consumed a lot of time and energy. Afterward, no matter how competent and qualified the new members were in terms of skills, experience, and knowledge, there was still the need to train them about how things were done at Rovio and teach them the internal "secret sauce." A good principle to have when hiring is to allocate a few hours in your daily schedule dedicated to settling in the new employees, answering their questions. This should ideally continue for at least the first two to four weeks depending on how fast the person learns and how much they have to digest. So, when your headcount jumps from 46 to 204 within a year, as it did at Rovio, you can well imagine the headaches that come with that.

It's a necessary process, and one many startups face at some point or another, after they achieve initial success. Nevertheless, it can be a struggle. All the time you spend training new people is time you cannot assign to other tasks. And when you are the company CEO, like Mikael Hed, or COO, like Niklas Hed, these tasks relate to important business decisions. Meanwhile, when your sales are so high, opportunities knock on the door every minute. If 2011 looked like a blissful year of success for Rovio from an outsider's point of view, inside it is remembered as the beginning of even more taxing workloads and challenges, reduced downtimes, longer and longer to-do lists, and time flying by ever faster. There was a continuous adrenaline rush and a constant feeling of catching up all the time, rather than being on top of things.

Before Rovio even selected, appointed, and trained its 150 new employees, it had to first locate them. It's not easy to find this number of talented, skilled, and highly motivated people. In that respect, having Nokia two blocks away helped a great deal. After building a world-dominating empire for the previous decade, Nokia was experiencing tough times and many of its people were in search of a fresh challenge. Not only did numerous top-notch engineers and programmers cross the street to join Rovio, but also a bunch of marketing and communication specialists, such as Saara Bergström, who joined to head the customer engagement efforts on owned media, or Philip Hickey, who joined soon after having set up the SXSW 2011 stunt as part of Nokia's team. Both would play instrumental roles in the following years. Wilson comments, "All in all, 25 people were working in marketing in our various offices. The addition of experienced people like Philip Hickey and Saara Bergström, who became the architects of our consumer engagement structure, helped [Ville] Heijari [the Rovio head of marketing] to move on to a higher level and focus on what he does best: strategy. He likes to identify patterns of what's happening in the world, and how we can leverage opportunities from that."[1] From this point on, although he held the title of head of marketing, Ville Heijari would manage the department in conjunction with Bergström, Hickey, and Wilson: He never moved forward with a marketing-communication campaign until it was refined enough for all other prominent figures in his department to be fully behind it. "We wouldn't put resources into creating something if anybody felt that it wouldn't work with a part of our audience or in an important channel," Wilson stresses.[2] Coming back to developers and engineers, Niklas Hed points out that the vibrant "demo scene" of homebrew coders in the Nordic region was also a great source for additional recruits.

As the brand went truly global, Vesterbacka needed to travel extensively to numerous countries to ensure *Angry Birds* stayed relevant everywhere. The U.S. had become such a big opportunity on its own that the Mighty Eagle couldn't represent the company stateside alone. To head its future Santa Monica office in California, Rovio hired Fox executive Andrew Stalbow, having been impressed with his work on the *Angry Birds Rio* collaboration. That same month, July 2011, another high-profile Hollywood executive got on board as special advisor: David Maisel from Marvel Entertainment. Maisel had joined Marvel in 1999 at a period when the comic business was in dire financial straits. He is credited with being the first Marvel executive to think up the idea of self-producing movies based on the company's portfolio of superheroes, rather than licensing out the rights to established Hollywood producers. He had started Marvel Studios, a subsidiary of Marvel Entertainment, to self-finance and develop films like *Iron Man*, *The Incredible Hulk*, and *The Avengers*, on which he served as executive producer. Maisel also had experience facing resistance from Hollywood. He vividly recalls the pushback he received at the Variety Venture Capital & New Media Summit in July 2011. "There were questions of 'Why are you betting on this?'

'You can't make a $100 million movie on your own.' 'Your last name isn't Spielberg.'"3 Ultimately, Maisel led the negotiation for Disney's acquisition of Marvel for $4 billion. His experience of uphill battles was something Rovio definitely needed if it wanted to fulfill Mikael Hed's own movie aspirations. In the newswire, Maisel was quoted as stating, "The business model, intellectual properties, and the franchise potential of *Angry Birds* give Rovio the most exciting prospects I have seen in the entertainment business since Marvel in 2003."4

Just before Stalbow and Maisel joined the party, Rovio demonstrated its Hollywood ambitions by acquiring its longtime vendor Studio Kombo. The Finnish animation studio which had been responsible for the *Angry Birds* animation cinematic was fully absorbed by Rovio as an in-house animation department. Lauri Konttori, a multitalented thinker who was very familiar with the *Angry Birds* backstory and universe, was promoted to creative director across all of Rovio's product lines. Rovio also beefed up the animation division by hiring additional talents such as head of animation Nick Dorra, who had previously run his own production company and had hired Kombo for an animated feature film just before that studio's acquisition by Rovio. Having seen the response of the fans to the *Angry Birds Rio* trailer, this expansion felt natural to everybody at Rovio, as Wilson recalls: "Some people were expecting the *Angry Birds* characters to actually show up in the *Rio* movie because of the tie-in, and they were very excited about it. This inevitably makes you consider the possibility seriously."5

Creating more video meant there would also be the need for more music and sounds than Ari Pulkkinen could possibly produce on his own. It was time for Rovio to hire in-house composers rather than freelancers, too. An acclaimed harpist and composer in Finland, Salla Hakkola, joined her brother Ilmari Hakkola, cofounder of Kombo and a Rovio veteran, to beef up the audio department. Ilmari lays it out:

> I pitched this vision that there should be a complete audio department. Rather than just one guy doing sounds for the game, there should be this hub through which music would be taken more seriously, because when you are looking at how much the company spends on game production, visuals and marketing and the little it is putting on music and sound—this must change. Sound is an integral part of the whole brand.[6]

Mikael Hed and Vesterbacka agreed this was a great idea, and Ilmari built up the department inside the company with his sister Salla, while also pursuing collaborations with musicians outside the company.

Salla Hakkola started breaking apart the original theme songs into little motifs that represented different story moments (the birds theme, the cue for the pigs, the heroic moments, etc.) as well as dividing the birds and pigs into two distinct styles. Salla explains:

> For the birds, we would use ethnic pipes, flutes, xylophones, while the pigs are heavier, clumsier while a bit more threatening too, so we would go with the brass: tuba, bassoon, trumpets, horns, etc. This mix made us double down on the Balkan style that had already viscerally inspired the original theme from Ari Pulkkinen. It's not trying to be fancy, it's fun, funky and ... wild. Perfect for the Angry Birds universe."[7]

At the beginning, the Hakkolas faced a bit of skepticism from others inside Rovio:

> We were very excited about our branding guidelines but some more senior people thought we had to go more

the traditional American Hollywood route. We even heard internally that some tunes sounded too Russian. But there is a counterargument to be made that music is a great way to take risks, because the worst that can happen is, if someone doesn't like it, they just turn the sound off. At the same time, if you deliver something signature, you can really differentiate and become really memorable. And in this way, it's a low-hanging fruit in the tree of brand-building and risk-taking.[8]

Niklas Hed encouraged the Hakkolas to persist and insist: "They don't know you. You need to prove your value to the others, he told us. Just keep pushing."[9]

New Ventures

Besides animation and music, consumer products were another area in which branching out had been proven to work. The Commonwealth plush toys were a huge success, as was the board action toy that Mattel had released earlier in January 2011. There, as well, Rovio expanded. Besides toys, Rovio now wanted to move into books. After all, it was partly through his hiatus in the comic book sector that Mikael Hed had developed his intention of building a brand. Looking at the big picture, reading was an activity that Rovio founders and key members were passionate about, especially as there was so much discussion in the media that gaming might be endangering this core skill. The Rovio management vowed to help reverse this trend.

The whole team consisted of avid readers, and they believed it was immensely important for them to read as much as they could, to stay abreast of the latest technological evolutions, newest business trends, and whatever helped fuel their imagination. They wouldn't be where they were if it wasn't for reading. Literature is also a founding pillar of the Finnish education system. Rovio seduced Sanna Lukander to join in as vice president of book publishing, in order to spearhead this daunting effort from ground zero. Lukander had had more than a decade's worth of experience in the field, mostly with Tammi Publishers, which was the third largest book publishing house in Finland. The first self-published Rovio book was a cookbook: *Bad Piggies' Egg Recipes*, released in October 2011, which was later awarded the "Best First Cookbook of the Year" at the 2012 Gourmand World Cookbook Awards.

Having Amazon and Barnes & Noble as existing partners certainly helped when entering the book business. To strengthen the relationship, Rovio let Barnes & Noble exclusively throw the second *BirdDay* party on December 11, 2011. At all points of sale, the kiddie playground areas were rebranded with *Angry Birds* visual assets, prizes given away, and a permanent area created for *Angry Birds* books, plush toys, and other goodies. Furthermore, just for that day, Vesterbacka convinced Starbucks to add *Angry Birds* cookies to the menu of the coffee giant's cafés located inside most of the Barnes & Noble stores. Marja Konttinen explains: "We wanted to test out the reception for edible merchandising. We don't have a chain of cafés, but they [Barnes & Noble] do. So it was really cool to give it a try with them. That's how you should be working with partners. You have shops in all the malls? We want to be in all those shops. We give you something in exchange that nobody else gets. But we want to get something out of it too."[10] Supporting the struggling Nook device at the moment Barnes & Noble needed help the most paid back big dividends when it came to the expansion of Rovio's physical merchandise. In 2012, a whole flurry of coloring books, comic strips, and arithmetic or alphabet learning books followed and were added to the same shelves. Over the following two years, the book department published hundreds of titles in over 30 languages. A monthly *Angry Birds* magazine was also published in many countries.

On October 20, 2011, Rovio celebrated Halloween again, after the tremendous results of the previous year (tellingly, many other developers tried to cram their own Halloween levels into game updates this time around). An additional set of themed levels was delivered in *Angry Birds Seasons* under the title *Ham'O'Ween*. The levels were accompanied by a four-minute cinematic that demonstrated Rovio's strong commitment to animation as a way to expand on the *Angry Birds* story. It also served as a grand introduction for a new character, Bubbles, the orange balloon bird.

The longest *Angry Birds* animation ever released at its time, *Ham'O'Ween* was used internally to lock a consistent art style across animation, games, books, and other products, once and for all. Before *Ham'O'Ween*, studio Kombo had created several shorts for *Angry Birds*, but the art style kept evolving and was a bit all over the place. Jean-Michel Boesch, the French art director who joined the team during the summer of 2011, used this opportunity to develop a base style that would ensure coherence and consistency across the board. The *Ham'O'Ween* animation has been viewed over 60 million times on YouTube, not counting TV ratings.

Last but not least, Rovio capitalized on the fans' many self-made costumes from the previous year, so this time around official *Angry Birds* costumes were made available. Beyond the revenue stream this brought in, easing the process of dressing up as your favorite *Angry Birds* character was a powerful viral branding tool. The whole *Ham'O'Ween* event was exclusively announced through the *Angry Birds* Facebook page so as to maintain Rovio's tight bond with its fan community.

Just two months later, the Rovio animation department released yet another animation cinematic, *Wreck the Halls*, this time to celebrate the holiday season update. This animation film was the first in Rovio history to be premiered on a TV station before hitting the web, when Nickelodeon aired it in the U.S., Latin America, and the U.K. on Saturday, December 17, 2011. For these two shorts, Ilmari and Salla Hakkola worked hard on creating distinctive scores, greatly expanding the soundscape of *Angry Birds*, and ensuring that each animation oozed its own atmosphere. Separately, Finnish singer Osmo Ikonen headed to the Espoo recording studio to lend his voice to the "Angry Birds Peace" song, which was used as the end-credits score for the *Wreck the Halls* animation at Christmas 2011, as a thank-you gift for the fans. Salla Hakkola, who coordinated the recording, remembers: "We played the song first internally to the whole team at the Christmas Party. Kaj Hed was so excited that he blurted out in broken English, with his arms in the air, 'I'm so amazing.' Mixing up 'I'm so amazed!' with 'It's so amazing!', carried away by his enthusiasm."[11] Ilmari Hakkola remembers this moment as the key to earning the other team members' trust: "Niklas came to us and said, 'Remember I told you that you had to prove your value to these people. You've done that tonight.'"[12]

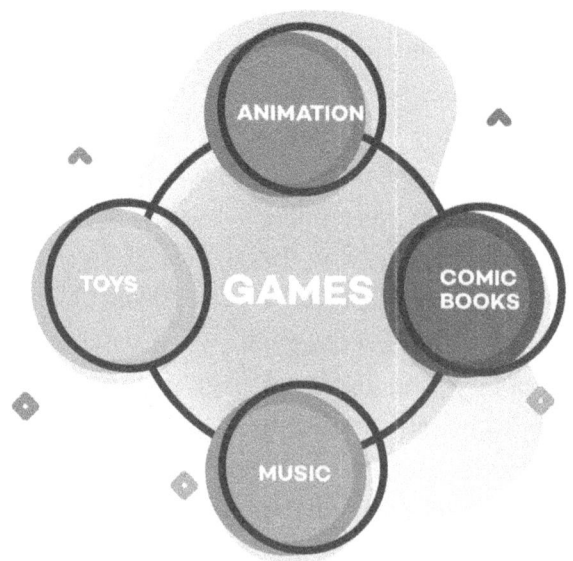

Rovio Products Divisions

The Triumvirate

From 2010 until mid-2012, CEO Mikael Hed and COO Niklas Hed, who were both stakeholders in the company, shared such a strong dynamic with Mighty Eagle Peter Vesterbacka that they practically managed day-to-day operations as a triumvirate. The three executives shared the same office space, separate from the other units. Mikael and Niklas discussed all key decisions and plans with Vesterbacka until a consensus was reached. They didn't completely disregard hierarchy but the level of trust established between them was such that it became secondary at times. In this triumvirate, there was a natural point of equilibrium between their different personalities, with each showing distinct strengths and weaknesses.

Of course, they were not insulated from the rest of the company and often gathered advice, information, and opinions from managers, directors, and employees. Furthermore, Mikael often sat in board meetings where he got to listen to the cold-headed warnings of his older and wiser directors. Ultimately, though, everything got discussed thoroughly between the three men.

All three were convinced that the triumvirate was the best possible structure to manage a small to medium-sized startup (we'll see later how it had its limits when the company evolved into a "big startup"). Based on my own experiences, I am in complete agreement. A one-man-show can often lead to autocracy and can end in a debacle. Having two leaders improves the situation, so long as the two persons don't share the same character profiles and have complementary skillsets. However, if there's a major disagreement between the two, they will find themselves without a mediator. That's where a third person can save a lot of time in reaching a consensus. There will be fights—in fact, there *must* be fights—but with a triumvirate they won't end in gridlock.

There were numerous clashes and disputes at Rovio in the early years of its growth and success. One thing that the triumvirate frequently fought about in 2011 and 2012 was the perceived arrogance Vesterbacka sometimes displayed in press interviews. "There were interviews where I was sitting next to him, and I would pause and ask myself, 'What did he just say?'"[13] says Matt Wilson. He made headlines with extravagant statements such as "There is no role model: Nobody has done what we're doing,"[14] "Console games are dying,"[15] "We've grown much faster than Facebook, Twitter, YouTube—you name it,"[16] and—hyperbole alert—"We are going to be bigger than Disney."[17] Part of his job was to seek exposure, grab headlines, coin soundbites, and generate buzz, and he knew exactly what he was doing. According to Vesterbacka himself, "One could take it as arrogance, but it positioned us as the hungry underdog. When you get compared to Disney or 'All of Television,' it is humbling in a way. But generally, in a 'David versus Goliath' situation, most people will tend to relate to and root for the challenger."[18]

In interviews and articles, Vesterbacka often put *Angry Birds* into the same bracket as some of the world's biggest brand names. Rovio and *Angry Birds* paled in comparison to legendary duos such as Nintendo and Mario or Disney and Mickey Mouse, and the conclusion was usually that Rovio wasn't there yet and there was still a long way to go. But the speculation was all about "Rovio vs. Disney," "*Angry Birds* vs. *Mario*," and even once, in *Forbes*, "*Angry Birds* vs. All of Television" (comparing respective consumption times). This all sounded infinitely more sensational and high level than if it had been "Rovio vs. Halfbrick" or "*Angry Birds* vs. [e.g.] *Temple Run*." It was brilliant public relations spin. By positioning the company as the underdog in heavyweight matches it couldn't yet win, Vesterbacka avoided the temptation of casting *Angry Birds* as a rival to other mobile counterparts. Through a wonderful smokescreen trick, he ensured that the brand was not only ahead of the pack but in a different league altogether.

Euphoria was another feeling that Rovians experienced as they become the center of attention during trade shows or fan events. Imagine walking around an industry event and, for the entire day, all your peers—often people you admire—approach you to say how much they love the game you represent and that you rock, by the way. When Vesterbacka walked on stage at Zeitgeist Americas 2011 to make a speech, skateboarder Tony Hawk was playing *Angry Birds* against Scooter Braun (Justin Bieber's and PSY's agent) on the giant screen. After winning the round, Tony Hawk welcomed the Red Bird T-shirt which Vesterbacka offered him as a prize, and bumped his fist: "Thanks a lot, man." Are you completely sure you could keep a cool head while adrenaline flows through your veins and you're bursting with pride?

When Vesterbacka got invited to the Finnish Presidential Ball on behalf of Rovio, he couldn't wear his Red Hoodie, as the dress code for men was formal. Instead, his wife got to wear a specially designed *Angry Birds* ball gown—the image went around the world, a first for the Finnish Presidential Ball. Subsequently, not a week went by without Vesterbacka invariably hearing some remark about the stunt in one country or another.

And what if the U.S. President Barack Obama was a fan of your game? Are you absolutely sure you could keep your feet on the ground if the leaders of the world were to shake your hand while praising your product? Come to think of it, *Angry Birds* may be one of very few topics about which the governments of Russia, China, and the U.S. are all in complete agreement. As one of the primary faces of the company, Vesterbacka got to meet all these heads of state. To say he sometimes experienced a confidence boost is an understatement.

The Red Hoodie Effect

There was also the Red Hoodie effect at play. It is to Rovians what the Superman suit is to Clark Kent. When Mikael Hed represented Finland in the Ernst & Young World Entrepreneur Award in Monaco for the global finals in 2018, there were over 50 top entrepreneurs from around the world as well as a bunch of world-class media present. Over two days, the reporters and the jury met the entrepreneurs. It was a very stylish event so everyone else was dressed in suit and tie. Mikael, clad in the Red Hoodie, had 52 interviews over one and a half days. Not even the founder of LinkedIn got that much attention. Sara Antila, the head of communications who had joined Rovio a year prior, had to stop journalists from interrupting interviews already on the go. Mikael had rock star status. In Monaco, Antila and Mikael Hed conducted a test to clock how long it took before somebody walked up to Mikael to talk or take a picture. It took 14 seconds. Generation Y kids call that peacocking.

In the flesh, Vesterbacka is a very accessible man, as demonstrated by the affection his colleagues have for him. Philip Hickey describes their work relationship, saying, "The best thing about Peter is he's always willing to listen to new ideas and to talk about how we can make things bigger and better. It's quite inspiring how he's very forward thinking. And he's a lot of fun. He keeps the job fun, and it's a very important quality that a lot of people overlook."[19] Rovians are also quick to point out that Vesterbacka is "crazy," but you can tell it is meant in a good way.

Niklas and Mikael Hed were closer to the production pipeline. They were therefore far more aware of the lead time necessary to polish a work-in-progress until the quality was right. They were also more aware of the underlying risk: potential failure to deliver. In contrast, Vesterbacka's focus was about striking the iron while it was hot.

The complementary nature of their skills are precisely what makes it so great that these three men found each other in business life. Eventually, through long-winded confrontations and heated debates, the three men always reached a better understanding of each other, and learned how they best functioned as a team. When that dynamic settles in, when trust is fully established between all three individuals, when personal attributes, strengths, and weaknesses are transparently established, then and only then can management really thrive. Patience is necessary from every party, though, because it can take a year or two to reach that level of osmosis.

One thing that has to be credited to the Rovio triumvirate is that they always swallowed their pride when their backs were against the wall and decision time had come. They always kept driving the company forward and never let their battles and doubts slow it down. Although things changed over time as the company grew in size and more people became involved with management, Rovio remained remarkably agile in the way it worked. The Heds and Vesterbacka also did their best to keep the window of opportunity as wide open as possible, since that happened to be the one thing they unanimously agree upon.

Vesterbacka wanted Mikael and Niklas Hed to build Rovio big, fast, and furious. Mikael Hed wanted to build big, solid, and reliable. They all had "big" in common. They were all ambitious visionaries. It was over pace and prioritization that they argued.

If you removed Vesterbacka from the equation, the company probably wouldn't have become so well known so fast in those early days. Peter, like Kaj, brought audacity, self-confidence, and ambition to the table. On the other hand, Vesterbacka wasn't a prophet—sometimes his predictions didn't materialize, as many Rovians have pointed out. If you were to remove Mikael Hed's clarity from the setup, unleashing someone like Vesterbacka without any boundaries or discipline, or with no one to contradict them, you may soon have a company that was going into buffer overflow. If you have a hard time convincing a colleague about something, it helps you rehearse and refine your discourse before you go out to persuade business partners or public opinion.

A One-Hit Wonder?

By the end of 2011, Rovio was doing a tremendous job at keeping its dirty laundry private. Despite the heated disagreements and the pressure of being in the spotlight, the public-facing shop window remained shiny and spotless. *Angry Birds* finished the year stronger than ever, and became one of the fastest, as well as cheapest, brands ever built.

In October 2011, Rovio published a press release announcing that its games had been downloaded 400 million times across all platforms. It also communicated that 30 million users played at least one of the games daily, and 130 million on a monthly basis. In November 2011, downloads reached 500 million. By December 16, 2011, when *the Financial Times* interviewed the company's marketing director, Ville Heijari, it was already 600 million.[20] By December 31, 2011, the tally was 648 million, 200 million of whom connected during the last month of the year. On Christmas Day alone, 6.5 million downloads of *Angry Birds* were generated out of a total of 242 million apps, accounting for a 2.7 percent market share.[21]

In the fiscal year 2011, Rovio generated €75.4 million (approximately $106.3 million) in revenue, a 1,000 percent jump from the previous year's total. Roughly 30 percent of that income derived from licensing royalties. T-shirts and plush toys were both selling extremely well, at a rate of 1 million units per month for each line, according to September 2011 reports.[22] Earnings before tax were €48 million ($67.6 million), a staggering 64 percent operating margin. Yet there were still many doubts inside and outside the gaming industry. Analysts suggested that Rovio was at risk of becoming a one-hit wonder. How could it top its phenomenal hit game? The *Angry Birds* fad might come to an end the following year, they warned. The bubble was about to burst. Benedict Evans, mobile analyst at Enders Analysis, told *the Financial Times*: "They have yet to show they can reliably produce a flow of hits. Disney is not one property, it's 50 properties."[23]

Behind the scenes, Rovio was already working on a bunch of leads for future growth. Among other tracks, China offered a bounty that the company, like many other successful developers of the time, had its eyes on.

CHAPTER TEN

Big China

In 2011, the U.S. was Rovio's biggest market in terms of income, but when looking at the daily stats, it became ever clearer that China was the fastest-growing nation in terms of device activations and app downloads. Apple was reporting huge iPhone and iPad sales numbers in the region, and Android was performing even better. Several local electronics manufacturers such as Lenovo, Huawei, Vivo, and Xiaomi were betting heavily on the Android OS by bringing out local smartphone and tablet models that were cheaper at retail than any other similar product on the planet. The big legacy carriers of the region, including China Mobile, China Telecom, and China Unicom, also supported the Android platform.

As with pretty much every other trend that occurred in the mobile app economy, Rovio spotted this one live in its own analytics. Matt Wilson candidly explains: "We see spikes in the market at the same time they happen, so we spot them pretty much when the manufacturers know, which gives us a couple of weeks' head start compared to analysts and press. Often, they report about something as if it was fresh news from this morning, and I feel like, 'Yeah, we knew that since last month ... Oh, but wait a minute, they didn't!'"[1] Knowledge-hungry people don't simply read the news—they also sift through stats.

When made aware of the situation, Peter Vesterbacka convinced the others to immediately give him the mission to go on and start the work in China, without delay.

First Moves

Rovio's first move in the region was to replicate its Android strategy by ensuring its apps were available on all screens and platforms. Due to a long-lasting feud with the Chinese government regarding censorship on search engines, Google was not officially welcome in China, which prevented it from running its Android Market (later renamed Google Play) for apps there. Many companies were trying to take advantage of this situation by rolling out their own Android app stores. As a result, there were no fewer than 400 Android channels available in China, which was about the same number as in the rest of the world combined. If you weren't already aware that China is its own universe, this simple fact might give you a clue. Conquering this unique country is not an easy feat for anyone, as Rovio was about to find out. China is so colossal that it makes the biggest of companies feel small and humble.

To serve all 400 Android app stores without wasting too much time, Rovio contracted a Shenzhen-based startup called iDream-Sky, which focused solely on the distribution of foreign mobile hits into "Big China" (a term that includes Taiwan, Hong Kong, and Macao). iDreamSky's services encompassed uploading the game to every store and negotiating feature placements and other promotions. Due to the exceptional appeal of *Angry Birds*, Rovio entered a nonexclusive deal with iDreamSky, while also retaining direct relations with the top three telecom operators: China Telecom, China Mobile, and China Unicom. As in the Western world, it was the free, ad-supported and iAP-enabled version of the game that was distributed to the Android ecosystem.

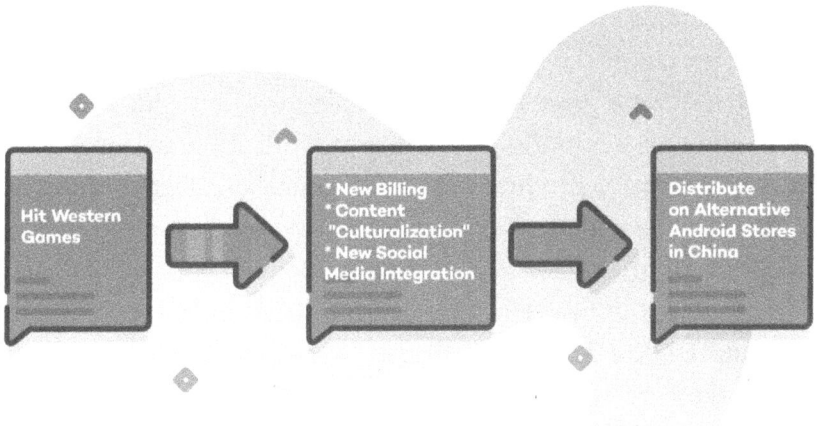

The Culturalization Process

Hired in the summer of 2011, Henri Holm, who had handled affairs in many Asian countries for Nokia, was put in charge of spearheading business development for Rovio in Asia. Holm started working on relations with key partners not only in Korea—with global manufacturers such as Samsung and LG Electronics—and Japan, the motherland of video games, but also in India, Thailand, Indonesia, and ... China. It was clear to him that the work in China alone was going to drain a considerable amount of time, energy, and attention from Vesterbacka and him in the coming months and years.

The first multi-pronged content effort specifically aimed at the Chinese market included a mix of digital and physical products. The most prominent prong came in the form of an update to the *Angry Birds Seasons* set within the scenario of a typical Chinese festive celebration called the Moon Festival (or, more formally, Mid-Autumn Festival). The extra levels featured a special version of the theme song that incorporated typical Chinese instruments and sounds. The update was made available to players worldwide, which globalized awareness of a holiday previously little known in Western countries. Back in Espoo, the newly founded comic department produced 16 digital pages of Chinese-style comic strips telling the tale of the Moon Festival from the *Angry Birds'* perspective. These were given away for free, along with the update.

In the real world, Rovio teamed up with PPW, a Hong Kong licensing firm, to produce branded mooncakes. It's traditional in China to offer mooncakes to your relatives or employees during the Mid-Autumn Festival. The item is about as popular as chocolate eggs during Easter in Western countries. PPW helped Rovio spread Red Bird Mooncakes to every major city in Greater China. The mooncake operation was a success, as the new game update resonated with Chinese fans and media. Bringing a touch of freshness into an ancient tradition, the mooncakes were in such demand that PPW would turn their production into an annual event.

Rovio also used the opportunity of the Moon Festival update to gain ground in the local social media landscape, opening and feeding accounts on popular social networks like Sina Weibo, QQ, RenRen, Youku, and Tencent Weibo. At this stage, the Chinese-language content was written in the Espoo headquarters, as Rovio counted a Chinese national, Tianyi Pan, among its marketing-communication staffers. Raised in Finland since the age of six, Pan's first encounter with the Rovio team preceded the company's existence. As a teenager in 2003, Pan was in the audience when Niklas Hed and his friends won the coding competition that led to the foundation of Rovio: "My friends and I actually voted for them!" Pan recalls.[2] Later on, while studying economics at Aalto University, Pan got into filmmaking with a group of friends. He crossed Peter Vesterbacka's path in 2009 when he pitched a film-related idea at a startup event where Vesterbacka was also present. Pan was thinking about joining a Finnish paper manufacturing company to work on his graduation thesis when he received a call from Vesterbacka. Pan recalls Vesterbacka telling him, "No, no. Don't go there. Come work for Rovio instead. We have this game, *Angry Birds* ..."[3]

The Piracy Problem

Shortly after the Moon Festival, Rovio authorized a special edition of Red Bird shoes with trend-setting Chinese online store Letao. The reception of the shoes was Rovio's first disappointment in the region. Although the announcement drove quite a bit of buzz, the shoes did not sell very well after the initial rush in the first 24 hours. This lukewarm reception, an anomaly in the *Angry Birds* bubble, was the first signal that Rovio faced a well-known problem in the Chinese market: rampant piracy and ubiquitous dirt-cheap counterfeit goods. All popular brands deal with this plague in some measure. It's hard to drive high sales numbers of consumer goods if the few official items that exist are drowned in an ocean of unlicensed items of all sorts, all changing hands for unbelievably cheap prices.

Let me share a brief instant of my personal life to help you grasp the extent of the problem. In November 2011, I was visiting former business partners in Hong Kong for a week. I had lived and worked there between 2002 and 2006 while I was marketing director of online retailer Lik-Sang.com. In Mong Kok, a popular neighborhood of Kowloon, there's a place called the Ladies Market. In the past, I've often used that street as one of my sources of information to determine "what's hot right now." There, the street vendors offer unlicensed goods of every kind, shamelessly exploiting the most famous and iconic characters and brand names. The range of copycat items on display is unique. Since the plagiarists are unhampered by contractual duties of any sort, they are free to do exactly what consumers demand, and at a faster pace than those working in the formal economy ever could. The only limit is their imagination.

The knock-off manufacturers and street vendors in the Mong Kok area of Hong Kong function with absolutely no administrative constraint. Economics is all that matters to them, which is precisely why that street is a good indicator of the pulse of the market. If you walk through the Ladies Market and count how many times you see Mario, Naruto, Goku, Hello Kitty, the Powerpuff Girls, Spider-Man, Master Chief, or Pikachu, it will give you a pretty good idea of the mindshare these brands currently enjoy. As I wandered through the Ladies Market on that particular day in 2011, I witnessed a sight I had never experienced before: One brand had organically taken over everything in sight—*Angry Birds*. It was everywhere. Red, red, red. Even *Gundam* had vanished to free up shelf space. *Angry Birds* towels, *Angry Birds* board games, *Angry Birds* plush toys, figurines, keychains, posters, flags, banners, magnets, clocks, watches, lighters, stickers, costumes, T-shirts, slippers, sweatshirts, pants, underwear—for miles on end. It was a total blitz. Meanwhile, the Chinese news reported that *Angry Birds*-themed attractions had popped up in some of the country's major theme parks, completely unauthorized by Rovio!

An optimist would concentrate on the fact that this proved the unparalleled appeal of the game in the region and that the window of opportunity for the brand was wide open. After all, imitation is the sincerest form of flattery. Although unlicensed and unwanted, the exposure served as a marketing vehicle, nonetheless. But Rovio was becoming aware that cleaning up the local market of knock-off goods would be a Herculean task. The key problem was that unlicensed, low-quality counterfeit items are extremely cheap to make. How could Rovio compete with them? How would customers differentiate official products from the clones? What is the incentive for a manufacturer to pay for the license royalty if that ends up making its product more expensive than the ubiquitous copies? These questions would eventually need answers, because consumer products had been a solid source of revenue in other markets and were a key part of Rovio's big plans for China.

The more Henri Holm delved into China, the more he reckoned that he couldn't possibly do this alone, even with Vesterbacka actively backing him. Holm was supposedly in charge of Rovio's movements across Asia, and yet China was proving to be a continent in and of itself, at least in terms of workload. Henri Holm and Vesterbacka started spreading the word at every Asian trade conference they visited that they intended to open shop in Shanghai, throwing out the fishnets to attract potential partners. Quickly, they received an interesting call from Paul Chen, an industry veteran with 20 years' experience under his belt.

A Guam-native, Chen had spent most of his life and career in Los Angeles. All his previous endeavors had had a hardware component tied to the product, which had led Chen to visit China-based factories on a very frequent basis for much of the previous decade. He knew the country—its idiosyncrasies and distinctive rules—very well. He also happened to speak and write Mandarin. Chen was officially appointed General Manager of China in February 2012. He was joined in his mission by Tianyi Pan, who relocated from Espoo to Shanghai at the same time, to get closer to his family.

Year of the Dragon

Chen and Pan arrived in China to find an office space full of furniture still under plastic wraps, shipped to them from Europe, to ensure both Nordic-level quality and brand consistency across all the international offices. Although the furniture was present, basic utilities were still not in place: There was no electricity, no internet, and no (vital) air-conditioning. For the first couple of months, Chen and Pan had to rent a service apartment with internet connection, where they could work together until everything was connected back at the base. Despite these hiccups, the pair hit the ground running, without worrying too much about either comfort or aesthetics.

China's complex bureaucracy unfortunately slowed down their ramp-up. Chen explains, "We had cubicles for 25 people, but we had no people."[4] In order to hire staff legally in China, Rovio first needed to register itself as a W.F.O.E. (Wholly Foreign-Owned Enterprise)—a process that takes anything from six months to a year and is heavy on paperwork. It took four months before two extra account managers were allowed to join the setup, through a governmental organization called FinChi. FinChi is a soft-landing services company owned by the Finnish government which helps Finnish companies set up shop in China by providing them with a temporary office space, a registered address, and administrative services if they need them—essentially, an executive suite environment reserved for Finnish companies. It would eventually take ten months to fully form the legal entity of Rovio China and start hiring a larger team, with a financial controller, a couple of lawyers, a social media manager, a game distribution manager, and a few more account managers and business developers.

The hiring process was not the only thing that slowed Rovio down in its expansion into the Far East. Adapting the business model to local rituals, laws, culture, and commercial conduct in China proved to be a steep learning process that required plenty of flexibility. For a company that was used to going against the grain and disrupting conventions everywhere it went, trying to achieve the same in China was sometimes difficult. Then again, if Rovio hadn't gone to China, business would have continued without it. This isn't a country that waits for you.

The conquest of the Chinese market has been a humbling undertaking, even with the advantage of having 40 million monthly active users in the country. Rovio's crazy growth numbers simply don't impress there. Over the last decade, figures like these have become almost ordinary in China. They are used to financial figures and audiences running into hundreds of millions and billions, and you sense this in any negotiation process.

Peter Vesterbacka, the big believer in the China opportunity internally, understood it would require some adjustments. In his view, the globalization of intellectual property (IP) is achieved through an aggregation of efforts toward cultural localization. At the opening of the Shanghai office, Pan distinctly recalls Vesterbacka declaring to the regional staff, "We want to be more Chinese than the Chinese." The Mighty Bird himself elaborates:

> What does it mean to be more Chinese than the Chinese? Obviously I'm not Chinese, and I didn't speak a word of Mandarin. So this meant we needed to hire local talent and we needed to deeply understand local culture. My favorite example is what we did with the Moon Festival. [...] We're not just bringing *Angry Birds* to China, at the same time we're bringing cool aspects of Chinese culture to the Western world. That's the kind of experiences I want to create.[5]

The big stunt they pulled on January 19, 2012 for the Chinese Lunar New Year was further clear evidence of that mindset.

Out of all the Chinese zodiac symbols, the Dragon is uncontestably the most popular. To celebrate the beginning of the Lunar New Year, the eleventh update to *Angry Birds Seasons—Year of the Dragon*—was entirely dedicated to Chinese culture, in terms of style, references, and storyline. Even some gameplay elements were adapted: for example, the Mighty Eagle was replaced by the Mighty Dragon as a one-off, and depicted as attracted to red koi rather than sardines. Gold blocks also appeared in the *Angry Birds* environment because the cliché has some truth to it: Chinese people tend to love gold and the prestige it implies. The update was once again accompanied by a free digital comic story, the previous one for the Moon Festival update having been so well received.

The main event of the show was clearly the animation cartoon put together to broadcast the new chapter in the story. Two and a half minutes long, it matched the quality, scope, and ambition of the *Ham'O'Ween* tour de force, proving just how judicious Rovio had been to acquire Kombo. Whereas the Moon Festival theme song had simply been a remix of the original *Angry Birds* tune with tiny Chinese touches added, the score of the *Year of the Dragon* piece was a unique composition, with which Salla Hakkola had plenty of fun going over the top. The result was a symphony of some of those very special instruments and sounds that China has to offer, standing out from every other track in the *Angry Birds* repertoire. The proof of all the hard work that went into this video clip, and at the same time of Rovio's commitment to China, is in the credits list: 65 talented creatives participated in the making of those 150 seconds. The cartoon was the second *Angry Birds* cinematic trailer to be premiered on U.S. television before going online, again featuring on Nickelodeon, as Rovio stuck to its habit of globalizing local events. The video has been seen an additional 33 million times on YouTube and has also made the rounds on Youku and Tudou, at the time the two leading video-sharing sites in China (which later merged into one single group). This was Rovio's first true 360-degree cross-media effort, telling the story through animation, music, online comic books, marketing, and gaming simultaneously. "It laid the foundations for the later global cross-media launches that we were planning for 2012. *Year of the Dragon* served like a practice run for that,"[6] Pan points out.

In terms of business development, too, the team couldn't have hoped for a better start, as Rovio nailed a big promo campaign with long-time partner China Mobile. In exchange for a timed-exclusive window of 24 hours for China Mobile against other national stores for the *Year of the Dragon* update on Android, the world-leading cell phone provider gave *Angry Birds* a free ride across all its owned media and various promotional tools to reach out to its 670 million subscribers. These benefits included full-frontal featuring on its Android App Store, a banner on its high-trafficked website linking to the game download page, and an embed for the trailer, as well as—the icing on the cake—SMS text messages sent to all customers. In social media, Sina Weibo (the Chinese Twitter/X) agreed to promote the trailer link atop all feeds to its huge user-base in exchange for being the first to break the news. Rovio also took to the streets, again with the help of licensing partner PPW. Whereas mooncakes are the customary gifts given during the Moon Festival, at Chinese New Year tradition dictates that relatives offer "red pockets" (*hongbao* in Mandarin) filled with presents to one other, while bosses hand out red envelopes containing a bit of cash to all their employees. For the Year of the Dragon, Red Bird pockets were produced and dispatched nationwide.

While traveling across the country to oversee all these operations, Vesterbacka made sure he emphasized the benefit of Rovio's efforts for the Chinese nation. Pan notes, "Whenever Peter talks to Chinese officials, you can be sure you'll hear him say, 'We showed the Moon Festival and the Year of the Dragon to tens of millions of people overseas.' That makes quite an impression."[7]

Lost in Translation

Rovio had made a big entrance in China, showing the kind of flair industry observers had become accustomed to. However, "wow" events and day-to-day business are very different things. While *Year of the Dragon* provided ace content for delivery at the macro level, the packaging and distribution at the micro level suffered a few hiccups in the early stages. From this point onward,

Rovio set out to deploy *Angry Birds* directly to Chinese Android channels. Since there were 400 such channels in China, all with specific requirements, the decision was made to focus on the top 20 during the first phase, as these represented 80 percent of the regional app economy. The problem was that, besides this deployment to the channels, you also needed a billing SDK (Software Development Kit—think of it as a mobile plug-in you can easily attach to your app without the need to program the extra features from scratch), to collect in-app purchases and micro-transactions.

Unlike in the West, ecommerce in China (as in many other Asian countries) doesn't revolve around credit cards. Many people don't have a Visa or MasterCard, but even for those who do, it's not the norm to input your digits into a mobile device to purchase something virtual. The most popular form of payment in the region at the time was carrier-based, customers either paying through SMS or charging the purchase to a monthly bill. Furthermore, to give all customers another, possibly preferred option, local distributors like iDreamSky, Yodo1, or Chu Kong also supported ePay (the local equivalent of PayPal), AliPay, and, subsequently, WeChat Pay. SMS payments and bill-to-carrier are payment methods that had become very popular in many countries, and Rovio provided them in its Android games extensively. Fortumo, a service provider from Estonia, enabled this for Rovio (among many other mobile developers) through an easy-to-implement SDK. Unfortunately, there was one country where Fortumo did not provide any solution whatsoever and that country was, you guessed it, China. For a long time, the builds of the games available on Chinese channels contained insufficient local payment options for in-app purchases and converted poorly from a monetization perspective.

Another area where Rovio suffered was copyright issues and brand protection in China. App developers won't be surprised by this revelation: "Hey, we all get massively pirated in China." But infringement goes way beyond apps and games getting cracked and shared on the internet there (that issue is rampant, and each company deals with it in its own good way, Rovio included). That's just the tip of the iceberg. Rovio was also facing novel kinds of hassle.

The company's big plans in China always relied on consumer goods as one of the pillars for monetization, given the success it had garnered with that strategy elsewhere. Facing an ocean of counterfeit products, it would prove to be difficult to work with licensees in the same way as in other areas of the world. The fight against piracy is a bit like the War on Drugs: You spend a lot of time, energy, and money containing it but you still know deep down that you'll never get rid of it. Rovio did invest in brand protection, factory raids, and local police cooperation, but tackling the problem only with a stick isn't effective; you need to dangle the proverbial carrot, too. If you want to sell goods in China, on top of fighting counterfeit goods, you need to give Chinese consumers an incentive to buy the official ones. And even before that, you need to give consumers a way to recognize the official products and tell them apart from the counterfeits.

Like many foreign brands before, Rovio adopted the tried-and-proven "official store" angle. This consists of opening branded stores in prime locations and getting the message across that official products are sold only in those stores, and that everything else is fake. This has proven to work remarkably well for many—for example, Adidas owns and runs over 7,000 shops in China. Disney has also followed the same path.

Rovio instructed licensing agent PPW to go out and find good locations in major commercial centers across China. Since PPW dealt with state-of-the-art venues, the protocol required that Rovio China and PPW prove they were the legitimate license-holder in China for the lines of consumer goods they were about to offer (such as clothing and plush toys) and for using the brand on the store front. This, ironically enough, in an effort to combat the presence of counterfeit goods in those prime locations.

As soon as Rovio filed the paperwork to extend its *Angry Birds*™ Chinese trademark into other domains beyond the category of "computer games," Rovio discovered that the brand was already registered in 70 of the 140 available categories, including the crucial "apparel" classification, by a multitude of different applicants. From a Western perspective, you might assume that all you needed to do was to put a lawyer on the case and oppose the registration on "first use" grounds. And Rovio did initially go down this route. When doing so, it convinced PPW to open the stores anyway and promise the local authorities that the appropriate documents would be produced within six months. Nine *Angry Birds* stores duly opened in good shopping malls in major Chinese cities.

Whether through delays with court hearings or lengthy turnarounds with paperwork, Rovio discovered how complex and protracted bureaucracy can be in China. With his eye on the clock, Paul Chen in the Shanghai office envisaged negotiating a buyout with all these so-called "trademark scalpers." This, after all, was the way most giant multinationals entering China dealt with this problem, he had heard. However, this procedure would also cost a lot of money. When you are active in so many categories, buying back all the different applicants can quickly mount up into the high millions. Not to mention the moral dilemma this poses: By undertaking these buyouts wouldn't you just be encouraging more trademark scalping?

Unfortunately, six months later, Rovio still hadn't recovered the *Angry Birds* trademarks in the apparel category and had also failed to produce the documents it had promised to the management committees of the malls. Call it unjust, ironic, or paradoxical all you want, the harsh reality was that Rovio ended up getting kicked out of its stores because it could not prove to be the legitimate license-holder of its own brand in malls where counterfeit goods weren't welcome.

Many other foreign companies have had difficulties penetrating the Chinese market, most of them much more powerful and wealthier than Rovio. Google is blocked by the so-called "Great Firewall of China," as are Facebook.com and CNN.com. The country didn't approve the official release of a Sony or Nintendo console until 2014. *World of Warcraft* also had administrative headaches when launching in the country. The closest point of comparison is Apple, which, when introducing the iPad in China, got sued by Proview Technology (Shenzhen) for copyright infringement. According to legal testimony in the ensuing court case, Apple had retained British lawyers several years before to set up a shell company, IP Application Development, to buy up rights to the name "iPad" around the world. Apple paid $50,000 to a Proview Technology affiliate in Taiwan for that company's iPad trademarks in various countries. When the iPad came out, Proview Technology (Shenzhen) said that the Taiwanese subsidiary was not entitled to conduct transactions regarding the trademark for China. Proview Technology filed a trademark infringement case against Apple in a Shenzhen court, and the case ended up in the provincial court. Apple vowed to vigorously defend itself and fought the lawsuit, but in vain. Things took an ugly turn when Proview sought injunctions forcing retailers to remove the iPad from shelves in two cities. Under pressure, Apple ended up settling the lawsuit and buying the Chinese "iPad" trademark for $60 million. Teck-Zhung Wong, a Beijing-based analyst with technology research firm IDC, commented at the time: "The settlement is great news for Apple. It just allows them to get on with business and stop being distracted. The new iPad has arrived so late to the China market that, if they drag it out any longer, Apple stands to lose quite a bit more."[8] In China, pragmatism prevails.

Rovio's trademark battles frustratingly dragged on for what felt like an eternity, to the despair of the marketers and business developers involved in the push to China. Despite the technical and administrative issues in the early stages, the efforts in China generated a lot of positive results for Rovio. To have a foothold in Shanghai helped organize local co-promotions and marketing stunts that would be otherwise unmanageable.

In the buildup to the London Summer Olympics 2012, Tianyi Pan orchestrated a collaboration with Coca-Cola China that involved viral animations and branded *Angry Birds* games. The theme of the campaign was that *Angry Birds* and Coca-Cola supported the Chinese Olympics Team. Rovio produced the video involving the birds and five top Chinese athletes selected for the promotion. A special web-browser game was developed especially for the occasion. Instead of shooting birds at pigs, you flung them at drum symbols that unlocked "beats," as Coca-Cola called them in the campaign. The earned beats could be exchanged for free song downloads.

In Hong Kong, meanwhile, Henri Holm scored another deal with the MTR Corporation, which runs Hong Kong's subway system. The MTR is crucial to Hong Kong life, with millions of people using it every day. For several weeks, the MTR Corporation was allowed to print *Angry Birds*-branded tickets. The idea behind this was that fans would want to collect the tickets, and that this would organically increase the usage of the subway service. Miniature plastic train cars that resembled *Angry Birds* characters were also produced in limited quantities. They could be purchased only in subway stations, the goal being, for MTR Corporation, to score coolness points among customers and increase their attachment to the service.

The largest-scale campaign in China was a collaboration with McDonald's which was negotiated by the team in the second half of 2012. The fast-food giant had been offering piles of cash to get *Angry Birds* in Happy Meals in some form or another for some time. The omnipresence of McDonald's restaurants was appealing, and Rovio sought a way to make a deal that ensured it brought genuine value to McDonald's customers and *Angry Birds* fans. Rovio took the "*Angry Birds* Magic" concept, which they had used earlier at Barnes & Noble in the U.S., to a whole new level. A geolocation-based system was set up inside the iOS version of the game, in order to detect whether a player was near one of the McDonald's restaurants in China. When they approached one of the flagged spots, the game alerted them that there was something special inside McDonald's, prompting them to enter. When they were standing at the right GPS coordinates, *Angry Birds* loaded a special game mode "courtesy of McDonald's." Those without GPS enabled could buy a collectible toy containing a special code over the counter. In five major locations, the Golden Arches were transformed into slingshots by adding gigantic plastic Red Birds on top of them and rubber handles attached to the bars of the *M*. Menus, posters, and banners were all themed for the promotion. and big fat plush toys were added to the decor. All 1,800 fast-food restaurants run by McDonald's in China took part in the campaign. McDonald's also committed to a spend in the advertising channels inside the *Angry Birds* games, for the ten-week duration of the operation. For this campaign, Rovio and McDonald's scooped the 2012 Effie China Award for Marketing Efficiency. The Effie Awards are internationally recognized in the marketing and advertising industries because the key criterion for selection is the effectiveness of the campaigns, measured by triggered sales and market share gained.

In Asia as a whole, the Rovio team also scored a significant exposure deal with leading broadcaster Fuji TV in Japan, in which Rovio agreed to show the company's Tokyo HQ building with its logo on top in the *Angry Birds Seasons* update *Cherry Blossoms*. They also organized a big event in Jakarta, Indonesia, for the launch of *Angry Birds Friends* on Facebook in February of 2012.

Jakarta happened to be the Facebook capital of the world at the time, with 17 million accounts in one single city. The game hadn't previously appeared on the platform because the technology was not ready to run it smoothly just yet. The game could run at only 20–25 frames per second (FPS) on Flash technology, which made gameplay glitchy. When HTML5 came out, the developers could now run the game at 30 FPS. In a big shopping mall, in front of the Indonesian media, as well as Bloomberg and Reuters, the team and the fans counted down from ten to zero until Kai Sauer, the Finnish ambassador to Indonesia, cut the ribbon to launch the game on Facebook. When the game appeared, the attendance was invited to come forward and be the first to try it out on the giant screen in the middle of the mall, with the Indonesian Minister of Culture and Education Mohammad Nuh kicking things off. All fans were also handed *Angry Birds* cupcakes and plush toys. Just over two weeks later, the game already had 3.9 million monthly active users and 930,000 daily active users on Facebook, according to analytics site AppData. Like all Facebook games, *Angry Birds Friends* was free to play from the beginning. To boost monetization, four new power-ups were introduced: King Sling, Super Seeds, Sling Scope, and Birdquake joined the Mighty Eagle. All could be earned through gameplay, gifted by friends, or purchased for prices between $1 and $40 on Facebook.

Lessons Learned

By the end of 2012, Rovio had 12 employees in China but still found it difficult to move at the fast pace it was accustomed to in other countries. All people involved in the big move are quick to confess that the Chinese market has often proven to be a tough experience. Nonetheless, like most foreign companies setting their sights on the Chinese market, Rovio doggedly learned the cultural differences and figured out the market practices along the way. Not everything in business has to be a mad rush: Speed is not the answer to every challenge.

Rovio's experience in China had and has wider lessons for the company. As Rovio matures, it must prove its capacity for endurance, persistency, and patience, which are equally important in certain circumstances. Vesterbacka concedes, "We're thinking and moving very fast. But when necessary, we are ready to take our time. It's important to persevere in China if we want *Angry Birds* to stay relevant in the long run."[9] In business, as in many other activities, it is important to learn how to dance to the beat of the drum. As we will see in the coming chapters, the ownership of local cells would prove to be a powerful asset in extending the *Angry Birds* message around the globe, especially when launching new titles.

In 2014, Rovio recorded its first administrative victories in China by securing back its trademark rights on some categories of consumer goods, and this while sticking to its principle of not engaging in buy-back, but instead staying the course of diplomacy and litigation. In November 2014, Rovio also announced that it had entered into an agreement with China's Guogou Group for the construction and operation of nine *Angry Birds* family entertainment centers across the country by 2018. *Angry Birds* theme parks were coming to China, officially this time.

Rovio's challenges with trademarking were far from being at an end, though, as, even today, several competing trademark applications in other categories are still pending arbitration. Nonetheless, Rovio's patience and persistence in China will likely end up paying hefty dividends in the long run, especially when you consider that 93 percent of the urban population in China has at least heard of *Angry Birds*. The sales of *Angry Birds* mooncakes during the Mid-Autumn Festival are a good indicator of the rising popularity of the brand, growing year on year to the point that they have almost become an integral part of the tradition.

CHAPTER ELEVEN

The Final Frontier is Space

If you've conquered the world and are still hungry, where do you go next? Rovio goes into orbit in 3 ... 2 ... 1 ...

It all started with a tweet. On March 27, 2011, in the middle of the initial *Angry Birds Rio* craze, Bob Jacobs, a spokesman for NASA, was sitting at his home office, "which is, you know, my kitchen table," he quips.[1] He was sifting through tweets mentioning @NASA—a routine task for him. "NASA launched a man to the Moon. We launch birds into pigs," read a tweet from game consultant George Bray. Somebody else riffed on this and joked about the fact that smartphones of today have more computing power than the machines NASA used to launch a rocket to the Moon in the 1960s. Jacobs emailed a friend: "What are they talking about, 'shooting birds at pigs'?"[2] The reply was almost instantaneous: "It's *Angry Birds.*"

Jacobs knew of the game but had never played it. He did his homework and installed the app. Falling immediately for the physics aspect of the game, Jacobs got in on the action and tweeted: "Hey, @RovioMobile, our computers are a bit better than they were in '69. We might be able to help you launch birds if you can find a pig in space." Peter Vesterbacka was sitting at the other end of the message that particular day, well awake. He rapidly fired off an answer: "@NASA Sounds good! It might happen in the not too distant future." Private messages followed. Phone numbers were exchanged. Jacobs describes their tweets, saying, "A lot of times the best ideas fortuitously happen by accident. I jokingly say around the office that it was a lame attempt at a Jedi mind-trick: 'You want to work with NASA. If you ask, we will help you.'"[3]

The pass from Bob Jacobs would soon reach the hands of a new Rovio employee. Delighted by the success of her previous collaboration with Rovio—the SXSW non-terrorist building attack she coordinated for Nokia—Marja Konttinen dreamed one night that she had filed a job application with Rovio and that it had been accepted. The following morning, she woke up and acted on the dream, and joined the company as an account manager a short time after. On her first day at work, she convinced Matthew Wilson that maybe the time had come to change their strategy vis-à-vis working with partners. She recalls telling him: "You remember when I called you? You said, 'Yeah, you can use our assets freely.' I think we should reconsider that one."[4] In some instances, she argued, it was fair for advertisers to pay for image rights, especially when production work for extra content was involved. On other occasions, where long-term partnerships were being nurtured, image rights were less important. Wilson showed Konttinen a full mailbox in which new enquiries kept coming in by the minute, and told her to have fun. He also casually mentioned that there was an opportunity for Rovio to work with NASA lying around ... She might want to pick that one up, too.

Konttinen arranged a conference call with NASA later that evening. On the other side sat Jacobs and Burt Ulrich, and they threw around some ideas for a game they could help Rovio develop. "They were giggling on the other side. And I was giggling on my side too," Konttinen says. "'Oh my God, I'm speaking with NASA and they're excited to work with us.' And they thought the same of us, like, 'Wow, this is so cool to talk with a game company."'⁵ When she hung up, Konttinen was brimming with excitement. Although it was quite late in the evening owing to the time difference, she went striding straight to the top management's offices in the hope of still finding the triumvirate working. They were, of course: The Heds were discussing strategy with Vester-backa and Petri Järvilehto, a luminary of the Finnish video game industry who had joined Rovio in February 2011 as Senior Vice President of PC and Console. Järvilehto's wealth of expertise and knowledge was very much appreciated by the Rovio management, who picked his brains on more and more subjects as time passed.

"I just had a really good call with NASA," Konttinen announced, as she barged into the room. "They had a lot of cool ideas. We could make a game set in space. And I think we should really do this if it's at all feasible."⁶ Konttinen barely had time to sit down before Järvilehto walked over to the flipboard and started sketch-ing a few planets. "Well, if we tweaked the engine, we could prob-ably implement microgravity."⁷ He kept drawing for two minutes before concluding: "Yeah, this is a cool idea. I think we could make it work. We'll look into it."⁸ Konttinen headed home and went to sleep. When she came back to work the next morning, a prelimi-nary screenshot was sitting in her mailbox. "IT'S WORKING," said the subject field. Petri Järvilehto and art director Toni Kysenius had run wild with the idea overnight. In fact, they had reactivated a project that Jaakko Iisalo and Kysenius had been tinkering with a few months before for the purpose of a hypothetical update, but which had been stored away deep on their hard drives.

Project "*Angry Birds Space*" was on.

Shoot for the Stars

After this revelatory first night, the rest of the game's construc-tion didn't go quite as smoothly. When Kaj Hed received the first test-build, he was extremely worried that he was looking at a flop. The art style was visually too dark. The team was trying to be too realistic, and this seemed like the wrong direction. Diagnosing the problem in retrospect, Lauri Konttori says:

> The first version of the game was really dark. It was black space basically. Kaj Hed was afraid because people might dislike the overall darkness. Hed saw himself as an *Angry Birds* user and he was talking to me as a user. He thought the graphics were going to turn people off. So we got the assignment from Petri Järvilehto to help Jaakko Iisalo's team by creating a brighter universe with more light, more colors, and cheerful characters that were more appealing. Space hadn't been explored in that way before. Our design team made it more colorful and casual, and the new batch of characters were designed in one day by Miguel Francisco.[9]

Worse still, as in the development of the original *Angry Birds* title, halfway through the development cycle, Niklas Hed wondered whether the game was feasible after all. Although there was some promise in the test-levels produced by Järvilehto and Kysenius on proof-of-concept night, multiple problems emerged when the design team tried to build on this vision. Many of the things they were trying out just didn't work well once coded. Luckily, lead designer Iisalo was left unaware of these fears. He recalls:

> I didn't know that they thought of canceling the project, neither *Angry Birds* nor *Angry Birds Space*. I only heard about it later. Fortunately nobody told me. It's better that way because I can go a bit "bi-polar," so to speak, when working on a game. When I'm stuck, I feel this is never going to work. And when I discover a little

nugget, I think it is going to be awesome. You create systems, and then you balance them. The job of a game designer is balancing. If they let me do my thing in my bubble, it's going to be fine. I've always had good producers, and people in between, that have served as a buffer and shielded me from the politics.[10]

As the development team struggled to get the birds flying outside the virtual stratosphere, NASA was preparing for a real-life Shuttle launch in July 2011. It was an historic moment—the launch of *Atlantis* STS-135 was the 135th and final mission in the Space Shuttle program. Rovio received invitations for the event via Konttinen. To her delight, all top managers were booked up for these dates, so she got to attend the event accompanied by her husband.

Here was an opportunity too good to be missed: Rovio improvised a teasing operation for the occasion, even though the unannounced work-in-progress game was still firmly under wraps at that point. Within three days, a special-edition T-shirt emblazoned with the slogan "Shoot for the Stars" was designed by Toni Kysenius and printed by Fifth Sun. A couple of boxes of the T-shirts were rushed out to Orlando just in time, along with a bunch of plush toys, of course. After all, the list of VIP guests included a veritable who's who of Hollywood stars, and there were influential friends to make over there. In the bus, Konttinen sat next to Optimus Prime, the giant robot-truck from *Transformers*, or at the very least an actor dressed for the part.

Once on site, Konttinen immediately took some pictures of the *Angry Birds* plush toys placed right next to the launchpad and emailed them back to Saara Bergström in the Espoo office. "If you want to post these on Facebook ..." Bergström ran with it and hinted at the fact that Rovio and NASA were working on something together with the caption "Greetings from Orlando." Later that evening, NASA officially tweeted a picture of the "Shoot for the Stars" T-shirt to all its followers, kicking off speculation in the media about what the collaboration could possibly be about. "I basically laid a T-shirt on my bed, took a snapshot, and tweeted the picture,"[11] remembers Jacobs.

In Orlando, Konttinen continued to have the time of her life among millionaires, Grammy Award-winning musicians, Hollywood producers, and Academy Award-winning actors. For the countdown, she was sitting a row behind the mission control NASA employees who had guided the original Moon landing. She was terrified when a slight malfunction occurred, as she had seen the footage of the *Challenger* disaster in 1986 and the *Columbia* tragedy in 2003. After the Space Shuttle launched successfully, Konttinen burst into tears and a senior mission control director turned to her with tears in his eyes as well. She remembers his words even today: "He said, 'That's the end of my career. This was my thing, the Space Shuttle program and sending people into space. And this was the last of them.' I lost it. That was really hard to see someone else's big dream end right there."[12] Although Konttinen was greatly affected by the whole event, her business sense got the better of her emotions enough that she didn't forget to leave a box of T-shirts near the exit for the departing celebrities—all the garments were gone in a matter of seconds.

On the same day, Konttinen coordinated an online event with another major partner to further raise awareness of the brand. Samsung was among the first wave of device manufacturers and telecom corporations to use *Angry Birds* in some of its ad campaigns during the period while Rovio had allowed everyone to run wild with its assets. As the clear global leader in electronics, with a 30 percent market share, Samsung was in another league compared to the other Android device manufacturers, and Konttinen viewed the South Korean giant as another potential long-term partner. Samsung was also one of the biggest global spenders in advertising. *Angry Birds Space* gave both companies an opportunity to try out their partnership on a grander scale. Rovio added value to the table for Samsung by showing the first ever gameplay footage of *Angry Birds Space* on a Samsung Galaxy Note device in the press release, as well as including the device in the first animation trailer.

Furthermore, Rovio agreed on what it calls a "character association" for the same device. Every time Rovio had added a new bird into the game, be it the Mighty Eagle, Terence (the big tough bird), Hal (the toucan boomerang), or Bubbles (the orange balloon bird), the reception from fans had been wild excitement. The audience for the backstory animation trailers of those new characters was always extremely high. As the entire flock was about to get sent into space, the game would introduce a completely revamped cast to the audience. Aware of the frenzy this would cause, Philip Hickey, who had been put in charge of digital marketing on *Angry Birds Space*, chose to drip-feed the new information. Hickey explains: "Between the announcement of the game and the game launch, every detail, tease, and piece of content was meticulously planned to take our fans on a ride with us to Space. I like to call this 'Marketing the Marketing.'"[13]

Each of the new characters would be introduced one by one on a daily basis, to maintain momentum in the press and across social media between the announcement of the game and the live date. Hickey and Konttinen were pretty much inseparable during the entire operation, constantly comparing notes and sharing each other's plans to see how the former's digital marketing plans could nourish the business development efforts of the latter, and vice versa. One of the new characters, the Lazer Bird, would be unveiled "in partnership with Samsung." In practice, this meant that the first-ever image posted on social media would show the new bird on a Samsung Galaxy Note screen and bear the slogan:

"Launching with Samsung Galaxy Note." The teasers and the 30-second backstory clip of the character also presented product placement opportunities for the device.

In exchange for all these goodies, Samsung committed to heavily promote the game across all its owned channels, stores, and media but also through a flurry of local campaigns in the U.S., U.K., China, Hong Kong, Germany, Scandinavian countries, South Korea, and the Philippines. The campaign included TV commercials, promotional events at retail or landmark locations, and a massive internet advertising spend. Samsung went out of its way to mobilize AT&T as a U.S. partner, displaying posters on the walls of all its shops. During the prelaunch ramp-up of *Angry Birds Space*, Samsung also agreed to provide Rovio with a prominent co-branded stage at key industry events covered by media.

Samsung also got *Angry Birds* on board for its smart TV gaming push, in September 2012, embedding the game prominently on all home flat-screens, and showcasing it in various global TV commercials and other advertisements at points of sale. This campaign would be about the original *Angry Birds* game being ported to Series 8000 Samsung Smart TVs, which supported motion control and camera-capture capabilities. At this time, Samsung was, on average, selling one Smart TV somewhere in the world every six seconds on average—it was certainly not a minor deal. As Konttinen says, manufacturers always have a new product to sell, and there's always a special feature for which they need a game to highlight the point in their commercials. By meeting these requirements repeatedly, Rovio found Samsung to be the synergetic long-term partner that Konttinen had hoped for.

Treading the "Exclusive" Rope

Its first experiments with exclusivity quickly made Rovio wary of the practice. Giving exclusivity usually convinces one partner to give you more exposure. At the same time, it carries the risk of alienating other partners. Furthermore, potential customers sometimes can find themselves collateral victims of your dealings if they don't have access to the particular service or network you are giving the exclusivity to. It's a dangerous game. For example, releasing *Angry Birds Rio* on Amazon 24 hours ahead of everybody else slightly damaged other relationships for a few weeks in 2011. After this experience, Rovio never gave an exclusive on a complete game launch, not even for one hour.

What Rovio put in place instead was a rotation system through which everybody got the big game at the same time, but some of them might get some exclusive extra feature or a couple of bonus levels. As Konttinen points out—and as we've already seen in the cases of Apple and Samsung— "Manufacturers always have a new device to push, and there's always a unique feature that they want to show off."[14] The job of the content marketer is to help them do just that. When someone starts playing that game, the important keywords are "rotation" and "bonus." The trick is to make sure you identify all your valuable partners and not to always give everything to the biggest one. Treat them with fairness and make sure that everybody gets their turn within a year or so.

The Shanghai team applied the same rotation system for timed-exclusive updates and bonus content with Chinese partners and providers, although in China this is harder to enforce. According to Tianyi Pan, "When you give something exclusive to a channel, you can be sure it will only take a few hours before pirate copies appear magically on other channels."[15]

If you are releasing a completely new game and want to maximize your chances for optimal exposure from all top platform-holders on Day One, the best method is to give them all a little exclusive. You give everybody the same cake at the same time, but you put a cherry on top on one side, and a chunk of pineapple on the other.

Simultaneous Shipping

Besides digital partnerships, Rovio was also keen to make further inroads into the physical world. *Angry Birds* was one of the first mobile games to tell its story through cinematic trailers. It was the first mobile game to branch out into merchandising and consumer products. Now competitors were following its lead. Rovio wanted to pioneer again by being the first developer to simultaneously launch a mobile game alongside a complete line of consumer products and animation—a full-blown cross-media launch in the manner of the biggest Hollywood franchises. Mikael Hed no longer wanted Rovio to be seen just as a games studio but instead wanted it to operate as an entertainment company. The *Angry Birds Space* launch would serve to demonstrate that intent to the marketplace.

As Business Head of North America, one of the first things Andrew Stalbow did was to reach out to Walmart, the world's biggest supermarket chain. Walmart owned around 8,500 stores in 15 countries. Its most profitable ventures were in North America, South America, the U.K., China, and Japan (under the Seiyu banner). Walmart already stocked inventory for *Angry Birds*-licensed items such as T-shirts and plush toys, which it purchased respectively from Fifth Sun and Commonwealth Toys. Stalbow wanted to step up Rovio's physical retail presence. And at the time, Walmart was also keen to extend its digital presence. Everything was set up nicely for a win-win partnership.

Stalbow concocted a tailor-made plan of action for the retail giant, using Konttinen's and Hickey's help, plus a bit of Vesterbacka's essence peppered here and there. The topline idea was to take the "Super Bowl clue" concept from the *Angry Birds Rio* collaboration and expand it, turning it into a proper treasure hunt. On the development side of things, four "Eggsteroids" bonus levels were hidden within various levels of the game. When *Angry Birds Space* launched on March 22, 2012, licensors ensured that plush toys of the new characters, T-shirts, and a flurry of books and comics accompanied the game's release. The Walmart inventory was manufactured and packed separately from the other production lines and bore exclusive tips on how and where to find hidden Eggsteroids levels, guaranteeing Walmart extra foot traffic and retail preference. The T-shirt was a limited edition incorporating a clue within the design. Another clue was added to each plush toy's hangtag, and still one more could be found inside the packaging of the *Angry Birds Space* Fruit Snack Box.

In return, Walmart brought out the big guns: a video wall with *Angry Birds* animations, pallets, branded security shrouds, and posters in its thousands of U.S.-based stores, a big media buy across traditional media (i.e. TV commercials), and PR efforts. Last but not least, Walmart took the opportunity to experiment with a bunch of digital advertising options: promotions through Facebook advertisements and animation pre-rolls on YouTube and other mobile ad networks. According to Konttinen, "We both tried new things we wouldn't have otherwise tried, because the other one was so credible in their field."[16]

T-Mobile also rallied at the eleventh hour to scoop the fourth Eggsteroid reveal. Every month Walmart printed out and dispatched a magazine catalog to millions of mailboxes stateside. If a vendor wanted to be featured in the so-called "Walmart Circular," there was a price to pay. Stalbow and his team really wanted to score that ultimate bonus, but the fee Walmart demanded was more money than he could have bet. Rovio had become used to the luxury of never having to directly pay for any advertising, and this had become crucial: The startup couldn't afford to pay for all these promotions itself even if it wanted to. To avoid doing that, Rovio kept creating cool exclusive content for partners to whom this had more value than cash. Konttinen called close partner T-Mobile and offered it the last-minute opportunity. T-Mobile gladly got involved, its logo was added, and it got the right to exclusively reveal the fourth clue to its audience.

These retail and digital partnerships ensured massive visibility throughout the launch window, but the thinking heads at Rovio wanted more. Mikael Hed, as always, wanted to eliminate the element of luck, which on the now ultra-competitive and increasingly volatile mobile platform had become an even harder task than in 2011, let alone 2010. By now, every garage developer and bedroom artist had flocked to the App Store, hoping to become a millionaire. There was also a massive exodus of talented developers, artists, and producers who were leaving AAA console development houses and publishers to go independent on mobile. Some of them moved due to the waves of layoffs that accompanied the tough financial times some of these major console gaming companies were experiencing; others because they were attracted by the new disruptive mobile phenomenon. Some of them scored big venture capital or angel investments fairly easily, as the mobile bubble was at its peak.

As for the major companies themselves, they didn't just sit and wait for their slow death, but tried to incorporate every hot property or back-catalog asset they had into the mobile gaming world, in some form or another. The year 2012 was a veritable gold rush for mobile gaming, and the scene more and more seemed like a Wild West. When *Angry Birds* launched in December 2009, the number of apps available was 140,000. By early 2012, this number had grown to 600,000. The number of game developers in the world was estimated at 60,000, and would reach a staggering 100,000 by the end of 2013. *Angry Birds* was partially a catalyst for this—its fast rise to global success and constant presence in worldwide media had a profound influence. Furthermore, Rovio was no longer the only superpower in town. Titles like *Cut the Rope* or *Fruit Ninja* had also passed the 100 million downloads mark and their licensed plush toys were also available through Commonwealth Toys. Competitors were keeping an eye on Rovio's every move and replicating them when they could.

The most dangerous threat of all for Rovio was the rise of a business model called free-to-play (F2P), also known as "freemium." As time went by, the price war between app developers reached an inevitable endpoint. Some games were just free to download, with incremental fees charged to core users for extra services or content further down the road. The first video game to utilize the model successfully was *Crazyracing Kartrider* by South Korean company Nexon in 2004. Nexon pretty much built its fortune using F2P in South Korea, Japan, and China, and the model had been on the rise in Asia ever since. In the West, it was only in 2011 and 2012 that in-browser casual gaming, social gaming, and mobile gaming combined to make the model utterly dominant. Consumers vote with their wallets, and by the first quarter of 2012, whether Rovio liked it or not, the verdict was uncontestable. Freemium games accounted for 75 percent of the 100 apps in the top-grossing charts, and, when you looked at the top 50 and top 25, the percentage increased sharply. All entries in the top ten were F2P, without exception. The original *Angry Birds* itself was right on the edge of the top 50 grossing apps, even though it still oscillated around the top five in the paid charts.

In that respect, the most eye-opening case study making the rounds was *Jetpack Joyride* from Halfbrick. The Australian studio had released *Fruit Ninja* in 2010 at $0.99 and had sold well over 100 million units of it in the first year. Anticipation for Halfbrick's next game was very high in the blogosphere and on social media. When it came out, critical acclaim and user ratings for *Jetpack Joyride* were even more outstanding than for *Fruit Ninja*. Halfbrick could also count on its 100-million-seller hit to serve as a cross-promotional vehicle. *Jetpack Joyride* quickly rose to number one in the Apple App Store paid apps charts and stayed within the top ten in the U.S., the U.K., Australia, and 80 other countries for the following eight months. No other new premium game sold better than *Jetpack Joyride* in that period.

And yet, *Jetpack Joyride* only triggered 1 million sales, a meager 1 percent of what had been accomplished with *Fruit Ninja* the year before. Paid games were dying. Halfbrick tried dropping the game to free in cooperation with partners Free App A Day and OpenFeint, who alerted tens of millions opt-in subscribers about it. Within 24 hours, another million users downloaded the game, doubling the installed base overnight. The spike was so mind-blowing that Halfbrick kept it free for a while. Six weeks later, in February 2012, Halfbrick CMO Phil Larsen told *Joystiq* that the numbers were sitting at 14 million and that 5–10 percent of the users purchased at least $1 of in-app purchases, which meant that revenue had actually increased since dropping to free.[17] Imangi echoed these results when communicating about its runaway success *Temple Run*, explaining that the daily revenue average had quadrupled after the game made the move from premium to freemium.[18]

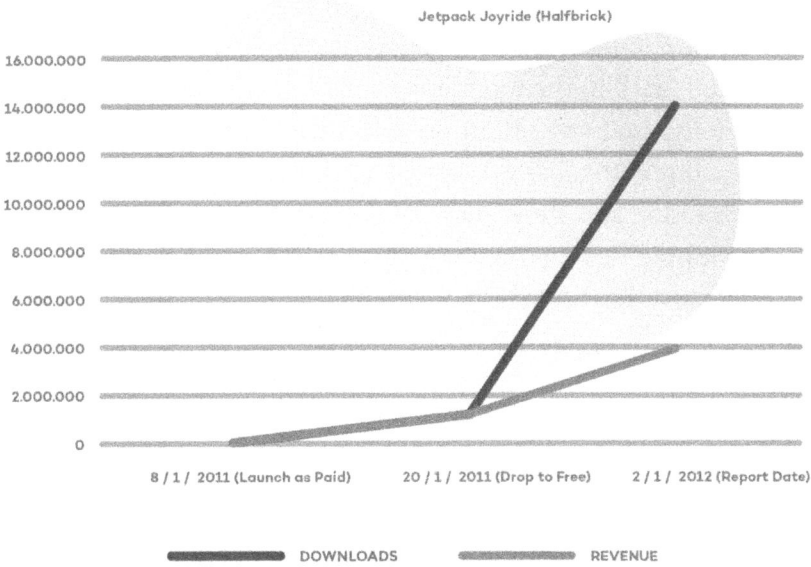

Jetpack Joyride Growth After Dropping to Free

The problem with free is that you can't compete with it. The $0.99 up-front that seemed extremely cheap last year now looked steep compared to all the perfectly good games that gave consumers a free trial. In fact, they gave more than a trial: Most users could complete the full game without spending a single cent. The free ride of the vast majority of the audience was subsidized by power-ups and shortcuts purchased by the more impatient minority. If you're dealing with a player-base in excess of 100 million, monetizing 1–8 percent of those users on a monthly basis is quite a lucrative business. It's what economists and businesspeople call "volume play."

Despite the hostile environment, Rovio chose to be confident in the staying power of the brand and took the calculated risk of going paid with *Angry Birds Space* again. Sales of *Angry Birds* and *Angry Birds Seasons* remained more than reasonable on iOS, and it was always easier to decrease price than to increase it later down the road. They decided to take the risk, yet they were seriously biting their nails over it.

As always, Vesterbacka encouraged the marketing-communication team to think about the impossible. The Fox collaboration had left a mark in the top managers' minds. They wanted to pull off a Hollywood-level stunt on *Angry Birds Space*. They wanted to come out with a bang. After all, to stay in the lead, you have to keep thinking two steps ahead of the competition.

As they pitched their wildest ideas in early 2012, Konttinen and Hickey found NASA to be a pretty good sport. "NASA had this big auditorium set up for us," remembers Konttinen. "We showed the game. We passed the iPad around the 25 attendees. They had the educational people, the public outreach team, some scientists—it was an amazing setup. And they were all really excited." At some point, somebody wrapped it up. "Okay, we just need Legal to prepare for contract signature." A brief moment of silence followed. "Legal?" the man asked again. Everybody stared at the NASA counsel, who happened to have the iPad in her hands. "Sorry!" the woman says, "I haven't been listening at all! I just love this game!"[19] There was contagious glee around the room as they all laughed to this ultimate proof of the quality of the game. A few minutes later, Rovio became the second Finnish company in history to sign the Space Act Agreement.

Go Big or Go to Your Home Planet

In February 2012, Konttinen and Philip Hickey called Burt Ulrich at NASA. "Hey there, we have this crazy idea," Konttinen recalls saying. "It's fine if you say we are bananas and laugh, but we just thought we'd check what you think. How about we launch the game from space?" Konttinen summarizes the ensuing dialogue:

"Sounds cool. When do you need it done by?"

"In two weeks."

"Let me make a couple of phone calls."

A few hours later, they received the green light, "Yeah, let's do it." Rovio now had a wildcard in its deck. "That was way easier than I thought," Konttinen readily admitted a couple of years later.[20]

The marketing team picked a date in the calendar for the big event. Philip Hickey and Saara Bergström then used the three-week countdown to raise expectations by teasing fans and media with content they had prepared in the pipeline. On February 16, 2012, Hickey's digital marketing campaign began with the first teaser video, showing only the face of Red Bird with light coming out of his eyes, revealing the logo and title, a date for the official announcement with international times listed for major cities (so as to magnify the sense of occasion), a link to the micro-site, and finally the bold tagline: "It's one small fling for a bird. One giant quantum leap for birdkind." Sci-fi sound effects scored the piece to build tension—no music this time. It was as mysterious as it gets. Six days later, the clip was followed by a spoof of the historic Moon landing footage, which happens to be in the public domain and therefore free to use. The team airbrushed the original images from the 1960s and added a slingshot and a red bird in the setting while also modifying the dialogue between the astronauts to reference the game. After ten days, another teaser was released. This one introduced the "Pigs in Space" and the tagline: "In space, nobody can hear you squeal."

Following up on Konttinen's special request, which had gone more easily than she thought, Hickey and Konttinen received an email from NASA astronaut Donald Pettit, a man who didn't quite have his feet on the ground. The email was entitled "Greetings from Space" and read, "Much fun it was making video for *Angry Birds*. I do hope you folks find my video scenes useful. I have many more ideas on educational science aspects of space that could be used in contraction with your game. [...] This could be a way to strategically put physics concepts into the young minds. I'm up here until mid-June."[21] NASA delivered a video file shortly after.

"We had written a script for five minutes of material show-ing the various key gameplay points in relation with space and physics, which is Don Pettit's area of expertise," recalls Konttinen. "We were lucky that he was up there because he's known to be an experimental scientist who does a lot of unorthodox videos about physics in a very approachable language. He read the script and ignored most of it. Instead he did 40 minutes of ad-libbed mate-rial. There's an amazing amount of stuff in there. He went really into detail with all kinds of cool physics-based experiments."[22]

On March 8, Rovio and NASA wrote a page of history together, by making *Angry Birds Space* the first mobile game to be launched in outer space. Astronaut Don Pettit addressed Planet Earth from the International Space Station, 242.5 nautical miles above Earth's surface, through YouTube. "I want to do some physics demonstra-tions that involve some of the things you might see in the *Angry Birds Space* game," he said. Whether it's the coolest or most sur-real piece of marketing video ever is still up for debate: Holding an *Angry Birds* plush toy in one hand, Pettit goes, "We need a pig." He blows into a green balloon and draws eyes, a mouth, and ears on it. "I'm not very good at art. It's a good thing I chose to be a sci-entist and an engineer rather than an artist, because I'd be starv-ing by now." Pettit then uses a bungee to simulate the slingshot and shows how zero gravity influences trajectories using the Red Bird, the green balloon, the bungee, and a couple of eggs. "Don't ask me how I got eggs in space," quips Pettit. Nice decoy attempt there, right? Forget the eggs—how did the Red Bird plush toy get there? That's what the fans want to know!

Realistically, the only way to supply a physical item to a Space Station is by sending a rocket. So when one hears that this all happened within two weeks, the practical skeptic objects, "Wait a second. Logistically, how did you get the plush toy in the astro-naut's hands on time?" Konttinen's answer to this question is possibly the most wonderful bit in the whole story: "The Red Bird was already up there."[23]

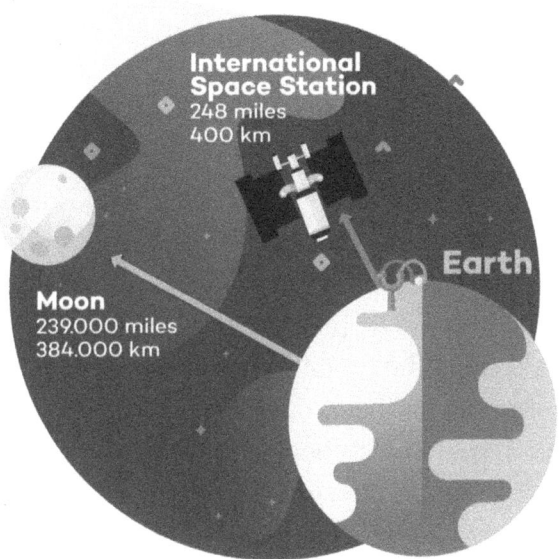

International Space Station Location

A few weeks earlier, the Russian Soyuz TMA-22 spacecraft had taken off on top of a Soyuz-U booster from the Baikonur Cosmodrome in the desert steppe of Kazakhstan, on its way toward the International Space Station. On board were cosmonauts Anton Shkaplerov and Anatoly Ivanishin, and NASA astronaut Daniel Burbank. As is customary on all spacecraft, the crew took with them a little quotidian plush item that would be used as a "gravity indicator." As it enters zero gravity, the plush item expands in size, which is a pretty good visual cue. When Anton Shkaplerov left home for this mission, his five-year-old daughter gave him a Red Bird to remember her by, as this was her favorite toy. Rovio had had nothing to do with it. In fact, Rovio only found out about it when NASA sent Konttinen the link to a news article on space.com. It got the team brainstorming and eventually they came up with the space launch idea. Amusingly, because it was taken up there by a cosmonaut, the Red Bird was the property of the Russian Space Program. A formal diplomatic authorization had to be officially filed by the Russian government to let Pettit use the plush toy in his video.

Pettit's presentation went instantly viral on YouTube. At the time of writing, it has gathered 31 million views on that network alone. It also got massively broadcast in world news on TV, in print, and in online media channels. Pettit told Konttinen that his boy was now very proud of his dad, not because he was an astronaut but because he made a video for *Angry Birds*. The cool astronaut also took the trouble to ship the remnants of the green balloon to Rovio, once he returned to Earth. The balloon still has a place of honor at Rovio's headquarters today.

To keep Rovio's promise with Samsung, the first in-game footage at the end of the Pettit announcement video was shown using the Samsung Galaxy Note as the display device. Furthermore, the press release wired to the media included a paragraph about the press conference being held the next day, March 9, in Samsung's booth at SXSW in Austin, Texas. This was the first time that the media was able to experience *Angry Birds Space* up close. Since all the journalists were playing on the Samsung Galaxy Note handed to them, all the pictures later published around the world would inevitably show the device as well. Astronaut Ron Garan even came on stage wearing his blue NASA flight suit. Konttinen was there, too. She says, "When I was showing Ron Garan how to play the game, he beat me on his first try! 'OK, that wasn't too hard.' Then a six-year-old boy arrived. 'Can I try?' And he immediately beat all our high scores. What was really cool is that the kids wanted to know all about the game, but they also wanted to know everything about space."[24] The booth was full of merchandising, and the trailer video was premiered on a giant screen. In the week leading up to the live date, the marketing team accelerated the dissemination of content in the press and in social media, at the rate of one video per day.

For launch day, the team had imagined yet another big stand-out idea: to turn Seattle's landmark Space Needle Tower into a giant 300-foot-tall slingshot aimed out into space, by hanging an enormous 35-foot Red Bird from it made specifically for the occasion. The idea was quite apt given that the architecture of the Space Needle was inspired by flying saucers. Since the idea was too big for the small startup to execute alone, Heijari and his team thought synergy and Konttinen brought T-Mobile on board. The partner helped them out in exchange for printing its logo on the slingshot band tied to the tower.

Because the Space Needle Tower is classified as an art installation, Heijari, Konttinen, Hickey, and Stalbow had to negotiate for weeks to secure approval from the building management team, the architectural firm, city officials, and T-Mobile. Even after it got the go-ahead, the execution of the stunt still presented difficulties. According to Hickey, "High winds would have killed the project immediately and with Seattle's high percentage of rainy days, all fingers were crossed. And all toes too."[25] On the night before the event, the weather conditions were so bad that some equipment got damaged during preparations. Heijari went for a drink that night, thinking, "Hey, it might not happen but at least we tried."[26]

At dawn, on March 22, 2012, the skies cleared up. Led by Andrew Stalbow and Heijari, David Doxtater's The Workshop LLC, probably the best professional climbers in the U.S., who were just back from a 12-hour job on an oil rig, went ahead with the setup. The process consisted of pushing a deflated Red Bird balloon through the two legs of the structure, then inflating it to full size after that. Hickey couldn't be present—he was at home looking after his overdue pregnant wife. He received a sudden

Skype message from Stalbow: "You won't believe this. I cannot even look. They put a hole in the bird."[27] The bird balloon had been ripped while still deflated, and the team only noticed while inflating it. The whole operation was compromised. Hickey didn't have time to say a curse word before his wife went into labor. He hastily drove her to the hospital.

Over in Seattle, Stalbow, Heijari, and the team on the ground didn't give up and managed to improvise a fix. They set up a giant sewing kit made of ropes, applied a crazy amount of rim tape designed for bicycle tires, and finished the job by sewing a giant patch onto the balloon. Up went the giant Red Bird. It stayed up there for the entire weekend, clearly visible from Seattle's highways. It turned out to be yet another image that made headlines all around the globe and got virally tweeted and retweeted millions of times. On her end, Hickey's wife delivered little Liam Anakin Hickey into the world. "What a launch day! Figuratively and literally," concludes Hickey.[28]

With all this commotion, it's no surprise that *Angry Birds Space* went straight to number one across all charts just three hours after being made available. It went on to beat the speed record of *Angry Birds Rio* by getting downloaded 10 million times in just three days. Consumer products also sold extremely well, turning the whole cross-media entertainment launch into a successful operation. *VentureBeat*'s headline read: "*Angry Birds Space* introduces the age of the mobile blockbuster."[29]

Even the company's book publishing department shared in the success: *Angry Birds Space: A Furious Flight into the Final Frontier*, the flagship title produced in collaboration with iconic magazine *National Geographic*, was already number one in the Science and Education books charts on Amazon, having been made available for preorder.

Mission Accomplished

When Mikael Hed stepped into the marketing-communications office to check how things were going on launch morning, he was surprised to find all the staff members silently gazing at their screens. Worried, Hed enquired, "How is it going?"[30]

Hickey turned to Hed and pointed at the screen, "Just check this out."[31] The number of tweets on the feed was so overwhelming that, while scrolling through, the team could see them only as a blur. When an operation succeeds far beyond expectations, it can happen that the sheer amount of feedback leaves you speechless and paralyzed—a short moment of bliss before you comprehend, realize, and get over what you have accomplished. After his own couple of minutes of contemplation, Mikael Hed looked up and addressed the room with a single word, "Yes!" Everybody broke into laughter, and the real work began.

The response from fans was very positive. The average customer rating was slightly higher than the 4.82 out of 5 that the original *Angry Birds* had enjoyed, and the number of five-star ratings obtained was higher than on any previous title. Game critics were unanimous in their praise, and reviews complimented the very high quality of *Angry Birds Space*. It was a home run and Iisalo's most accomplished *Angry Birds* title, by his own admission.

Even gaming divinity Shigeru Miyamoto, creator of gaming classics such as *Mario* and *Zelda* among other Nintendo games, gave it a nod when he told a panel of European journalists in Paris that *Angry Birds Space* was his favorite game of the year.[32]

Iisalo, nicknamed "Nintendo-Jaska" by his childhood friends, was over the moon with the compliment: "It's awesome. It can't get any better than this really. At the same time, *Angry Birds* is so popular that it's almost hard for me to grasp how famous it has become. It feels like I'm almost looking at it from outside; it's a bit unreal. The commentary from Miyamoto-san, it feels a bit the same to me."[33]

Angry Birds Space spread around the world like a pandemic. The published video content garnered so many view-hits that Rovio ended up being the most visited channel on YouTube in Week 22 of 2012. The game racked up 100 million paid downloads within 76 days. The momentum contributed to the breaking of an even bigger milestone, one that eclipsed all others: On May 9, 2012, Rovio attained its one billionth download for the *Angry Birds* series across all versions and platforms. The achievement was so big that a casual tweet from Rovio sufficed for the news to reach every major media outlet around the globe within minutes, the time it takes for an article to be quickly jotted down. This was a first for the entire video games industry. Some analysts reacted with disbelief. A few jaws dropped. The record was eventually authenticated by Guinness and included in the *Guinness World Records 2013*. Rovio had made history.

Mikael and Niklas Hed now owned the brand they had been dreaming of just two years before. *Angry Birds Space* validated Mikael's vision for the company, and Rovio Mobile was rebranded as Rovio Entertainment, making the company's intentions crystal clear. With its own animation department, its books division, its reactive marketing-communication division, and its capacity to get consumer products to market on time for a game launch, Rovio had ceased being just a game studio and had truly become an entertainment company.

The celebrations didn't last long, however. They never do at Rovio. New company goals were immediately voiced. Citing Coca-Cola as a role model, Peter Vesterbacka declared: "Let's become a permanent part of pop culture. Coca-Cola serves one billion drinks a day. Their business is physical. It shouldn't be too hard to get to one billion fans connected digitally every day."[34] It was around this time, too, that Vesterbacka coined a new company metaphor, used to motivate the latest recruits and to keep current employees hungry:

> I tell them that you can walk on water. People's natural reaction is to say that it's impossible. But it was supposed to be impossible to launch a game with Hollywood, impossible to launch a game from space, and impossible to get to a billion downloads. At some point, all team members start believing that they too can walk on water, because nobody has proven them otherwise. And, you've been to Finland; you can see that here in the winter the sea is frozen anyway![35]

A Rover Named *Curiosity*

"So why did NASA want to partner with a small game company?" Iisalo pondered this question out loud during a brainstorming session with the agency. "I have one question to be honest. Why are we here? Why do you want to work with us?" he asked.[36] They answered with a smile across their face, Konttinen recalling their response: "You're helping us to talk about [our projects] to the big world. We're doing a lot of stuff that nobody is interested in and you're able to make those kids excited about it too."[37] It was a win-win partnership: Rovio made NASA cool and relevant for 21st-century kids, for whom the Moon landing was something old hat and dull, while NASA gave Rovio the touch of class that comes with being associated with an iconic institution and backed them on the scientific aspects of its venture. Together, they were pioneering fresh ground.

In an interview with *Federal Computer Week*, Bob Jacobs, the NASA spokesman behind the original tweet, acknowledged: "The value [of the collaboration] for NASA is in getting people excited about science and space technology. We see it as a mutually beneficial relationship that allows us to get NASA mission information into the game."[38] Jacobs later told me, "In the past, we've sought out partnerships that you'd think were common sense or naturally aligned, but didn't work."[39] It's really necessary for both sides to get the vision at the same time and to see how it could be advantageous for both. Game developers also need to be:

> willing to think outside the box just a little! Usually, requests we get from video game companies are about making a first-person shooter game about NASA astronauts going to space and killing a bunch of things, which of course we don't do. One of the struggles that we have as communicators at an agency like NASA is that you don't want to diminish the serious risks and the science, you don't want to do anything too frivolous, but we also don't want to eliminate the fun out of what we do. All of us here at NASA fell in love with space because of a movie or a TV show that we saw in our childhood.[40]

Both on the web and on mobile, the top ten most visited pages on the *Nasa.gov* website in 2012 all related to *Angry Birds* according to its Google Analytics. The gap between these pages and the rest was vast. "This is one of the most popular platforms in the world and it has links in it that drive people to NASA information and NASA content. We would be foolish not to explore this opportunity," Jacobs emphasized.[41]

In fall 2011, NASA had launched a rocket into space with the objective of landing a rover named *Curiosity* on the Red Planet nine months later. During spring 2012, Iisalo, Konttori, Konttinen, Hickey, and Mikko Häkkinen met with scientists, engineers, and researchers from NASA for a big brainstorming session about what could be added to the game to update on the *Curiosity* project and the upcoming Mars landing. "We asked them to give us the equivalent of a 'Mars for Dummies' crash course, because that's what we were," says Konttinen.

"We learned all those amazing facts and took a lot of notes. We took all this inspiration and brought it back home to make a game update that would release on the day the *Curiosity* rover was supposed to land on Mars, hoping that nothing would go wrong. We have actual stories, actual facts disguised as fun. And that was behind the drive for *Angry Birds Space* all the way: How much science can we pack into a fun little game?"[42]

In the *Red Planet* update, *Curiosity*, along with older rovers from the 1980s like *Viking* and *Phoenix*, guest-starred. There was even a digital comic available in the game showing all the technical steps involved in the rover landing. Konttinen shares an anecdote highlighting the effect of these little extras:

> One day, our art director, Toni Kysenius, was taking his kids to kindergarten, and this boy comes running over. "Toni, Toni, did the pigs really take the rover? I saw the comic!" I found that really amazing. Five-year-olds care about a machine on another planet and they want to know what's going on. So they're going to pay much more attention to the news, and when they're going to hear about the mission at school, they'll say, "Oh yeah, I know the rover. I heard about it in *Angry Birds*." When those kids go to school, they're going to start from a very different perspective than ours. And hopefully in 20 years we can see a different generation of astronauts and engineers. That's astronaut Don Pettit's message. "If you want to be like me, you need to learn your math. And there are cool ways to do it."[43]

Another neat addition in another update was the new electric guitar cover of the theme song that replaced the original edition. A month earlier, as he was perusing the morning press, Hickey read an article about Slash, formerly of Guns N' Roses. In the interview, the legendary guitarist raved about the game app he was obsessed with—*Angry Birds Space*. Hickey asked Robin Squire, community manager at Rovio, to check Twitter, and Slash had indeed been tweeting a lot lately about losing levels narrowly or getting three stars. Rovio placed a call to the artist's manager, and soon a Skype call with Slash was arranged. From the other end of the line, a few minutes before taking the stage at a concert in Brazil, Slash covered the theme song on his guitar for Hickey and head of audio, Ilmari Hakkola, who were both completely incredulous about the situation.

Hakkola remembers: "I had social anxiety when talking to stars, and he started by saying, 'Let's keep it short, guys. This is Brazil, anything could happen.' I said 'Okay. Hello, Mr. Slash.'"[44] A few exchanges later, they agreed to co-record a new theme song with a Slash solo in the middle of it. Slash himself explained the context on YouTube: "They asked for something a little bit different, but it weren't specific as to what they wanted. So I made a few versions, and it was a lot of fun to do while I was on the road. I was really thrilled when I came to the version that I really liked and that they really liked. It was a pretty exciting little process."[45] The guitar solo was added into the game, and Slash was later thanked for his collaboration with his own Slash Bird. A limited-edition T-shirt was printed by Fifth Sun and the fans swarmed on it. Slash explains: "When they sent me the Slash Bird, I was over the top. So cool-looking. Because I come from an illustration background, it's one of the coolest things that people have been able to take my image and do all sorts of cool things. Yeah, I was pretty elated about that."[46]

Over the Moon

Rovio, meanwhile, won the highly competitive 2013 NASA Honor Award for its outstanding work on *Angry Birds Space*, which the agency was over the moon about. Speaking of the Moon, the Mighty Eagle might soon be heading there or even to another planet, having successfully performed a series of tests at the Marshall Space Flight Center. In this case, however, *Mighty Eagle* refers to a robotic prototype lander that NASA named after the famous character. "Everyone thought it was more interesting than the official name, Warm Gas Test Article (WGTA)," comments Jacobs.[47]

Both sides carried such a lot of pride for the joint effort that the game continued to receive live ops updates and campaigns for years after, perhaps the quirkiest one being *New Horizons* in 2015 when NASA's space probe flew by Pluto for the first time in history. Kai Torstila, head of product marketing at Rovio Entertainment, remembers: "Pluto had been declassified from a planet to a dwarf planet. We pushed people to petition in *Angry Birds Space* to 'Make Pluto a Planet Again' and there was no limit to how many times a user could click. The petition gathered over 50 million votes!"[48]

Marketers and entrepreneurs have an expression they use a lot to explain success stories in a nutshell: "The planets were aligned." There will never be another marketing blitz that wears the line better than *Angry Birds Space*.

CHAPTER TWELVE

With Bigger Success Come Bigger Problems

After the all-round success of *Angry Birds Space*, one could be misled into thinking that the skies at Rovio were permanently cloudless. They were making it, they were rich and famous, and life was easy, right?

Wrong. Stagnation being the entrepreneur's worst enemy, every company faces challenges as it tries to move up to the next level. The magnitude of problems tends to grow in proportion to the stakes in play, or, put more crudely, the money. Similarly, the faster you expand, the more likely it is that there'll be friction along the way. Rovio was not immune to this. After all, a company is an ensemble of human beings. And human beings are flawed. No one is perfect.

The year 2012 was an incredibly busy one at Rovio. Even with 250 employees, the startup was still desperately understaffed given the workload. It urgently needed more people. Meeting and hiring new recruits one by one became too slow of a process for Niklas and Mikael Hed. They accelerated the pace with a couple of big moves. They opened new development offices in Tampere, some 110 miles (180 km) to the north of Helsinki, as the city is known to have a pool of talented people, some of whom wouldn't consider moving to Espoo. Another office soon followed in Stockholm, with pretty much the same reasoning in mind. To avoid having to spend time assembling the team themselves, Rovio's top management delegated the hiring process and the daily management of the Stockholm office to a highly experienced studio manager, Oskar Burman, formerly with Electronic Arts. Burman rapidly hired Patrick Liu from EA Dice, who made the jump from creative director on *Battlefield 1943* to creative director on *Angry Birds Seasons* at Rovio Stockholm. *Angry Birds Seasons* was a recurring service that required a lot of weekly work to keep it fresh. It was better kept away from the core team, so that the latter could focus on the next big games. Rovio also acquired the game development division of Finnish middleware startup Futuremark. The employees there were already well trained and skilled and had a good dynamic—they were ready to go, which would save time. A vice president for mergers and acquisitions, Teemu Huuhtanen, was also hired to deal with the assimilation process and to keep watch on other possible targets.

Too Fast, Too Furious

If the addition of enthusiastic fresh blood helped in keeping up with new market demands and opportunities, it didn't change the fact that some of the original members of staff were exhausted. At some point, too much work is just too much. In video game development jargon, when nearing a deadline, teams often go into what is called "crunch time" mode: sleepless nights, hazy days, no weekends, a stench of sweat all around, typing lines of code, drawing and shading characters at the speed of light. This had become the status quo since the launch of *Angry Birds* in late 2009. "Crunch time" was routine, and not just for the developers or creative types, but on the business side of things, too. Rovio was going nonstop. Senior Character Designer Miguel Francisco remembers the times: "The rhythm became really hell. We had more and more animators and artists joining the department, but we still needed to work hard to maintain the consistency and the overall quality. At least we never had to put out really low-quality material. We always stopped this from happening."[1] Konttinen adds: "When I was traveling with Peter, Mikael, or Andrew Stalbow, I learned very quickly that I needed to bring my own food and sleep wherever I could, such as on a taxi ride. These guys, unless you pass them some snack, do not even eat on business trips: 'We don't have time for breaks.' I'm half their age and I can't even keep up with them."[2] There's a limit to what the human body can endure though. The Spartan warrior lifestyle comes at a hefty price once you reach that limit.

After two and a half years of constant rush and hyper-growth, some of the Rovians who were there from the beginning needed a break. A few even experienced what psychologists call "burnout." Burnout is the career-centric version of a nervous breakdown. While the latter leaves you questioning your very existence and not wanting to do anything, the former is mainly about work. The last thing you are thinking of before going to sleep is a work-related thing. The first thing you are thinking of when waking up in the morning is also a work-related thing. There comes a point when the brain makes too many rapid decisions and wants to just shut down. No more decisions, please. The only way to escape that terrible mental state is to get away from it all. Far away. This rang alarm bells inside the company and most members of the original battalion were put to rest for a while. Matthew Wilson, for example, was rewarded with a five-week holiday to recharge his batteries.

Revitalizing tired members of the team didn't solve the core of the problem, though. The workforce was too large for the company to continue to be managed in the same way. There were too many people asking too many questions and requiring too many decisions for just three men to handle, and so the corporate structure went through a reshuffle. The company was divided into different units, each with a head of department: Games, Animation, Audio, Books, Consumer Products, Marketing-Communications, and New Business Ventures (referred to internally as "The Greenhouse"). At the top of the pyramid, the Executive Management Team (EMT) ruled over them all yet allowed the divisions to interoperate within the same building in Keilaranta, Espoo, as they saw fit, without needing any form of approval. Mikael Hed's plan with the new structure was to organize processes in a way that prevented chaos yet enabled the company to stay as agile as possible despite its size.

Rovio Executive Structure

In each department, Mikael Hed tried to replicate the triangular management structure that had worked so well for the company as a whole till that point. In every division, power was shared between a creative-centric professional, a finance and economics expert, and an operations specialist. Hed told the *Wall Street Journal*: "We've divided up our departments into smaller, more independent studios—we call them tribes. Each tribe has their own [profit and loss sheet], their own management, their own targets, and they all focus on different types of products."[3]

At the top, Mikael Hed was supported by legal counsels, human resources, a chief financial officer, and others. Mikael also kept regular meetings with his corporate board of directors, among whom his dad, Kaj Hed, remained as the chairman and majority share-holder. Furthermore, Mikael also oversaw the cross-media storytelling as, according to Niklas Hed and Lauri Konttori, he happens to be blessed with a natural knack for consistency. If you look at the credits list of the early cinematic trailers, you will systematically find Mikael Hed's name among others under the "Story by" title. Mikael Hed admits to a true passion for the creative process and wanted to stay involved as much as time allowed. Konttori confirms, "Mikael loves to create new stuff and be close to the excitement."[4]

Head of North America Andrew Stalbow's and Petri Järvilehto's roles grew in importance, after they had proven themselves to be highly competent, reliable, and trustworthy on projects of every scale and scope. As for Peter Vesterbacka, since he is at his best when delving into everything that's going on, he was granted the freedom that you would give a player wearing the number 10 shirt in soccer, moving between all these departments like a free agent. For every big project he wanted to start or big idea he brought home from one of his international meetings, he had to go through the department heads so they could evaluate its feasibility and importance.

The problem was nobody was entirely suitable for assuming the role of head of consumer products, so this temporarily remained as part of the responsibilities of the COO. After returning from his holidays with a clear head, Niklas Hed came to the realization that he didn't want to be the COO anymore. He had founded Rovio to make video games. Now he had been cornered into an operational role because he did it well and because there was nobody else around to pick up the slack. Hed wanted to resume a more creative role. He says:

> We used to do products 90 percent of the time. Then I found myself doing something else 90 percent of the time. I realized that this [the COO position] was not the

role I wanted to do. I don't have a big ego and I don't need a big title. What drives me is to make the best entertainment products. That is the best contribution I could ever give. So I wanted to go back to that. It's not just games; it's all these bits and pieces that make up entertainment and how to tie them together to make a universe.

The problem worsened when Rovio fumbled on who to appoint as Niklas Hed's successor. At one point, the COO position was held by a person with a full-steam sales profile, which was not the right match. All in all, it took a year until Rovio dubbed Teemu Suila as the replacement for Niklas Hed as COO. In the summer of 2012, just before Niklas stepped down as COO, Rovio scooped the LIMA Awards for "Best Licensed Program of the Year" and "Best Character/Toy Brand Program of the Year," while Commonwealth also won "Best Character/Toy Brand Licensee" for its plush toys range.

Structure the Message

Around the second half of 2012, Sara Antila joined Rovio as head of communication and set about implementing a ten-point plan. The implementation of this plan took more time than its writing did, however. Everything was so fast moving, so agile and so reactive at Rovio. She was jumping on a train that was not only already in motion but also pretty much running at hyper-speed. The pace at which opportunities came in, and the sheer number of media requests Rovio received in a day, was a lot to manage. They had to be reactive, responding minute by minute. Planning while "running."

Furthermore, when she interviewed all the key Rovio people to find out what level they were at with regard to public relations, she found out that, despite the massive coverage the company had successfully attracted, most were lacking in knowledge of the field. Up until this point, the company had just been winging it. In that sense, the results they obtained and the impact they had were all the more remarkable. But this also explains the many slipups that occurred. The positive consequence of those slipups was that Antila found people to be very receptive to her advice. It's always very helpful for a communications advisor when those they are advising are open-minded and ready to improve.

Toward the summer of 2012, Antila set up a new communications system. Its centerpiece was a simple bullet list of key points that needed to be conveyed when talking about a given topic in an interview, reflecting the key messages of the company at large. Key messages define the voice and persona of a company, so they don't change all the time. Although they do get updated and finetuned over time, some of these messages will persist for years.Having a set list allows an employee to take the lead in a debate or interview rather than acting passively. A question is often an opportunity for the interviewee to say what they really want to say, so long as they know how to dance around it correctly. Training also prevents everybody from speaking off the cuff or about their own opinions, which can lead to confusion and sometimes contradictions. Key messaging is not about putting exact words or prefabricated sentences in someone's mouth—the style and tone are left to the speaker—but making sure that the interviewer comes away with the "takeaway points." What information should stick in people's minds after they've finished talking to you? And it must be the company's message, not an individual's message. In a way, the key messages are a safety net. If an employee feels trapped at any point, they can fall back on these messages to parry the curveball questions. In politics, it is the cornerstone of spin-doctoring. And because they are the company's key messages, all top company deciders have to adhere to them.

Externally, she also slowly repositioned one of the most visible characters in the company, Peter Vesterbacka, as the "freethinking guru," as the brand evangelist who spoke about the future in striking metaphors and visions. She clarified the border between his views and the company's views in the public eye: Vesterbacka was an interesting character who worked for Rovio, but Rovio was a company, an ensemble of individuals and talents, and it had values on which it stood as well as a corporate identity.

Antila also ensured that a mixture of voices and faces represented the company at trade fairs, conferences, and seminars. And they always came bearing gifts. It's common practice for Rovians to appear on stage with dozens of plush toys on hand. At the end of their presentation, they would send their audience out on a high by throwing the toys at them one by one.

People so often complain about people "talking the talk without walking the walk" that it has become a cliché. Rovio was walking the walk. In fact, it was running the rush. Antila helped the company shape the accompanying message, as well as bring consistency and clarity in internal communications. As a result, the goals, values, and vision of the company became more transparent. With several hundred people joining the company in such a short timeframe and working together in offices around the world, good internal communication was no small matter. It was the glue that held Rovio together. It was the basis for a positive collaborative atmosphere. It ensured everybody was moving in the same direction.

Vertigo

Another problem the company faced was the risk (and constant fear) of disappointing and underwhelming fans whose expectations just kept growing. It's human nature to always want more and better. We can't find satisfaction in the status quo.

After the release of *Angry Birds*, Rovio became much more cautious about its output. Many prototypes for potential new titles were canned at the incubation stage for not being of high enough quality. There was even a game into which €500,000 of development money had been funneled, before it was canceled because it was not heading in the right direction.

Until it could find its next spark of genius, to fill the gap Rovio proceeded through acquisition. Indie developers Noel Llopsis and Miguel Friginal had cooked up a wonderful little physics puzzle game called *Casey's Contraptions*. Rovio acquired the studio, pulled the game off the App Store, and prepared a rebranding that launched in July 2012 under the title *Amazing Alex*. More pertinently to the topic at hand, the physics engine and the algorithmic code acquired in the *Casey's Contraptions* deal also laid down some useful principles for the physics-based spinoff title *Bad Piggies*, which further enhanced the *Angry Birds* universe by focusing on the swine side of the conflict. A lot of the calculus and mechanics necessary for the *Bad Piggies* game had already been refined for *Amazing Alex*, which saved considerable time on development. The marketing-communication team released a teaser in August 2012 promising that "Something Pig is Coming," while opening a new Twitter account for the piggies to express themselves on social media. A *Bad Piggies* Facebook page also launched, with 200,000 fans liking the page prior to launch. This gave the game a head start when chasing chart positions on release date. Some video teasers quickly followed on YouTube, in which the pigs learned how to build things by watching archival footage such as the Wright brothers attempting to fly airplanes.

Everybody thought that *Bad Piggies* would be just another slingshot game, in which you got to fling the pigs at the birds. Rovio didn't mind the confusion: It only gave the gameplay trailer more weight. To release this trailer, Rovio partnered with Yahoo, the company once synonymous with the internet in the late 1990s. A no-show in the early mobile wars, Yahoo.com was still the third most visited website on the planet at the time, behind only Google and Facebook. The best way to work with a nonmobile company with massive internet traffic remained the good old-fashioned news scoop. Yahoo was given a 24-hour exclusivity window for the video, which unveiled how *Bad Piggies* is played: You get to help them build shaky, rickety vehicles and then try to drive them through one tricky level after another. The clip was displayed as a main news item on the Yahoo front page in the U.S., Europe, and South Korea, helping it shoot up to be the second most discussed video of the month on the network.

On September 27, 2012, *Bad Piggies* hit the Apple App Store and Android. Featured by Amazon, Apple, and Google, and benefiting from the usual cross-promotional vehicles and social media push, it took the number one spot in three hours. As always, Rovio prepped up some spectacular launch events.

Konsta Klemetti had joined the marketing-communication department as marketing manager. He arrived from leading digital agency Valve but prior to this had worked for creative agencies, with a long career in the music industry, mostly with MTV Europe and Music Export Finland. While working on the *Bad Piggies'* launch plans, there was a Pink Floyd reference that a colleague, Les Spink, brought up during a brainstorming session and which Klemetti couldn't get out of his head. The cover of the progressive rock band's album *Animals* (1977) showed a giant pig floating above the iconic Battersea Power Station, on the bank of the Thames in southwest London. Klemetti convinced Head of Marketing Ville Heijari that it could be cool to reenact this. He contacted the management at Battersea Power Station and got redirected to the approval department. After looking at a price list for various possibilities, he booked a takeover date. He then called a specialized company to make a giant Green Pig balloon and tie it to the top of the building. He also coordinated a lighting company to project the green logo of *Bad Piggies* on the side of the building and to light up the balloon itself. The stunt was visible along the whole Thames waterfront of southwest London and was covered on television, while also generating buzz on social media.

Since the appeal of the spinoff brand was naturally slightly lower than for the main *Angry Birds* titles, Klemetti couldn't find a partner to co-sponsor the stunt. For the first time in *Angry Birds* history, Rovio financed the operation itself, finding it too cool to pass on. The whole stunt cost approximately €100,000. It would be impossible to measure the conversion rate of such an offline campaign accurately, as opposed to online advertising, which offers very good tracking analytics, but it's not about that. It's about brand recognition. When a stunt works, it builds a connection between the brand and the fans. It's something tangible, something real that you can see with your own eyes, and that's kind of priceless. It builds real brand equity.

In the U.S., Barnes & Noble respected tradition by playing the *Bad Piggies* trailers in its 800 front windows and putting the game on the screens of every demonstration device in its retail outlets. The Rovio team in China was on the ball, too. Finally set up as a real company, with a real team in a real office, the subsidiary created a series of events with China Mobile in Shanghai. On the iconic Bund waterfront, facing the upscale Pudong area of Shanghai, the telecom giant helped Rovio display its *Bad Piggies* trailer on the largest television screen in the world, covering the entire side of the gigantic Citigroup Tower looming over the riverside. The trailer ended with the words: "Download with China Mobile."

China Mobile also threw a big launch party in another venue. In the streets, a Red Bird truck and a Green Piggy truck were constantly chasing each other, zooming through neighborhoods throughout the city. In Hong Kong, a partnership with Nissan was arranged. The Japanese car manufacturer was busy promoting its new electric vehicle, the Leaf. There was a connection through color: Both brands were decisively green. On launch day, hundreds of Nissan Leaf cars, disguised as Bad Piggies for the day, drove around the peninsula, with passengers handing out merchandising to citizens along the route.

On the lookout for a big event in Asia, Henri Holm reached out to the mayor of Taipei through a mutual friend. Making a compelling case, he convinced the mayor to let Rovio decorate Taipei 101, the city's tallest skyscraper, with green piggy lights. The mayor granted his approval free of charge, after Holm pointed out that the footage would make the news around the world. The only provision was that the word "TAIPEI" was included as part of the message. Holm got Taiwan's leading telecom corporation, Far EasTone, on board, in exchange for providing its digital Android store with content. To help spread the campaign to every neighborhood in Taiwan, Far EasTone completely rebranded all its 200 brick-and-mortar stores nationwide. *Angry Birds*-clothed women also handed out 10,000 *Bad Piggies* helium balloons on the sidewalks in front of every shop. The skyscraper stunt itself shone across the Taipei skyline and was visible from all over the capital.

The development team also incorporated a neat viral tool inside the *Bad Piggies* game that facilitated the spread of user-generated content on YouTube. The idea was borrowed from the *Amazing Alex* project, another example of added value from the *Casey's Contraptions* acquisition. Since the game was about building vehicles from nuts and bolts and then heading out on wacky rides, with millions of different scenarios possible, every attempt to clear a level was a unique experiment. As a result, failing in *Bad Piggies* was not frustrating. Konsta Klemetti points out, "That's very rare in gaming and I find that really cool."[5] Making failure fun and a kind of success was the whole design philosophy according to lead designer, Markus Tuppurainen. Hence the slogan: "Bad Piggies Never Give Up."

The mindset was embraced by the music department as well. Salla Hakkola worked on several versions of a track that ended up not fitting the bill as the *Bad Piggies* theme song. She still remembers the heart crush: "I was so excited because it was my first theme song composition, so I was really sad when the decision was made to cut it, only two weeks before the release of the game. It's part of the job and it still happens to me to this day, but this was my first time facing such a situation."[6] Ilmari Hakkola adds to the story: "Petri Järvilehto had doubts all along. I just sat on a piano and went nuts, playing something tragicomic against the clock. It was then re-recorded properly, using piano, mandolin, accordion, and a high whistle as the main instruments for the final theme song."[7] Fail fast. Fix faster.

Within the game, *Bad Piggies* enabled users to record their failed attempts and upload them to YouTube in a couple of taps, thereby ensuring a barrage of fan videos on the channel. This was something that the fans had already been doing a lot in *Angry Birds* anyway, under their own steam; making it easy on them through plug-in EveryPlay (later acquired by Unity 3D) was a great way to fuel the trend. It took only a few days before a fan-led community site appeared on the web, under the pigineering.com domain name. The site rapidly collected more traffic than even the official badpiggies.com page. Rovio could count on a very reactive fan base. A year later, Pigineering would merge with AngryBirdsNest.com into a mega-community where bird-lovers and pig fans share stories, content, and scores to this day.

The customer support team was led by Ric Thorneycroft at the time. To Thorneycroft and his colleagues, connecting with fans was a serious business. It was no longer just about troubleshooting or finding technical solutions. The team was constantly brainstorming to think up cool ways to keep customers in love with *Angry Birds*, or to make them fall back in love with it. They enjoyed thrilling individual fans by going way over the top with the "Surprise and Delight" mantra—just to see their gasping and gawking reactions.

When Rovio organized social media competitions, the first prize was frequently something that "money can't buy," such as a miniature 3D model of a level that the graphic artists had sculpted and painted for the winner. One of the most touching fan-related events was undoubtedly Ben Levi's wedding proposal to Melissa Swift. Ben had emailed Rovio from Australia with the crazy request for it to create an *Angry Birds Friends* level especially for his proposal. Rovio got back to him. To his surprise and delight, they were going to do it with the cameras from *The Huffington Post* hidden inside the restaurant where the proposal was to take place. On the day, when Melissa finished playing the special level, the words "MEL, MARRY ME" appeared in the virtual skies, and Ben went down on one knee. In tears, she said: "Oh my God, I'm actually gonna die!" before adding, "Of course I will." Ben won the level with three stars.

Another very moving time for the whole team was when an email came from a fan explaining that his mother had terminal cancer and that she only got her beautiful smile back when her family put an iPad with *Angry Birds* in her hands: "Thank you for bringing back joy into my mother's life."[8] On a similar note, a worried dad emailed in when his son, a huge *Angry Birds* fan, was about to have open-heart surgery. The web development team coordinated a special edition of the Facebook game *Angry Birds Friends*, bearing the name of the little boy as a watermark in the corner and playable only through his account. It also included a personal message, to build up his courage before he went into the operating theater. It's hard to imagine better customer support!

As might have been predicted, the spinoff never quite reached the same heights as *Angry Birds*, *Angry Birds Rio*, *Angry Birds*

Seasons, or *Angry Birds Space*. Nevertheless, by surpassing the 100 million downloads mark by the end of 2013, *Bad Piggies* was still within the top 1 percent of all-time successful game apps. It was a decent feat by Rovio's standards, but an outstanding achievement from a broader perspective. Creatively and artistically, *Bad Piggies* also presented Rovio with a great chance to expand on the piggy side of the universe. The refresh on their mischievous looks opened up new opportunities in consumer goods licensing, and also laid the foundation for another lead that Rovio wanted to pursue in the future: to turn its animation production into a proper cartoon series. And for that, it needed to flesh out the antagonists. Furthermore, *Bad Piggies* was a more complex game than *Angry Birds*, with gameplay nuances aimed at a more mature audience.

Such back-to-back operations also kept the momentum at a maximum and the marketing-communication team on its toes, as they were about to launch its fourth number-one title within a single year—maybe the biggest of them all ...

CHAPTER THIRTEEN

The Galaxy Far, Far Away

During the development of *Angry Birds Space*, the team started toying with the idea of having content updates introducing new levels set in the universes of sci-fi classics such as *Star Trek, Battlestar Galactica, Star Wars,* and *Plan 9 from Outer Space.*

Since everybody wanted to partner up with it, Rovio could choose its dream partners, even among those who hadn't reached out yet. Head of North America Andrew Stalbow picked up the phone and called the company at the top of Rovio's list: Lucasfilm. The talk immediately took a very positive turn. The top executives at Lucasfilm had seen what Rovio and Stalbow had pulled off with Fox on *Angry Birds Rio* and were impressed. Lucasfilm had partnered with many different brands—LEGO *Star Wars* immediately comes to mind—but, as Philip Hickey notes, "I don't know if they ever paired with a brand as young on the market as we were."[1] It soon became apparent to everyone at Rovio that such a massive opportunity deserved more than a game update. It was worth a full game. All other possible sci-fi partners were rapidly forgotten and the excitement at Rovio was such that it went all in with *Star Wars.*

One person didn't share in the enthusiasm. With *Angry Birds Space,* Jaakko Iisalo felt he and his team had already delivered the best possible *Angry Birds* game. Like a few others, he was at the end of his tether. He was getting tired of *Angry Birds* and wanted to work on something new. It didn't help that, although he liked the movies, Iisalo was not necessarily the biggest *Star Wars* geek on the planet. He remembers: "I told my boss that I didn't want to do it."[2] A couple of days later, Petri Järvilehto sat down with Iisalo to calmly talk things through, and eventually convinced him to do just one more version of the *Angry Birds* game.

They also made a compromise stipulating that Iisalo would pass on the torch before moving on to his next project. Iisalo designed *Angry Birds Star Wars* in conjunction with his protégés, Sami Lindqvist and Kimmo Sorsamo, with the goal of preparing them to lead the next *Angry Birds* games. Iisalo added one further condition: To lessen his workload, he needed somebody very familiar with the *Star Wars* universe to handle the characters and their attributes. Fans of the *Skywalker Saga* since childhood and familiar with its lore, Art Director Toni Kysenius and Character Designer Miguel Francisco had the honor of taking on the responsibility.

Free as a Bird

One good surprise for Iisalo and his team ended up making the experience much more pleasurable than expected: Lucasfilm granted them total creative freedom. Kysenius confirms this in *Hatching a Universe*: "I assumed that there would be limitations. I was concerned we wouldn't get a say in the design. But it turned out to be amazing, because it was clear that they were as excited to be working with our brand as we were to be working with theirs."[3] Salla Hakkola was even given freedom to have fun with the iconic John Williams themes: "We decided to give it our distinct Balkan style. The first internal demo was actually produced using only recorders and flutes in the intro; it pretty much sounded like the school kids' version of *Star Wars*."[4]

Obviously, it was imperative that the launch strategy would be cross-media. As with *Angry Birds Space*, the launch had to be orchestrated across every department. Consumer products were a top priority, and Rovio collaborated for the first time with global leading toy-manufacturer Hasbro, Lucasfilm's favorite licensee for decades.

In the summer of 2012, Andrew Stalbow hired Naz Cuevas into the Santa Monica branch and put her in charge of consumer products and retail strategy for North America. A top executive in the U.S. for over 20 years, Cuevas had studied business law and worked in sales and marketing for Warner Bros. and Univision, in consumer products for Fremantle Media, and even in video game console accessories for Naki in China. In short, she is a citizen of the world, an important quality for a global-thinking company: She is of Indian descent, speaks English, Spanish, and Portuguese fluently, and has developed the Latin American market for several of her former employers. She had also worked on numerous brands including Marvel, *Harry Potter*, FIFA World Cup, *Looney Tunes*, and *The Powerpuff Girls*.

Luckily for Rovio, which was beginning to overextend its licensing activities exactly at this time, Cuevas did a fantastic job at protecting the *Star Wars* license while it was in quarantine. Cuevas still remembers her first day and Stalbow telling her, "You manage the most important territory that we have. However, the most important task you have today is to focus. That is the number-one challenge that Rovio has, because everybody will want to work with Rovio. You need to be able to say, 'This is where I need to go.'" Cuevas also clearly recalls his last sentence: "Right now the Lucas relationship is the one to nurture."[5]

Stalbow and Cuevas decided to team up with Toys "R" Us as a special retail partner for the *Angry Birds Star Wars* operation. *Angry Birds* was already present on the shelves of the global toy chain, through Mattel, Commonwealth, and a few other licensees. Hasbro product lines gave it the opportunity to take things to another level, ensuring massive in-channel advertisement in its 879 American outlets, later expanding into the extra 885 stores it had in 35 other countries. To seal the relationship, Cuevas and Stalbow, in accordance with the marketing team, agreed to hold the press conference for the official announcement in the Toys "R" Us Times Square flagship store. Hickey explains:

> It was paramount to keep things confidential with our partners. Leakage greatly damages the ability to make impactful launches. Most leaks actually come through production processes. Because those go to retail and you may have at least five people away from the original company and you never know what happens. Every partner had a super NDA (non-disclosure agreement) and they did an amazing job preventing leaks. The extra precautions they took to keep it secret were unprecedented.[6]

Hickey had good reasons to want to protect the unveiling from leaks. He was working on a cool digital plan in which he had a lot of faith. That wasn't the case for everyone inside Rovio. He recalls, "Many people were asking me, 'Are you really sure about this?'"[7] Hickey's line of thought was that they had already made the biggest event possible with *Angry Birds Space*. But with this one, why not go the other way and make the smallest announcement possible? *Star Wars* was such a massive brand on its own, *Angry Birds* was heading toward that status ... Match them up and you'd have a huge entertainment headline. When you have something that big, there's no need to hype it up and make it bigger. No need to "push" anything to the media. This kind of news was big enough to "pull" the media toward you.

On Friday night, October 5, 2012, Rovio casually dropped a simple three-second animation as a GIF file, the simplest animated file format on earth, very popular with the "meme" community on the internet. The GIF showed Red Bird with Luke Skywalker–blond hair, wielding a lightsaber. The text was a tease about a major announcement planned for the following Monday in the Toys "R" Us Times Square flagship store. It instantly went viral.

The following Monday, October 8, 2012, the store on Times Square was ready for the press conference, *Angry Birds Star Wars* imagery plastered across the facade. Hasbro, Commonwealth, Fifth Sun, and others had all worked around the clock to have prototypes and samples of the consumer product lines ready on time. Paul Southern, VP of licensing and consumer products marketing at Lucasfilm, told U.S. business magazine *Fast Company*: "Both Rovio and Lucasfilm have worked with 50 licensees in more than 100 countries to develop items from toys to apparel and bedding."[8] There was even a giant 2 by 2 meter plush toy of the Chewie Bird—the gigantic red-colored bird, Terence, meets the character Chewbacca from the original movie—sitting on a pedestal in the middle of the room. Besides media, thousands of fans lined up as early as 8 A.M. for the big event, which was massively covered internationally and generated a lot of excitement on-site.

Hickey and the marketing-communications team had kept the gameplay footage under wraps because they wanted to replicate the same "Marketing the Marketing" strategy as with *Angry Birds Space*, by pacing the material distribution at a sustained tempo. If the unveiling of "New Species" characters had generated excitement, Rovio could only speculate about the level of anticipation there would be in fans waiting to see how the *Angry Birds Star Wars* breed would look. First came Red Skywalker and Stella

Organa, followed by C3PYOLK and R2EGG2, Chuck "Ham" Solo, and Chewie Terebacca, and, of course, the characters from the climactic battle of the original movie, *Star Wars Episode IV—A New Hope*: Lard Vader and Obi-Wan Kaboomi. They were all there, stylized either as bird or pig. The final trailer, which was published on November 7, revisited the cult *Mos Eisley Cantina* scene through three minutes and 30 seconds of animated comedy. The game launched 24 hours later and immediately climbed to number one, after just 150 minutes of being available. It paralleled the *Angry Birds Space* sales curve, downloaded 10 million times within three days.

The merchandise was already available by October 28 so that the new costumes would be in shops in time for Halloween, and sales figures were huge. Hickey recalls, "Hasbro are the masters at making things collectible. They know how to put the right sets together, they know how to have an unbelievable offering for 'starting kits'— and the mad collectors know exactly what they want, what completes their sets, and what the exclusives are."[9] The Piggy Death Star special edition of classic game *Jenga* reached the number-one spot in the Toys category of Amazon.com, while the now-traditional *National Geographic* tie-in achieved the same in books. Over at Barnes & Noble, the numerous *Star Wars*-related books in existence were brought together with the *Angry Birds* line into one prime-located mega-aisle.

Mega Launch

The eye-catching mega launch event this time took place in Shanghai, with the Chinese team showing the boys back in Finland that they too could pull off crazy stunts. There was one location in the city that was reputed to be impossible to get: the Oriental Pearl Tower. Owned by the Central People's Government, it used to host the public radio offices. Nowadays, it has become a tourist attraction. The Oriental Pearl Tower is the second most visited tower in the world, behind the Eiffel Tower in Paris.

Through connections and introductions, Paul Chen got in touch with the director of the iconic building. The director and his staff all played *Angry Birds* games and were aware of its popularity. Two months before the launch of *Angry Birds Star Wars*, Chen was invited to a meeting, during which he understood that money was not the motivation: Oriental Pearl Tower has become the beacon of China and what they were after was fame. To catch up with the Eiffel Tower in terms of global recognition, the Oriental Pearl needed to appear in a lot of movies and other placements with high visibility—such as *Angry Birds*. A verbal deal was struck on the following basis: Rovio could do its press conference for the *Angry Birds Star Wars* launch in the building, but the Pearl Tower must appear in an eventual China-based update in *Angry Birds Seasons*. Hands were shaken. To facilitate the operation, Rovio was even introduced to an events company that was renowned in the area. Rovio China started sending invites to the press and media and organized a competition through Sina Weibo in which 50 lucky fans would be invited to the select party. They made sure to include a couple of "ultra-fans" who had sent Rovio some pictures of their *Angry Birds*-themed wedding.

Chen and Pan were hellbent on turning this unique occasion into a major event, to make up for the fact that the *Star Wars* brand was not as popular in China as it was elsewhere. After all, the original trilogy had never been officially released in Chinese cinemas. The tower itself was turned into a giant red lightsaber. The conference commenced with a 30-minute staged ceremony involving a laser show and an epic lightsaber duel between Obi-Wan Kenobi, played by Paul Chen, and Darth Vader, played by Shanghai-based actor Frank Zhang. This was followed by an introduction to the characters and in-game footage on a giant screen.

The ceremony ended with the ultra-fans couple being invited on stage to be gifted giant plush toys that were almost as big as them. After the presentation segment, the crowd was invited to have fun in six different sections, including a real-life replica of the game, a stand with people explaining how to make *Angry Birds* characters out of clay, a Hasbro booth with its full lineup of toys, and a stall stocked with edible merchandising. About one hundred press and media turned up, including all the big national television stations, giving the *Angry Birds Star Wars* launch a lot of coverage. Combined with the ongoing ten-week campaign with McDonald's, the event gave *Angry Birds* a lot of momentum in China at this time.

Angry Birds Star Wars stayed at the number-one position in the App Store charts for three months in a row. Such a feat was no longer thought possible in 2012, with the days of the original *Angry Birds* being long gone. But, irrefutably, the best reward for the *Star Wars* fans within the Rovio team was the fact that George Lucas wore a "Pig Vader" sweatshirt at the 2012 Formula 1 U.S. Grand Prix in Austin, Texas, on November 18. Coincidentally, *Angry Birds* was also present on the track during that race, on the Lotus F1 car of Kimi Räikkönen and on the helmet of Heikki Kovalainen, driving for Caterham—both the drivers being Finns.

The December 2012 rush took Rovio's monthly active users number to an all-time high, with 263 million people playing an *Angry Birds* game that month. On Christmas Day alone, *Angry Birds* games were downloaded 8.5 million times—out of a total of 15 million new device activations. Across the whole Christmas week, from December 22 through December 29, the figure grew to 30 million. When Disney published its numbers to impress people with how many millions of apps it had sold during Christmas week, across its entire portfolio, Rovio was astonished to discover that its own figures were much better. It issued a blog post with an infographic showing that every second mobile device activated during that Christmas week had *Angry Birds* on it. In total, by December 31, 2012, lifetime downloads of all *Angry Birds* games surpassed 1.7 billion. On the back of four number-one chart-toppers within a single year, total consolidated full-year revenue grew by 101 percent, amounting to €152.2 million. Earnings before interest and taxes (EBIT) were €76.8 million, up 64 percent on the previous year, while the employee headcount had grown from 224 to 518 within the calendar year.

The Christmas Tree Effect

Each year on Christmas Day, *Angry Birds* enjoyed a massive boost in downloads. This can be explained by two factors. The first is that many children received iTunes gift vouchers under the Christmas tree, which they got to spend as they saw fit, sometimes on games they had wanted to buy for a long time. The second and more significant effect came from the millions of iPads and iPhones that were given as gifts and therefore activated on Christmas Day. The fresh blood boosted *Angry Birds* more than any other app series because of the strength of its marketing during the whole year. *Angry Birds* was pretty much to mobile what Yahoo or Amazon has been to the web in its early days—the first words you typed into the blank field because they were the first ones that popped into your mind. And if nothing came to mind, it was *Angry Birds* sitting at number one when you first wandered in the App Store charts. The newcomer might not yet know much about their new device but they knew there was *Angry Birds* on it.

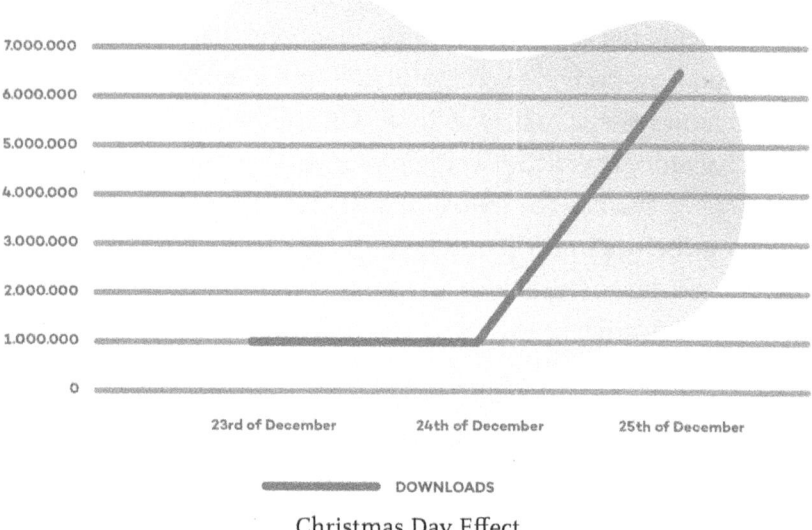

7.000.000			
6.000.000			
5.000.000			
4.000.000			
3.000.000			
2.000.000			
1.000.000			
0			
	23rd of December	24th of December	25th of December

DOWNLOADS

Christmas Day Effect

Join the Pork Side

The reception for *Angry Birds Star Wars* was so strong that Lucasfilm wanted to make a sequel, this time based on the prequel trilogy from the motion picture series. "As casual games grow as a category and mobile devices grow as an interface, it's going to become more important for us in the future," Paul Southern, VP of licensing and consumer products marketing at Lucasfilm, told *Fast Company*. "Our partnership with Rovio helped us to understand a little bit more about how they achieved that success."[10]

Hickey has vivid memories of the atmosphere around the table when they met to talk about the possibility of a sequel at the San Francisco premises of Lucasfilm. He recounts: "In the original kick-off meeting for *Angry Birds Star Wars*, we were just five people in the room. For this brainstorming about *Angry Birds Star Wars II*, the room was full, with over 50 persons sitting in, and they had to turn people down owing to lack of space. We literally couldn't fit everybody in the room."[11] After the meeting, the visiting Rovians—including an excited Kysenius, who sometimes dressed in a custom-made Jedi outfit for Star Wars Celebrations— were treated to a tour of Skywalker Ranch.

The extra attention meant increased pressure on the approval process, with more people looking over the different elements of the second game. This was particularly palpable on the art front, with the characters going through multiple rounds of edits. Miguel Francisco was trying to focus on other projects and let other artists take over the second *Star Wars* collaboration, but he was soon pulled back in. Typically for him, Phil Hickey went maverick. "All of a sudden, Phil pops to my desk and whispers to me, 'Look, don't tell anyone we are doing this, but I need you to give a pass to the character designs, because the deadline is approaching and we are not getting assets approval from Lucas.' I promised him to give it a try."[12] All of Francisco's character designs got approved within 24 hours. For many, there seemed to be a mental association between the *Angry Birds* signature style and Miguel Francisco's personal touch. To this day, freelance artists booked by Rovio are regularly shown Miguel Francisco's designs as references for the style they should aim for.

The biggest challenge was to find a big new thing that would wow the fans, in order to justify the sequel. Hasbro came to the rescue with an idea that made perfect sense for the project. In fact, it was the logical next step for which Rovio had been unknowingly preparing for the previous three years by exploring both the merchandise route and the fast-track education the company had hawked about the entertainment world.

In February 2012, Hasbro entered a master-licensing agreement with French company Les Éditions Volumiques and a proprietary technology called "Zapped" on which the small startup held patents. Volumiques had developed a system that looked and sounded like magic at first: You put a physical item on the touchscreen of your tablet or smartphone and the object transfers data to the app and triggered an in-app action. The whole thing relied on mini QR codes. Hasbro had first used this technology in semi-interactive editions of its classic board games such as *Game of Life*, *Monopoly*, and *Battleship*, introduced at the 2012 New York Toy Fair. The technology was refined by adding a small pedestal on which the object had to be placed to connect with the app. The pedestal was essentially a small covert magnifier which meant that the size of the QR code was reduced to a minimum, making it less visible and thereby increasing the "magic." Hasbro branded the concept Telepods.

Telepod Patented Tech

By using Telepods in combination with *Angry Birds Star Wars II*, players were able to add new playable characters into the game after purchasing them in toy format. The game business fed the toy business, which in turn fed the game business again; the cross-platform compatibility was truly circular. Rovio had already developed both sides of the universe, the physical and the digital, extremely well. Telepod technology offered it a way to tie in both sides and blend them into a single extensive experience. It was a brilliant model, both from a user and economic perspective. It served as a great way to tap into that unbelievably large and rich cast of characters and creatures that appeared in the *Star Wars* movies, much to the delight of Thomas Lundström, Rovio's product development manager, who was put in charge of designing the range of Telepod toys (during his years at Rovio he only ever wore either a *Star Wars* or an *Angry Birds Star Wars* T-shirt). It was also a harbinger of the future, according to Naz Cuevas, who adopted a forecast she had heard from Stalbow: "We believe that in two to three years, the smartphone will be the remote control to your entertainment life," she said.[13]

From a development perspective, the Telepod concept increased the pressure on Sami Lindqvist for his first *Angry Birds* game as lead designer. It was essentially two games in one. The game had to be playable in full without the Telepods and still offer a wonderful experience. When you incorporated Telepod characters, the game had to evolve without breaking the balance. There was a lot of layering around that onion.

On July 15, 2013, a joint press release from Rovio and Hasbro officially announced the game as well as the Telepods. Over the rest of the week at San Diego Comic-Con, Hasbro set up a massive booth to introduce the Telepods to the public. The toy line's interactivity with the game was also demonstrated on iPads and Android tablets. The demonstration generated a lot of buzz among the Comic-Con crowd.

The San Diego festival had become the ultimate geek-chic celebration, bringing in over 130,000 visitors every year, a lot of whom come dressed cosplay-style for the occasion. From famous comic superheroes to TV shows, sci-fi movies, animé, and manga, everything with a cult following was represented there. So much so that "It's very hard to cut through the news,"[14] says Hickey, and achieving that was a milestone by itself.

The booth was packed with parents and kids, a throng of *Star Wars* cosplayers, the biggest American media, and even the actor behind Darth Maul, Ray Park, who paid a visit to check out his Telepod doppelgänger.

The online "Marketing the Marketing" campaign gradually built anticipation in the six weeks leading up to the launch on September 19, 2013, and Hickey dared to dream of what his *Star Wars*-obsessed inner child would love to see. Robio's social media manager Robin Squire performed a bit of research on Twitter and found out that two actors who had starred in the *Star Wars* series played *Angry Birds Star Wars* and sometimes tweeted about their fondness for the game. Squire tweeted back to Peter Mayhew, the man behind the Chewbacca mask, and Daniel Logan, the actor who plays Young Boba Fett. They both agreed to do the ribbon-cutting for the unveiling of their character on Twitter on the relevant day. Though each had a solid following on Twitter to help spread the word, this was not a ploy to gain numbers but rather to build credibility with *Star Wars* fans.

Since the main tagline of the game was "Join the Pork Side"—the game was the first in the franchise to let you choose whether you want to sling birds at pigs or pigs at birds—who better than the emperor of the dark side himself to invite you in? Hickey, who still owns many of his childhood *Star Wars* figurines (his wife calls them "his dolls"), whose son's birth name is Liam Anakin Hickey, and whose dog is named Lando, reached out to Ian McDiarmid, the actor who has played Emperor Palpatine in all six movies. Hickey humbly enquired whether the Scotsman would loan his iconic voice to the animation trailer.

McDiarmid had never done anything like this before. Although he had heard of *Angry Birds*, he had never played the game, so he asked for a little time to investigate. After performing a quick background check, he agreed to meet the crew at their recording studio. Philip Hickey was starstruck: "To have the original Emperor invite you to join the pork side took it to another level. He was such a professional. It was so much fun to make, and the video turned out great with that unique *Angry Birds* blend of humor. What an honor and what a blessing to have somebody like that participate in such an idea. It was pretty awesome, man!"[15]

Besides the honor of meeting McDiarmid, it was also a special moment for Rovio as it was the first time in the history of *Angry Birds* that a pig's voice would be heard out loud. "It's a special moment for pigs too," quipped Ian McDiarmid when he was informed of the fact.[16]

While reading the script, McDiarmid couldn't resist telling the team a crispy on-set anecdote about the original 1977 shooting in which the Emperor's chair didn't stop at the right place when he turned around to face the camera. In the "Behind the Scenes" excerpt available on Rovio's YouTube channel, McDiarmid remembers: "They mechanized it, of course, but it never stopped exactly where we wanted it to. So George [Lucas] told me to do it myself. And I just did this [McDiarmid pushes on the floor with the back of his heels]."[17]

Once published on YouTube, the *Join the Pork Side* video built instant street cred with the fans, and went on to generate 7 million views, 17,610 likes, and 1,088 comments in its first months of availability, ranging from "I was like, is that Ian McDiarmid? And then no effing way it was. Beautiful" (Ryan Malin) to "OK. I am really not an *Angry Birds* fan. But, this was too funny not to share" (Ricardo Garza).

In the seven days leading up to the live date, the marketing-communications teams went for broke on all owned media, sharing new details and material to the press every single day. The unveiling of the characters on Twitter took place as scheduled. Although Peter Mayhew (aka Chewbacca) was undergoing knee surgery during this time, he didn't let that get in the way, tweeting the link to the Chewie bird video on YouTube from his hospital bed. To highlight the fact that players could choose to play as bird or pig, each character, depending on which side they rooted for, bore one of two hashtags in the right corner of the video clip: #JoinThePorkSide or #MayTheBirdsBeWithYou. This schism encouraged fans to pick a side. Such an action creates much more loyalty than simply retweeting about a game's title.

Aside from social media, Rovio also worked to ensure that members of its existing player-base were on the edge of their seats. In the week leading up to the release of *Angry Birds Star Wars II*, big updates were pushed out for three previously released *Angry Birds* titles. It started with *Angry Birds Star Wars*, the most relevant title for conversion purposes. The *Mission Endor* content expansion pack was added to the game. *Mission Endor* focused on the *Return of the Jedi* movie and completed the arc of the original trilogy, just in time before *Angry Birds Star Wars II* would dive into the prequel episodes. After that, new levels were added to *Angry Birds Space* and to *Angry Birds Classic*. Releasing those updates boosted the levels of daily active users across all these games. People who had finished all the levels available and moved on to other games came back when the App Store alerted them that there was a new version out. By drawing players back, engagement levels peaked right at the moment a massive digital advertising campaign was going to be splashed out for *Angry Birds Star Wars II*. It also served as a reminder to fans that when you invest 99 cents in an *Angry Birds* game, you tend to get plenty of free extra content over time for that dollar. This reminder was timed to coincide with the precise moment players were to make the decision whether to shell out a dollar for *Angry Birds Star Wars II*, which fancily launched with the video trailer featured on the NASDAQ Jumbotron in New York's Times Square.

As launch week neared, Hickey, Bergström, and Squire became increasingly worried about the fact they were going head to head with one of the biggest video game franchises of all times: *Grand Theft Auto*. *GTA V* was set to release on Tuesday, September 17, 2013, with *Angry Birds Star Wars II* following two days later, on Thursday, September 19. Facing a sequel that had been anxiously anticipated by fans for years, there were legitimate concerns that by Thursday gamers not playing *GTA V* would be watching the *GTA V* "Let's Play" video on YouTube. If you had another video game launching that same week, there was a serious chance of being drowned under the tsunami. Phil Hickey vividly remembers: "We felt a bit under pressure. Nobody had spent more money on a game or its marketing, no other game has been awaited for this long, with such high expectations. So we could not really compete but we needed to stay relevant and win the attention of the internet."[18]

With their typical rebellious and irreverent approach, the team figured out a way to turn the situation to their advantage with a very low-key but also very bold twist. They simply created a spoof asset that looked like a cover of *Angry Birds Star Wars II in* classic *Grand Theft Auto* style, from the font of the title lettering to the color code, to the cutout outline of the character heads on the poster, and the style of the character heads themselves— everything looked like it was a *Grand Theft Auto* cover, except the title clearly read *Angry Birds Star Wars II*, and the character faces in the vignettes looked like Chewie, Darth Maul, Mace Windu, Anakin Skywalker, Jar Jar Binks, General Grievous, Princess Leia,

Red Bird Skywalker, and so on. The spoof image was posted on the *Angry Birds* Twitter account on 17 September, the day of the *GTA V* launch, to catch some of its traffic and ride its coattails instead of getting buried. The tweet read: "If you play one blockbuster sequel this fall play GTAV, but if you play two, play #AngryBirdsStarWars2@RockstarGames."[19] Cheeky. Maybe even a bit risqué as a brand association for Lucas, though ... especially if maverick Hickey dropped the asset without asking for prior permission 48 hours before posting, as per agreements. Hickey remembers the fallout very well: "Someone from Lucas called. I've never been yelled at so much in my entire career. But a few days later, after seeing how well the post performed in data with extremely favorable press, another executive at Lucas decided to put the matter to bed."[20]

It was no longer a surprise that millions of Day One downloads quickly drove *Angry Birds Star Wars II* to number one in all digital stores. The groundbreaking achievement was elsewhere this time. Within the first 30 days of sale, Hasbro sold through 1 million Telepods, on the back of a top-notch TV commercial campaign. By May 28, 2014, less than a year later, Telepod toys would lead to a total of 30 million scans inside *Angry Birds Star Wars II*. Compared to the digital numbers, which often run into the hundreds of millions, and even billions, this may not seem all that impressive. But the logistics behind physical products are much more complicated than in the virtual world.

Let's assume that your prototype is approved for mass production. In the case of an app, it is submitted through the platform-holder's certification process and, within a week, it's ready to go live or you get a report of bugs to fix. Once live, it becomes available within seconds to anybody who taps on it and pays the required fee (if any) through a digital payment method, in 177 countries. How many you sell doesn't affect your workload—the servers of Apple, Google, or Amazon take care of everything for you. As for inventory, the pool is infinite and yet there is never any excess stock since units are reproduced at the exact moment they are purchased, without using any production material whatsoever.

In the case of a physical product, mass-production is done by hand in factories. Every stage of production takes time and the turnaround for such a massive amount can easily take a few months. All these products must then go through quality-control and quality-approval stages (which basically consists of trying to break the thing). They are then packaged in a retail-friendly box or blister clamshell, and then in carton boxes, appropriately marked with barcodes for warehousing and customs purposes. They are then shipped to their main markets on cargo boats. The "ocean freight" part of things can take up to a month when it comes to deliveries to North America or Europe. Then they go through customs. Depending on the target country, there can be taxes and tariffs to pay at that stage, and definitely paper-work to clear. Once the product is in the country, it still needs to be delivered from the distribution center to the retail sellers' warehouses by truck. Another trucking waltz follows when the retail chains break down the stock between their various stores. In each point of sale, employees put the goods on shelves and the promo material where it's supposed to be displayed. At this point, the "sell-through" can finally begin: Those 1 million toys are then picked off shelves, scanned through, and paid for at the counters. That's the supply chain being managed. To be able to deliver 1 million toys to kids in 30 days takes a half year's prepa-ration, a couple of emergency planes for replenishment, and a crazy rush for store employees at participating stores. Santa Claus's life isn't easy.

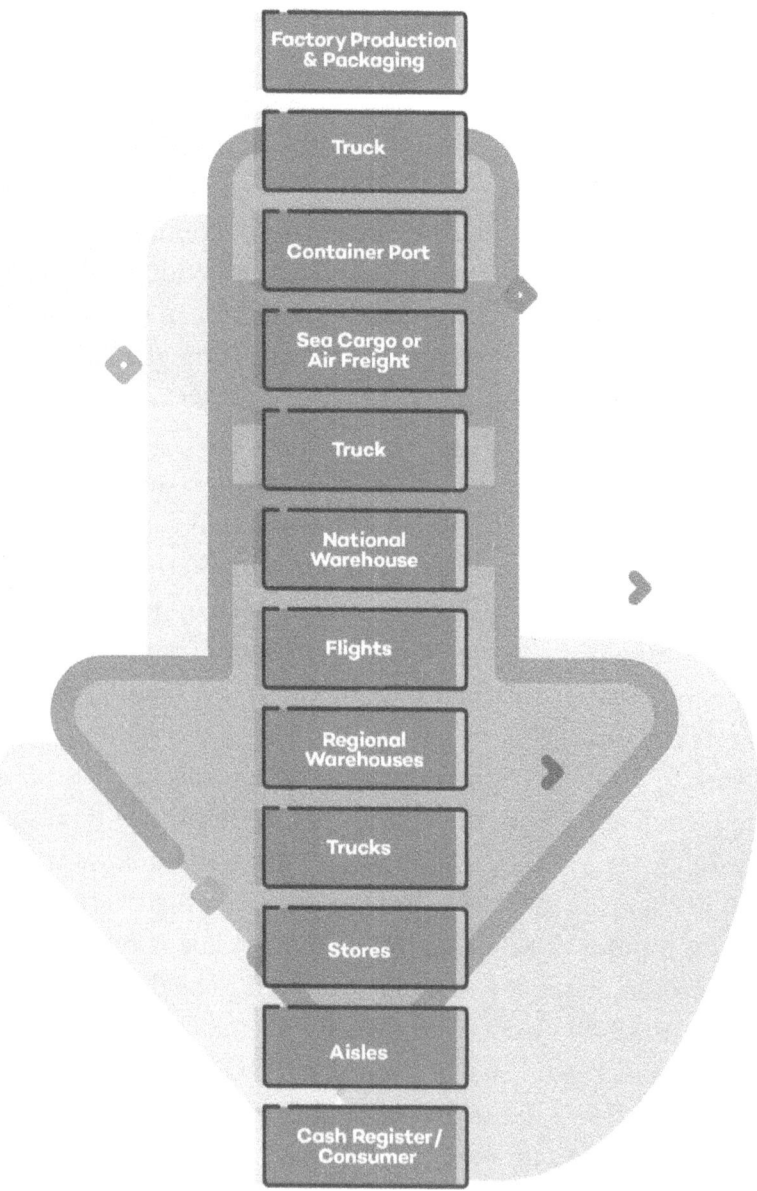

Logistics Supply Chain

Some licensing deals are nothing more than a brand name slapped on a product. *Angry Birds Star Wars* turned out to be the perfect win-win partnership. *Star Wars* was an iconic global brand, very strong in Europe and America, especially with mature gamers and the male demographic (as proven by the skewed stats: Most *Angry Birds* games were played by a 50/50 percent male/female audience while *Angry Birds Star Wars* was played by a predominantly male audience). On the other hand, the universally appealing *Angry Birds* helped Lucasfilm introduce the *Star Wars* brand to today's kids, boost its popularity with women, and give it a nice bump in China. As in the case of the *Angry Birds Rio* collaboration, it also gave the partnering brands a huge social media presence and direct engagement with fans through web and mobile. Learning this know-how was strategically crucial for Lucasfilm, as shown by its renewed approach to social media and mobile landscape after the collaboration. As for fanboy Phil Hickey, his profile picture on Facebook shows the late great Carrie Fisher and Mark Hamill posing together with his children and wife for the first family picture of new-born Finn at the 2015 Anaheim Star Wars Celebration. For a man who grew up playing with the Kenner *Star Wars* action figures, talk about coming full circle—he is now part of The Family as much as they are part of his extended family.

In many ways, *Angry Birds Star Wars* felt like a passing of the baton between two generations, a match made in heaven. The best evidence for this is that "some kids posted their disappointment on social media when they went to the theater to see the new *Star Wars* movie and there were no birds in it."[21]

The New "4Ps" of Social Business Marketing

In the 1960s, E. Jerome McCarthy, a marketing professor at Michigan State University, defined the four pillars of marketing, or the 4Ps, in his influential book *Basic Marketing*.[22] The 4Ps are as follows: Product, Place, Price, Promotion. According to David Amerland, writing for *Forbes*,

> Its legacy created a technocratic culture—one that focuses on the product's attributes, neglecting its value and appeal to customers. It's a long-standing military truism that generals always fight the last war. In the 21st-century marketplace, goods are commoditized. Technical attributes have become mere entry-level requirements—they're not the outstanding reason why consumers choose to buy a product. A growing force of customers—social customers—are resistant to promotion, looking for value beyond price.[23]

In July 2012, Kimberly Kadlec, Worldwide VP of the Global Marketing Group at Johnson & Johnson, redefined the 4Ps by coining the new 4Ps of the digital era: Purpose, Presence, Proximity, and Partnerships. It's not that the old 4Ps have become completely irrelevant and should be ignored. It's just that, except for "Product," which Kadlec acknowledges to be the very basis of any business, they have become secondary or, at the very least, a bit passé. In simple terms, they're not enough anymore. Consumers expect more from brands given the technological means and communication tools at their disposal. "The first one was purpose, which is really an augmentation to the traditional price. It's not just what things cost anymore, but the value they bring," adds Kadlec. "That could be value in terms of education, in terms of making the world a better place. The second was presence, and it really brings the traditional promotion into the social age of media. The next was proximity—anytime and anywhere media allows us to be everywhere all the time. The new place is the everyplace."[24]

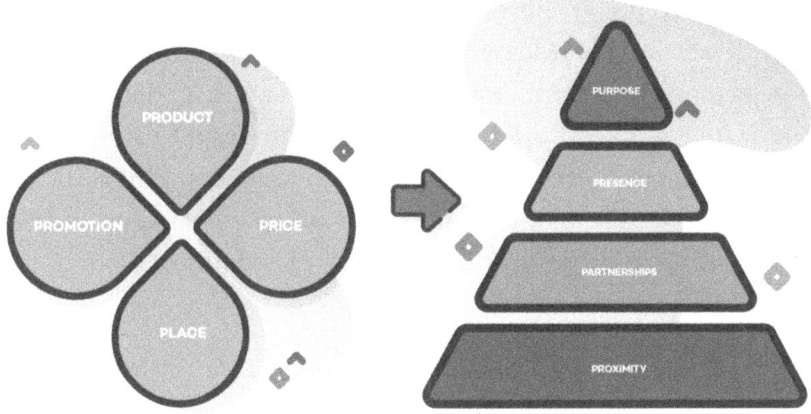

The Old 4Ps and the New 4Ps

As for Partnerships, this expands and speeds up your capacity to innovate and do things you couldn't do on your own, it opens up new markets at minor cost, and ensures rapid gains in credibility through brand association.

"Businesses that succeed in getting near their customers begin to produce exactly the kind of goods and services that customers want," Amerland writes in *Forbes*.

> In return, customers reward such businesses with their loyalty and brand evangelism. This approach turns every paying customer into a marketing point and every business into a socially conscious hub. In the 20th century, marketers depended on academic thinkers like [E. Jerome] McCarthy to help create the models they'd put into practice. But in the fast-moving world of the now, forward-thinking companies are at the forefront of change: They're seeing first-hand the transitions in their target markets.[25]

Indeed they do. When he ran into the new 4Ps theory for the first time, Konsta Klemetti found in it reassurance that the Rovio marketing-communication department was definitely on the right track. "We had been implementing and running this model organically for years!"[26] he exclaims. When Philip Hickey and Robin Squire met with the Rovio account managers over at Twitter and Spotify, they heard a similar validation: "Rovio is the poster child of content marketing."

CHAPTER FOURTEEN

Red Bird Goes to Red Square

To keep wowing the fans globally, Rovio had to keep coming up with more and more local stunts. What better place than Red Square in Moscow to keep Red Bird ever red? The pristine Red Square is Russia's most sacred space, overlooked by the eastern walls of the Kremlin. Looking at the device activations and download numbers in 2013, Russia looked like the new China. It was emerging fast, and, given the significant size of the population—almost 144 million—represented a substantial opportunity for growth. When Peter Vesterbacka first asked to set up an *Angry Birds* show in Red Square, the answer he heard was "impossible." That's precisely what you should tell him if you want him to restlessly pursue something.

The Russian Connection

Vesterbacka's attention had first been directed toward Russia back in 2011. During a busy week of traveling in July, he had a meeting in London with Digital Sky Technologies executives Yuri Milner, who was an investor in Facebook, and John Lindfors, formerly of Goldman Sachs. In the taxi to the airport, he received a call from Lindfors inviting him to join the Saint Petersburg International

Economic Forum the following Friday. The timeframe was too short. "There's no way I could get the visa on time,"[1] answered Vesterbacka, who was aware how complicated visa processes can sometimes be. He recalls Lindfors saying, "'This shouldn't be too hard. The president [Dmitry Medvedev] is inviting you there.'" Vesterbacka asked for more details. CEOs from all the big Russian tech leaders, such as Yandex or Mail.ru, would be there, as well as Daniel Ek from Spotify, Jim O'Neill, the Goldman Sachs economist who coined the B.R.I.C.S. acronym, and President Dmitry Medvedev himself.[2] There was one problem: That same week, the Mighty Eagle was due to travel to the U.S. for two days, then to Munich for a day, and then Barcelona on the Thursday. In which city, then, should he pick up the visa? Lindfors came back to him later that night. As the visa couldn't be arranged through local embassies, if it wasn't too much hassle for him, would it be okay to send Vesterbacka a private jet to pick him up in Barcelona? Vesterbacka candidly remembers:

> It was my first experience on a private jet ever! I had to make a stop in Moscow to pick the visa up there. Visa formalities in Russia are such that, even when the president is involved, it can be challenging. When landing in Moscow, we got stuck in a traffic jam of private jets! We arrived in St. Petersburg at 2 A.M. But they had given me a crew visa, so when I exit the airport, it's through a back-door and I'm there in the middle of a dark street with nobody in sight. My driver is waiting on the other side of the airport and I have no clue where I have to go.[3]

When he arrived at the event, clad in the ever-present Red Hoodie, Vesterbacka quickly realized the trip had been worthwhile when President Medvedev grabbed the microphone and said: "Before we talk politics, I want to thank Rovio for creating *Angry Birds*, for giving a huge number of Russian officials something to do in their free time, but also in the working hours—which is okay by the way."[4] Later on, Russian media types and journalists surrounded Vesterbacka, asking whether he was surprised that the Russian president had started talking about *Angry Birds*. He responded: "Look at our panel: seven guys and a lady all wearing dark suits, and one guy wearing a red hoodie and red shoes. What do you expect your president to talk about when he glances at the room?"[5] The next day, it was all over the Russian media. Needless to say, Vesterbacka made many powerful allies for Rovio on this trip.

In 2013, one of the multiple local licensees with which Rovio entered into an agreement was a beverage distributor that would bring its line of *Angry Birds* drinks to Russia. As they brainstormed about possible launch stunts, Vesterbacka found out that one of the key persons within the distributor company had relations in the Kremlin. A couple days after the meeting, Vesterbacka received an email introduction: "Talk to this man. His name is Igor."[6] No last name, no extra details—Vesterbacka felt like he was in a cliché scene from a James Bond movie. He broke the ice with a joke, "Let's throw a picnic in Red Square."[7] His local partner immediately wrote back to him, "Peter, you can't do that. It's a holy place!"[8] Vesterbacka clarified that he was kidding and specified his real plans, setting the wheels in motion.

Quickly, Vesterbacka found an ally in his own marketing-communications team to help him execute the ambitious vision. Kai Torstila had been recruited at the beginning of 2013 by his former colleague at Nokia, Philip Hickey. Torstila's first win after joining Rovio was to convince Simon Pierro, the internet magician from Germany, to come and perform iPad-based tricks with *Angry Birds* and *Bad Piggies* plush toys on the *Angry Birds* YouTube channel, on the occasion of the "Carnival" update in *Angry Birds Seasons*.

At the time, influencer marketing was not yet a thing and the creator economy was nascent, albeit growing rapidly. It was still possible to convince skilled and talented YouTubers with low audiences to come and perform "at production cost + exposure" on a more trafficked outlet like the *Angry Birds* channels. Nowadays, such a proposition would be considered offensive to creators.

A Day to Remember

On June 23, 2013, Rovio and its Russian partners attached themselves as sponsors of a classy yearly event in Russian society: High School Graduation Day. At the end of each school year, the 6,000 brightest students in Russia are invited, along with their families, to a red-carpet ceremony in their honor in Moscow's Kremlin. The 2013 event saw the *Angry Birds* drinks being distributed for free to attendees throughout the day and a giant *Angry Birds*-branded stage was built. The hall was decorated with thousands of Red Bird balloons, a quaint babushka choir hummed the *Angry Birds* theme song a cappella, and dancers dressed up as *Angry Birds* soda cans performed comic routines around Red Square.

Kai Torstila also concocted a very fitting gift for the students to remember the day. Torstila explains:

> How can we make sure that we didn't put too commercial a stamp on the celebration? How can we add a positive surprise element to it? We figured out that the Russians don't have a traditional costume for graduation day. So we looked into the country's hockey culture. In the Russian league, but also in the NHL [National Hockey League in the U.S. and Canada] and in the World Championships, the winners always receive a championship cap. So we wanted to create this cap

that was something they would wear with pride. Like, you're a World Champion.[9]

Five thousand Red Bird caps emblazoned with "MOSCOW GRADUATE 2013" were handed out—something with long-term emotional value tied to it. Torstila had doubts about his idea until the very last minute. He says, "We were wondering if this would go through with the girls who are dressed in their most elegant Versace outfits and have been to the hairdresser for hours. 'At least we'll have them for the guys,' we thought. In the end, every single student wore it. We totally ran out of the batch of 5,000 in a matter of minutes."[10]

Looking at the thousands of students wearing red caps and drinking *Angry Birds* soda, Vesterbacka couldn't resist the urge to give a speech. With his colleague Natalia Salonen, head of business development in Russia, by his side, he walked up to the man holding the agenda clipboard and confidently informed him that it was time for his speech. The man looked at the agenda, and protested that no such speech was scheduled. "How can there be no speech scheduled?" Salonen objected in Russian. "He's from the creators of *Angry Birds*. Of course, he should make a speech!" A short while later, Vesterbacka was standing on stage in his Red Hoodie and delivering an improvised speech to the 6,000 graduates to wish the teenagers the best of luck in their future careers.

The day ended with fireworks—all red, of course. "After this stunt, Russian friends who came to the event told me, 'Now I truly believe you that there is nothing Rovio can't do.' Since then, Russia is one of our fastest-growing markets."[11] The Angry Birds soft drinks also ended up outselling Coca-Cola drinks in Russia and Finland in 2013, leading to a larger-scale production and distribution deal with the Carlsberg-owned Baltika Breweries in 2014.

To support the real-life event with a digital happening, a new update was added inside the original *Angry Birds* game, which was now almost four years old and decidedly refusing to die. The update, called *Red Bird's Mighty Feathers*, was all about Red Bird receiving special powers from the Mighty Eagle, which introduced a twist on the gameplay. These new attributes were necessary as Red Bird had been tasked with facing the continuous waves of Bad Piggies contraptions (this was the first time that the *Angry Birds* and *Bad Piggies* universes had come together so symbiotically).

The next morning, a montage of the live celebrations at the Kremlin was added to YouTube. It started with a Red Bird plush toy peeking through the window of a car driving through Moscow. These little touches matter a great deal to Torstila. He comments: "We always tried to inject some humor into our stuff. There's a huge sense of irony in the stunts we pulled. Sometimes the audience took it too literally. We were not trying to be pompous. We just loved going big!"[12] The occasion also showed its effect on *Angry Birds'* presence on VKontakte (VK.ru), rapidly boosting community subscriptions on the most popular social network in Russia.

In its pursuit of building a global brand, Rovio has always been ready to go the extra mile to surprise and delight fans everywhere.

CHAPTER FIFTEEN

Becoming a Channel

Rather than continuously supplying content to third-party platforms and channels, Mikael Hed wanted Rovio to keep building its own channels—to eliminate the middlemen, and to keep bringing increased value to the community. In that respect, the most notable move of 2013 was certainly the roll-out of *Angry Birds Toons*, a 52-episode-long animation series.

Already back in 2011, Lauri Konttori remembers that Niklas and Mikael Hed had clearly singled out the creation of their own animation cartoon series as their primary motive behind the acquisition of Studio Kombo. He remembers: "The very first question in our meeting was, 'How would you feel about making a TV series?' They knew it meant hiring more people, and they were adamant about it. They were ready to take over the world."[1]

When ex-Marvel Studios COO David Maisel visited Rovio headquarters for the first time, Konttori remembers his surprise at the fact that *Angry Birds* didn't have a "story bible" in place. In Hollywood, that's one of the first things you would create. Mikko Pöllä, who joined Rovio from the production company Moskito Television, had been put in charge of the task. He fleshed out the characters with backstories, created a universe around Piggy Island, which is the environment in which the birds and pigs live, and listed the dos and don'ts of the brand. In the entrance lobby of the animation department is a huge sculpture of Piggy Island enclosed in glass. It contains every area and level ever created for *Angry Birds* within a single location.

There Are No Words to Say ...

Although pigs and birds had started expressing themselves in words in the comics and books, it was decided that the cartoon series would remain dialogue-less, much like the previous animation shorts produced by Rovio. No talking means that there's no need for localization when you are about to sell the rights to a new territory, which in turn makes distribution easier. Nick Dorra, head of the animation division at Rovio, argues that it's also easier to produce timeless material this way. He points out: "You are less tempted to factor in dated references."[2] It was also decided to keep the format short to ensure that the material was ideal for mobile consumption. This also facilitated sales to multiple channels, markets, and partners, since it was easier to find a spot for it within a television schedule, for example, not to mention that it encouraged reruns. Each episode was two minutes and 45 seconds in length.

The lack of dialogue does make the screenwriters' job harder, though. This may sound weird at first; after all, they don't have to write any dialogue. They do, however, still need to convey emotions and create a story arc in a way that the audience can follow and understand. If it were so easy to express yourself with shouts, grunts, and gestures, language wouldn't exist. The animation team watched a lot of references for inspiration, including Charlie Chaplin movies, *Tom and Jerry*, *The Pink Panther* animations, and *Road Runner* cartoons, to name but a few.

One contemporary TV series caught the team's attention more than any other: *Shaun the Sheep*, the U.K. stop-motion animated children's series produced by Aardman Animations. Mikael Hed has never made it a secret that he's always been a big fan of Aardman, and he professes his love for their work whenever a journalist leads him onto the topic of the *Angry Birds* cinematic trailers. Dorra agreed that *Shaun the Sheep* had nailed the format on the head. They started checking the names of the writers on IMDB.com and contacted them to try to lure them into the project. According to Dorra, "We heard from them that in the beginning they were facing exactly the same problems that we were facing. So, we were able to get ahead a little bit by using their expertise on that."[3] Once they tracked him down, Richard Hansom, the script editor on the series, became the key connection. "He had a network of freelance writers with whom he had been working on *Shaun*," tells Dorra.[4] Hansom and his team handled the screenplays for the first dozen episodes as freelancers, instilling a routine and the basic foundations. Once these were in place, French author Anastasia Heinzl moved to Finland and stepped in as lead writer for the remainder of the season.

Once they had enough material ready, with the remaining pieces at various stages of production, Rovio set a calendar date for the launch of the *Angry Birds Toons* episodes about five months later. It did this without asking any television channels whether they were interested. This was wildly unprecedented. Usually, the timeframe between pitching a program and it being broadcast was two to five years with the big networks. Traditionally, animation studios presented the idea on paper first, asking for production money and a distribution deal. They would start work only when they had secured these and leave all the decision making, intellectual property, and exclusivity rights to the network, which essentially acted as the producer.

Since Rovio was financing the whole production process, it only needed the channels and networks to broadcast the content. Still, expecting big TV stations to clear space in their schedules with only five months' notice before airtime was very optimistic on Rovio's part. Mikael Hed, however, had an ace up his sleeve that gave him tremendous leverage. In the same way that Rovio had instantly received massive reach for its launch trailers, and later for its plush toys—by simply showcasing them within the *Angry Birds* apps to millions of active users—Hed wanted Rovio to distribute every episode inside the games. In essence, the games would become Rovio's own video distribution channel.

This served multiple purposes. First, it added further value to the app for the fans. Dorra explains, "The main idea behind the channel was to give insane value to our fans in an app that you only buy once for less than a dollar."[5] Second, it gave users a reason to spend more time in the app. And when you reach the audience size that Rovio enjoyed, users' time is pretty much the only thing you are competing for. Your competitors are basically any form of entertainment available, whether it's TV, cinema, music, sport, or Facebook. Humans can't quite manage to do everything they like doing every day, because time is limited. Sometimes people need to sleep or work. Time is the only valid currency when you play at the top table of the entertainment industry. Once you have reached a critical mass, you have the capacity to build and own the container that serves to propagate your content, rather than putting it into other companies' pipelines and driving traffic their way. Finally, it served the purpose of recouping the investment by collecting revenue stream via the pre-roll ads that were shown at the beginning of every episode. The ad-based model worked very well, and Rovio decided to make it the pillar of its Toons channel.

Advertising revenue was now so crucial for Rovio, which already had a huge inventory on Android, that in September 2013 the company undertook to slowly build its independence in that domain. Rovio worked with all the leading agencies in every region, but envisaged becoming its own agency in the long run. With that in mind, Michele Tobin was poached from Millennial Media in August 2013 to head up advertising sales.

In the few months prior to *Angry Birds Toons* going live, Rovio stealthily started adding the Toons channel to every game in its portfolio. Although the entire infrastructure was installed, it kept the icon hidden so that users didn't notice any change. Making the channel visible to users across all games was only a flip of the switch away.

With the unveiling of the in-app Toons channel fast approaching, Rachel Webber, VP of the video department, assigned her team the task of contacting every channel and network that could be a potential partner, in all key territories. By setting a firm release date for March 17, 2013, Rovio twisted around the power balance. Its pitch might be summed up as: The train's leaving, so how can we get you on board? The proposal implied that while it was important for Rovio to have the networks on board, its channel would launch anyhow. Despite the difficulties and the unusually tight timeframe, channels in many countries made tremendous efforts to make any adjustments and be on board as launch partners, either from day zero or as quickly as possible thereafter.

Toons Goes Live

On Saturday, March 16, 2013, the partner TV channels began transmitting *Angry Birds Toons*. They enjoyed a head start of 24 hours to maintain the value of the content they had purchased. Partner stations included FOX8 in Australia, JEI TV in Korea, ANTV in Indonesia, Cartoon Network in India, MTV3 in Finland, the Children's Channel in Israel, 1+1 networks in Ukraine, Gulli and Canal J in France, SUPER RTL in Germany, TV2 in Norway, Canal 13 in Chile, and Gloob in Brazil. Furthermore, two strategic alliances were formed with alternative digital distributors. In the U.S., Comcast ensured video-on-demand availability through its Xfinity players. A global deal was also set up with long-time partner Samsung, which added the *Angry Birds Toons* channel to all its smart TVs, with embedded ads all over the menu screen. Each episode appeared on the Samsung network immediately after airing on television, slightly ahead of the in-game channel. In exchange, Samsung committed to a large 360-degree promotional effort including commercials, media buys, channel marketing, and even flash-mob events to raise awareness about *Toons* and its free availability to all smart TV owners.

Of course, Rovio couldn't broadcast on every earthly channel from the start. The short timeframe meant it was difficult to attract certain partners on time. But considering that respecting convention would have made Rovio negotiate with each of these stations one by one, with a two- to five-year plan laid out in front of them, it became obvious that cutting corners aggressively and applying pressure had saved a considerable amount of time. To appear on so many screens, in so many countries, within such a short timeframe must be seen for what it is: a remarkable tour de force. When reporting on the stunt, *Variety* headlines read: "How Rovio just played Hollywood with *Angry Birds*."[6] In the article, Marc Graser, *Variety*'s editor, elaborated:

> It's primarily a surprise to Hollywood, which has lauded—and been envious of—Rovio's ability to launch a new major moneymaking franchise that's not based on an existing property, but was unaware of the ability for Rovio's apps to also serve as an outlet for other original programming. Not bad for a company that was

considered just a game maker that lucked out with a cute slingshot game involving grunting pigs and squawking animated birds.[7]

Speaking to National Public Radio (NPR), Andrew Stalbow developed the concept of "doing Hollywood in reverse," pointing out that entertainment franchises usually started with a TV show or a movie, then made consumer products based on them, which might include video games. This time, the big entertainment franchise started with a game. "I'd say it's a business model inspired by somebody like Disney,"[8] Stalbow concluded. In moments of triumph, it's acceptable to be a tad defiant.

On Sunday, March 17, Rovio flipped the switch and made the Toons channel appear on the menu screens of all Rovio games, generating immediate fan engagement, with millions watching the first episode of the new animation series. Handpicked advertising partners included Paramount Pictures, Sony Pictures, BlackBerry, and Activision Blizzard. The latter has been a partner of Rovio since bringing *Angry Birds Trilogy*—which combines *Angry Birds Classic*, *Angry Birds Space*, and *Angry Birds Rio*—and *Angry Birds Star Wars* to consoles in brick-and-mortar stores on physical disks, and splashing out on a large TV commercial campaign for these in the U.S. and Europe. Every week, a new episode of *Angry Birds Toons* hits all channels—in games, on televisions, and on digital platforms.

Over the following months, a bunch of extra television stations joined the party and *Angry Birds Toons* started airing on Cartoon Network Japan, and other channels in Thailand, Italy, the Middle East, the Philippines, Eastern Europe, Greece, Canada, Poland, and New Zealand. The early ratings were robust everywhere.

October 2013 marked another milestone: Already very profitable through ad revenue in apps alone, the Toons channel surfaced directly on web browsers, adding "shareability" functionalities for social media under the domain name Toons.tv. This came a couple of weeks after Rovio announced that 1 billion video views had been generated within the games alone, not accounting for ratings on television and alternative channels. Vesterbacka was right when he had joked at the Helsinki startup conference, Slush, in 2012: "The first billion is always the hardest."[9] Compared to the hard work that it took to get to 1 billion downloads with the games, getting to that point with the video business almost seemed easy.

The success of the new venture was such that many other seasons of *Angry Birds* animations have been produced, and other companies also looked to get their content featured on Toons.tv, which is the ultimate proof that you have indeed turned into a proper channel. The first partners to jump onboard were National Geographic and Hasbro, which makes original series for its *Transformers*, *My Little Pony*, and *G.I. Joe* brands. Hollywood giants Sony Pictures and Twentieth Century Fox have also promoted their blockbuster releases through this new vector. Dorra observes: "Look at what we did with Sony on *Cloudy with a Chance of Meatballs 2*. Instead of just showing the trailer, which is not such great value for the fans, we created a sponsored channel in which actual excerpts from the movie were featured while it was in the theatres. It's still a promotional vehicle for Sony, but it's much more interesting for the fans."[10] Sony Pictures also scooped the rights for the DVD and Blu-ray editions of *Angry Birds Toons* and released the first season in December 2013, just in time for Christmas.

With yet another "game-changer" achievement under their belt, Mikael Hed and his team had, as he had forecasted to *Variety* two years earlier in 2011, successfully built the first entertainment franchise to come out of mobile.

Bad Piggy Records

Besides animation, games, books, and consumer products of all kinds, Rovio is also the proud owner of a music label. The first time Rovio helped promote the sales of a new song on iTunes was in August 2012. The manager of rock band Green Day reached out to see if there could be a cool collaboration to promote their new single "Troublemaker." As a result, Rovio added Green Day-branded levels into *Angry Birds Friends* on Facebook, and finishing those levels allowed gamers to unlock the song and listen to it in the game. Moreover, the band members of Green Day—Billie Joe Armstrong, Mike Dirnt, and Tre Cool—were all present in the game in green piggy form. The stunt created quite a buzz on social media and in music circles. "It's something unpredictable but in the end it's right, I hope you had the time of your life."[11]

Separately, Rovio also teamed up with musicians to make songs that had nothing in common with the original *Angry Birds* theme, and which the company released on special occasions, like the "Peace" mentioned earlier for example. These songs, however, were never available for sale and were for YouTube purposes only. Konsta Klemetti, who has roots in the music industry, attempted to connect the dots ... He contacted the electronic music act Major Lazer. This New York collective, formed by Diplo, Walshy Fire, and Ape Drums, was enjoying great success, and Klemetti was particularly fond of its sound. Their career manager happened to be a friend of a friend.

As was customary by now, Rovio was working on a special event to celebrate Halloween 2013. The theme for that year was Zombie Pigs and, for the first time, special-edition consumer products were put in stores especially for the occasion, in addition to the traditional *Angry Birds Seasons* update and the animation short. To make it truly and fully cross-media, Klemetti wanted to have a music single released simultaneously. He ran the idea by the head of audio, Ilmari Hakkola. The latter composed a brand-new track called "Shuffle & Spawn." The title found inspiration in the 1980s, and you can clearly feel the influence of Michael Jackson's "Thriller." Major Lazer remixed the track on its YouTube channel under the title "Moombahton Mix."

Klemetti's intent was to make "Shuffle & Spawn" the Official Halloween 2013 theme, and he plugged it everywhere he could—as the theme of the four-minute-long Halloween short, but also as the main menu track in *Bad Piggies* and *Angry Birds Friends*. The novelty was that the song was also available for sale in MP3 format on iTunes and Amazon. Furthermore, 1,000 copies of a limited-edition colored vinyl record of the Major Lazer collaboration were printed; one of those copies, autographed, still hangs in the Rovio offices.

Bad Piggy Records went on to release other records, such as Saara Aalto's "Reach the Stars," bilingual in English and Chinese, put out in celebration of the Lunar New Year, or the Christmas carol "Ode to Snow" in 2012, continuing the "Christmas Peace Song" tradition started by Salla Hakkola and sung by Ernie Sabella, the voice of Pumbaa in Disney's *Lion King*. For Salla Hakkola, this remains her favorite collaboration from her entire time at the company.[12]

In 2016, for The Mighty League tournament anthem, Salla Hakkola also teamed up with Finnish DJ hero Darude for a remix of his "Sandstorm" hit mashed up with the *Angry Birds* theme song. In addition to the 45 million views the video clip attracted on YouTube, the upbeat EDM track also allowed the *Angry Birds* tune to regularly be heard in the clubs.

CHAPTER SIXTEEN

From 100 Days to 100 Years

By the turn of 2014, the brand was still very strong, as proven by the presence of *Angry Birds* in news coverage surrounding the National Security Agency, in which the game was used as an example of how the agency allegedly leveraged mobile apps for gathering data (although Rovio denied any knowledge of this matter).[1] The brand also made an appearance among the fantasy characters and celebrity athletes invited by Barack Obama for the prestigious Presidential Easter Egg Roll—an iconic event held by the First Family on the South Lawn of the White House and attended by hundreds of American children. No other mobile game character had previously been represented in the Easter Egg Roll.

Nonetheless, it was becoming ever more clear that, after five years of furious growth, the time had come to shift the focus of the company—from 100-day sprints of launching products, shipping updates, and growing sales toward the 100-year marathon of maintaining the value of the brand.

Spring Cleaning

After a year of approving too many licensing deals, Rovio wanted to corral the merchandising side of things. Teemu Suila took over the role of COO in the second quarter of 2013, after an 18-year career at neighboring Nokia, and quickly observed that somebody needed to separately assume the management of consumer products. Naz Cuevas, who had done a tremendous job with the *Star Wars* license stateside, was promoted as global head of consumer products and relocated from sunny Santa Monica, California, to cold Espoo, Finland.

Before getting to grip with the tens of thousands of different products being made, Cuevas worked on changing the company mindset regarding merchandise. Here she focused on introducing a brand identity, something that hitherto had only been developed and nurtured for games and animations. The people in top management were all native to the digital world and had been applying to the physical side of the business the same model that had proven immensely successful for the games. The problem was physical goods are different from virtual ones. The way we consume physical products depends more heavily on cultural, sociologic, and macro- and micro-economic factors. Mexicans don't eat the same food as the Chinese, who don't wear the same clothes as the Americans, who don't love the same art as the French, who don't earn the same salaries as the Japanese, who don't share the lifestyle of the Filipinos, who have different expectations about durability than the Germans, and so on. The *Angry Birds* hockey sticks that sold well in Scandinavia and in Canada were redundant in Spain or Brazil. Commerce may be global, but the world is full of colors, tastes, and rituals that are not always unified or standardized—that's what makes it a wonderful place. Nevertheless, all these parameters and variables are very important to keep in mind when manufacturing real-life goods. "The quality of the product needs to reflect its price, and vice versa,"[2] Cuevas sums up.

More importantly, Cuevas wanted to change a key point when it came to quantity: "Obviously you'd want 'E-equilibrium' between supply and demand. But this rarely happens. What will happen is that you produce too little or too much. Which one is better?"[3] A newcomer in the licensing business coming from the digital side of things would tend to go for too much, since the licensee pays royalty on wholesale anyway, whether it sells the entire production or not. This means that the licensor will make more money and the fans will have a lot of goods to choose from. Cuevas toned down that impetus: "That's actually not good for the brand. The signal you are sending out to the market is that you are in this for a short period of time. That it is not an ever-green brand that's built to last for a hundred years. It's a cash business. You're in and out. In my opinion, if forced to choose, it's better to produce a bit less rather than too much."[4]

Once she had the right mindset implemented at the strategic level, Cuevas took a full quarter to delve into product lines and categories one by one. "I performed a complete business review on our current licensees, per category, per territory," she recalls. "I looked into all our licensees thoroughly. I wanted to see and touch all the products."[5] This is quite an undertaking, given the sheer amount of distinct *Angry Birds*-related items that were being made in the world. In Scandinavia and North America, there was just too much stuff out there and the market was flooded. There were contradictions, a lack of connection, and sometimes even cannibalization (when products compete with each other). Sometimes, it was very hard to find the relation between the licensed item and the original core product.

This didn't mean that Cuevas immediately broke with licensees that manufactured rejected products. Although she could probably have bought out of many of the contracts, Cuevas preferred to nurture and revisit relationships instead. After all, she says, "The licensees haven't done anything wrong."[6] They were simply lacking guidance, so Cuevas ensured that they received this in the future. She first set up a proper structural approach to procedures and protocols. She created a set of key documents such as a brand deck (including how to present, pitch, and sell the brand), a deal memo setup, and an enhanced MLA (Merchandise License Agreement), and, armed with these, revisited each business venture with each and every licensee, while setting up an appropriate auditing process. Cuevas explains: "Rather than letting the licensee carry on doing business as usual, we cater to them, so it's a tailored program. We share the specific assets and style guides that would be appropriate for each category. They continue to exploit their contract in all its rights but we do it in a way that is respectful toward the brand."[7]

Rather than letting everybody dance in their own little corner of the stage, Cuevas choreographed things to act in synchronicity. She communicated thoroughly with the licensees, to make sure not only that their products were good in themselves but also that they were complementary to the rest of what was available, building synergy, symbiosis, and harmony across the product lines.

As an example, *Angry Birds* vitamins sitting alone on a shelf full of chewing gum might come across as a brand slap. Put it alongside a personal care range that includes ice packs, bandages, toothpaste, and a toothbrush that encourages kids to brush their teeth longer by playing the *Angry Birds* theme song for two minutes—"Now it's Mom-approved," Cuevas happily concludes. "It took us two years to refine the vitamins and personal care kit to the point where it was appropriate at last."[8] When you're positioned as a family entertainment brand, being Mom-approved is essential. The games are for everybody. Dad might prefer the *Star Wars* mashup. The son might be into the Telepods (and probably doesn't understand why Dad keeps some of them in their original shrink-wrapped packaging "for later"). His sister may be sleeping with the plush toys. At the end of the day, it doesn't matter what they want if Mommy says, "No." "We see Mom as our super fan. We want to make sure that we are in line with her,"[9] Cuevas emphasizes.

After nine restless months of dedicated hard work, by the beginning of 2014, Cuevas finally had the infrastructure in place, and the right team to execute it. Three new VPs of consumer products had joined to work under her: one in charge of Europe, another to fill her old shoes in North America, and a third to spearhead efforts in Asia and Latin America.

Exercise Regularly

Peter Vesterbacka, meanwhile, had started the year casually by kicking off the new season of the Brazilian soccer league. To hype up Brazilian fans about an update to *Angry Birds Rio*, tied to the release of the *Rio 2* movie, local business developer Fernando Vasconez put Vesterbacka on the *futbol* pitch, kicking off a Brazilian pro league soccer game with former World Cup legend Zico in front of 55,000 cheering supporters in the legendary Maracanã Stadium, Rio de Janeiro, in January 2014.

The Rovio marketing teams had an eye on expanding the brand's stadium presence as well as location-based entertainment activities. "We saw sports, which are very community-based and have all-year-round events every calendar day of every year, as a great platform to maintain the momentum of the brand over a potentially infinite period of time,"[10] explains Kai Torstila. The sports market was after all the only entertainment sector that had remained bigger than gaming in terms of annual revenue generation, making it an attractive arena to look for brand expansion. Whereas since the early 2010s gaming had surpassed in size both cinema and music combined, the sports market remained two and a half times bigger than gaming, and continues to be so to this day.

Also in January 2014, Hockey Bird, originally designed by Tony Kysenius for the IIHF World Cup 2012 in Finland and Sweden, became the official mascot of the NHL, showing up in the stadiums of ice hockey pro league games across the U.S. and entertaining the crowds during the breaks:

> We already had a contract signed with Finnish company Applause, who are among the best in the world at crowd activations in stadiums. Rebirthing Hockey Bird felt like the best way to work with the NHL. It led to a funny moment at the Chicago Soldier Field Stadium, where I was attending under a snow blizzard, and the fans of Chicago Black Hawks felt that Hockey Bird looked a lot like he was one of the Pittsburgh Penguins they were facing that day.[11]

After scoring quite a few stunts in Brazil with his colleague Igor Burattini—including a virtual reality exhibition at the Rock in Rio Festival, having the linesmen disguised as red birds during the Tennis Rio Open, and securing the licensing rights for the Ayrton Senna Bird in *Angry Birds Go!*—Vasconez started becoming instrumental in more international dealings with the sports world. Under the aegis of Miika Lundgren, VP of business development, Vasconez supported Torstila in working out the details of the collaboration with the NBA in *Angry Birds Season*, which started with the *NBA Ham Dunk* update that coincided with the start of the NBA season on October 9, 2014.

A second episode followed during the NBA All-Star Game, featuring an exclusive bird inspired by NBA Hall-of-Famer Larry Bird. Layup pun intended. Torstila remembers that the comedy was what won Larry Bird over. "When we reached out to him at the time, Larry Bird was the head coach of the Indiana Pacers and really not into doing endorsements. But he thought it was too funny to pass on. As an NBA fan myself and as a marketer who knows the importance of the NBA and its reach internationally,

I was completely over the moon about this one."[12] One thing Torstila was blue-eyed about until this deal is how complicated it is to secure good footage and still imagery of an athlete in action even after you secure name, image, and likeness (NIL) rights from him. First, you need to clear the rights with whoever photographed the image or filmed the footage you fancy. You can broker it through Getty, Shutterstock, and other photographic licensing rights banks. In this case, Rovio cleared footage directly owned by the NBA. But then you need to make sure you blur or cut out any other players or recognizable faces from the public in the backgrounds. Then there is the jersey issue: you need to white-label that in Photoshop, too, since you don't have a licensing deal in place with either the Boston Celtics or Team USA just because you signed with Larry Bird. Anybody who has had any experience in exploiting NIL licensing deals with athletes in practice knows the pains and tribulations I'm referring to.

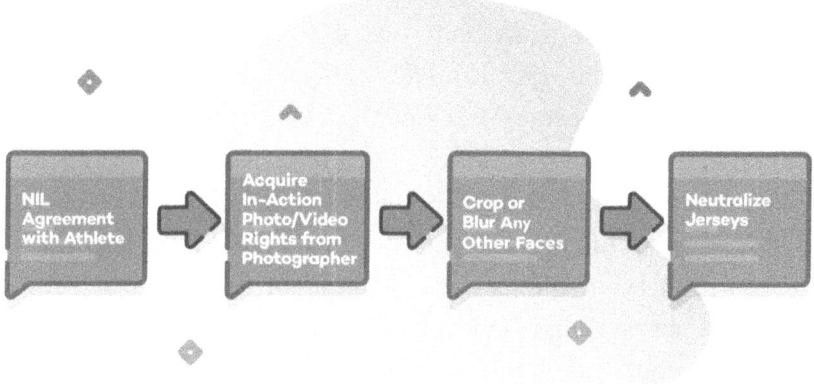

How to Clean Licensed Imagery

The deal was expanded into a full-year collaboration, with promotional events and in-game live ops in *Angry Birds Seasons* matching each other for every NBA match played overseas during the year's calendar of fixtures. "The international match levels were something available to all players without cost, and it made a lot of sense with our strategy in *Angry Birds Seasons* because we saw it at the World Tour title and we wanted to bring more sporting calendar tie-ins as excuses to revisit certain cities with new basketball-themed levels."[13] There were also paid level packs tied to each NBA team, tapping into the fandom of each of these teams and scoring social media posts from some of them in the process. "If you were a Knicks fan, you had to have the Knicks levels, and so on for all the other teams,"[14] Torstila says. To cap it off, Vasconez would later seal a deal with New Era to make a limited run of *Angry Birds* x NBA caps. Torstila still wears his to this day, "They were so cool and so high quality. I made sure I scored a few for myself from the warehouse."[15] Swag attack.

Ahead of the 2014 FIFA World Cup in Brazil, but later postponed to aim for the UEFA Euro 2016, an *Angry Birds* soccer game was also soft-launched under the name *Angry Birds Goal.* Although the game had very enjoyable gameplay, and the business development team had several co-marketing deals lined up for it, the game was ultimately canceled because of poor key performance indicators. We came this close to getting a Cristiano Ronaldo Bird!

After the NHL and the NBA, Rovio officially partnered with the NFL as an official licensor and partner of Super Bowl 50 in 2017 for an event that saw the helmets of the teams becoming available across *Angry Birds 2* and *Angry Birds Epic*. In September 2017, in what was a three-year deal, *Angry Birds* also became the official shirt-sleeve sponsor of Everton F.C. in the English Premiere League, the most viewed European football league globally, drawing huge audiences not only at home and across continental Europe but also in the Middle East, China, Southeast Asia, and many other areas of the world. The deal also involved pitchside signage for *Angry Birds 2* and other *Angry Birds* games around the stadium during the 38 games of the regular season.

More U.S.-centric, in October 2018, *Angry Birds 2* became the first "Eye in the Sky" sponsor of the Chicago Bulls, another iconic red, angry animal logo, setting up the brand at the top of the backboard in the United Center.

During their world tours wearing the Red Hoodie, Vesterbacka, Torstila, Vasconez, and other Rovians could play *Angry Birds* mid-flight by simply touching their in-flight entertainment screen. On April 14, 2015, Rovio entered a deal with travel industry connectivity provider Global Eagle Entertainment, granting Global Eagle the right to customize *Angry Birds* for seat-back entertainment systems. At the time, Global Eagle had a catalog of more than 150 titles in its Air Games portfolio and 20 years of experience in providing casual games for airline seat displays. The company provided licensed and in-house-designed games to over 100 airlines around the world. The deal is still in place to this day, and *Angry Birds World Tour* remains playable on many airlines around the world, although Global Eagle has rebranded the company name to Anuvu. Over the last decades, I've spotted the *Angry Birds* in-flight edition being played on board Air France, KLM, Avianca, American Airlines, British Airways, Cathay Pacific, and Iberia airplanes. Angry Birds can't fly, so being available to humans slingshotting from one city to another is an amusing achievement!

Perhaps not as shiny a partnership as those with the big American leagues, there is an undeniable long-tail value in such a "quasi-permanent" multi-year deal, with ubiquitous placements in areas where there is a constant flow of family traffic. "Quasi permanent" because, when considering the cost of setup and the cost of removal, both parties will tend to renew such deals in perpetuity.

In the same vein, the licensing partnership struck with Topgolf is also of a quasi-permanent nature, and for the same reasons. Founded by twin brothers Steve and Dave Jolliffe in Watford, UK, in 2000, the Topgolf franchise offers a family-friendly "fun night out" approach to the sport and has grown considerably over the years, leading to a US$2 billion acquisition by Callaway Golf Company in October 2020. Topgolf operates a network of 100 locations scattered across the U.S., and 110 other Topgolf locations worldwide, in the U.K., in Australia, China, Germany, Mexico, the UAE, and Thailand. Since 2020, the *Angry Birds* experience has leveraged the Topgolf proprietary Toptracer ball-tracing technology to let visitors launch *Angry Birds* characters Red, Chuck, and Bomb with their golf swing, to smash down structures and defeat pigs on the virtual outfield. What's great is that the slingshot mechanics are a natural fit for golf gameplay. "What Topgolf has developed with its Toptracer technology is highly innovative and aligns with the physics-based challenges that can be discovered in *Angry Birds* mobile games. The resulting experience is a familiar but uniquely branded experience that we're excited for our fans to take a swing at,"[16] said CMO Ville Heijari. A range of golf-centric merchandise has also been manufactured, such as *Angry Birds*-themed golf balls and hats. The partnership won the Best Licensed Product award at the Licensing International Awards 2021. It may not turn heads like a spectacular launch from space, but it's not every day you get to do a big tentpole event, and so it is important for the marketing mix to have such steady vehicles that drive recurring flows of business every day. Such activities help keep the routine baseline on an ever higher trajectory between the "hockey sticks" in the analytics curves.

Race to Zero

Despite Rovio maintaining its success with premium mobile games for longer than thought possible, the pressure to get into the free-to-play (F2P) arena eventually became inevitable. To succeed as a staying power in mobile gaming, Rovio needed to assimilate the paradigm shift that the video games industry had been going through since 2012, with F2P now the dominant business model in the digital distribution era. Billion-dollar maker *Clash of Clans*, made by neighboring developer Supercell in Helsinki, was becoming the new industry success story and its financial model was built entirely on "in-app purchases." By late 2013 and 2014, it was clear that the *Angry Birds* franchise had to adapt or die trying.

Matthew Wilson expands on this:

> I ranted against paid user acquisition back in 2012 during a public panel at the Casual Connect trade conference, but the market had changed a lot since. The reality is it had become impossible to break out a new brand without spending any money on direct user acquisition during those days. The top dogs were spending so much money to get to those top positions that you couldn't compete in the U.S. charts without spending a certain amount. I wish it wouldn't be this way, but unfortunately the depth of pockets was becoming increasingly important.[17]

As the mobile market matured, barriers to entry arose. If it cost between $4 and $8 to acquire each user because of the increased competition on the advertising front, then it became paramount to increase the lifetime value (LTV) of the acquired user. This only worked out if you built sophisticated in-game economies that would monetize users regularly, while still retaining them in high numbers. Easier said than done.

The first foray of Rovio into this brave new world was *Angry Birds Go!*, which is pretty much to *Angry Birds* what *Mario Kart* is to *Mario Bros.* It's a racing game co-developed in partnership with Exient, in which you get to drive ridiculous karts with the *Angry Birds* and *Bad Piggies* characters. It marked the entry of the franchise into semi-3D environments, and more importantly it was also the first *Angry Birds* opus to be fully designed as a freemium game.

Unfortunately, the *Angry Birds Go!* in-game economy didn't prove robust enough to sustain the game's position in the top-grossing charts for very long. As we got into 2014, *Angry Birds Go!* gradually fell down the charts and didn't prove to be the immediate dominant force Rovio hoped it would be, and this despite amassing a pretty decent 250 million installs over the following years. There was still a lot to learn for Rovio on the freemium monetization side of things, and a lot of work to do before getting to the same levels of revenue as the top dogs in the category.

By the beginning of 2014, Rovio had grown into a sizeable multinational company that employed 798 people in offices spread across five continents. Rovio's total consolidated full-year revenue for fiscal year 2013 amounted to €156 million, a meager increase of 2.7 percent compared to fiscal year 2012. Due to the sharp increase in R&D investment and staff costs, profits decreased compared to previous years, to €36.5 million before tax. When these numbers came out on April 28, 2014, the *Wall Street Journal* pointed out that, during the same fiscal year, Supercell and King had monetized considerably more from their respective F2P titles *Clash of Clans* and *Candy Crush Saga*. At the time, both these games were each generating no less than $1 billion per quarter.

King and Supercell had undoubtedly done a better job at maximizing the immediate digital monetization inside their hit video games. On the other hand, Rovio's investments during that same year demonstrated a different mindset altogether: diversification of activities, nurturing the brand and culture, hiring of people with a wide spectrum of skills (beyond gaming), and building a foundation. By focusing their time and resources doing all the above, Rovio undeniably made less money from games short-term than it could have.

In response to this stagnating revenue growth, Rovio laid off 130 employees in October 2014, with another 260 made redundant in August the following year. "We did too many things," admitted Pekka Rantala, CEO of Epassi Group, in the official announcement. After growing to 800 staff members at its peak, Rovio had to reduce its employee count to a leaner 400, in two waves of layoffs.

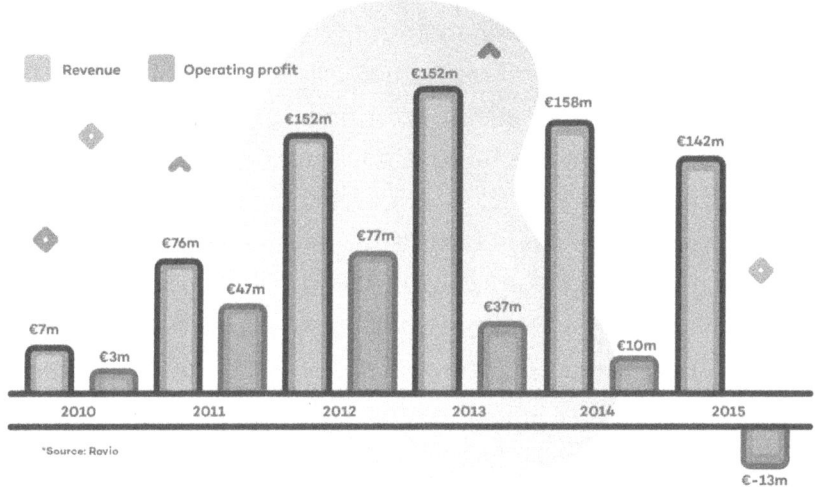

Rovio Financials Before Movie Release

The number-one priority of the company in 2015 had to be F2P mobile games. Wilhelm Taht joined in the middle of 2015 to reshape the vision for the games department, actively spreading the universe into as many popular and lucrative gaming genres and categories as possible. After *Angry Birds Go!* in the racing category, *Angry Birds Stella*, resolutely aimed at the female demographic, and *Angry Birds Epic* as a casual card-based role-playing game, strongly aimed at Asia, came *Angry Birds Fight!*, a sort of puzzle and number-based combat system clearly aimed at competing with the number-one game in Japan at the time, *Puzzle & Dragons* published by Gung Ho. Anecdotally, Rovio had already acknowledged *Puzzle & Dragons'* success by teaming up with Gung Ho to add the *Angry Birds* flock as playable characters in the game. *Angry Birds Fight!* aimed to further grow the aura of the characters in Japan through a game that was completely tailored to this market, both in mechanics and style. The motherland of video games was one of the few territories where there was still room for growth and Rovio could count on a new licensing partner over there on the consumer products side of things, as *Angry Birds* was now represented by Sanrio Far East Ltd., the subsidiary agency of Hello Kitty maker, Sanrio.

Rovio also covered genres with more global appeal, as with *Angry Birds Pop* in the "bubble pop" puzzle genre, which even saw Shakira Bird appear as a playable character in December 2015, based on the world-famous music icon. Earlier in the year, in March 2015, on the occasion of the Mobile World Congress in Barcelona, Fernando Vasconez, well connected with the football world, organized an encounter between Peter Vesterbacka and Gerard Piqué, better known for his daytime job as a professional footballer for F.C. Barcelona and the Spanish national team, but who at the time was also moonlighting as CEO and founder of mobile development studio Kerad Games. After the energized meetup, Piqué gratefully invited Vesterbacka and Vasconez to attend the Barcelona team training session at Nou Camp the following day, and then to have dinner with his then wife ... Shakira. After taking a selfie with Lionel Messi for his Instagram account during the day (what? jealous, me?), Vesterbacka sat down with Shakira and Piqué and, according to Vasconez, that's where the contagiously passionate Vesterbacka convinced the singer to appear in the game's universe and also to let Rovio publish her own game, *Love Rocks*.

Love Rocks didn't stick around for long and went quickly through the Peak–Drop–Vanish cycle. Steve Porter, who was hired by Phil Hickey the year before and took over the role of Robin Squire as head of community marketing, comments on the important lessons learned for the company:

The Shakira game and campaign was a wakeup call for many internally that the days of relying on brand only were numbered. We needed to care about the full funnel, and especially the product: retention, product–market fit honed through soft launch, live-ops, player motivation, and segmentation strategy—the complete package. It's undeniable that Shakira had a strong brand (even Mark Zuckerberg gave the launch trailer a like on Facebook)—but the game did not reach its audience despite her support, and did not have a viable product–market fit.[18]

Don't Call It a Comeback

The most significant game release of the year 2015 was undeniably *Angry Birds 2*. After years of resistance not to go into numbered sequels, Rovio felt it was about time. The development of the title has been led by Patrick Liu, who joined the company from DICE in 2012, where he had worked on the famous *Battlefield* series for EA. After a year of work on *Angry Birds Seasons* updates, Liu took on this big mission with his team at Rovio Stockholm near the end of 2013. A freemium reimagination of *Angry Birds Classic* gameplay, the game first soft-launched for a few months in Canada under the stealth title "Under Pigstruction." When KPI performance was deemed acceptable, *Angry Birds 2* launched globally on August 6, 2015 under the fitting campaign hashtag #StayAngry, racking up 1 million downloads in 12 hours and instantly becoming the number-one downloaded game on Apple App Store in 100 countries, as well as the most downloaded game of the day on the Google Play store. Three days later, it passed the 10 million installs mark, becoming the fastest game to do so at the time. At the time of writing, only four games have reached this milestone faster: *Super Mario Run, Pokémon Go, Clash Royale* and *Candy Crush Jelly Saga*. Two weeks later, after a successful launch in China across all domestic Android stores, *Angry Birds 2* had reached 30 million downloads.

Notably, the marketing mix included a flurry of performance-based advertising and paid user acquisition on the same networks as all the other F2P publishers, such as Facebook, Unity Ads, AdColony, and even TV commercials bursts financed by Rovio itself rather than partners. This was a stark departure from the "we don't pay for advertising" policy that Rovio had had in place from 2009 up until 2014, an era during which the company relied exclusively on owned media content and earned media through partnerships and barter deals for its growth. Steve Porter confirms this:

> "In the transition between phases, there were certainly challenges in biz dev as the power of the brand alone wasn't enough anymore to secure significant investment support from platforms. Anecdotally, I recall one partner telling me that, with a Rovio meeting, you were never quite sure if we'd come to buy or sell. However, by 2016, product and marketing performance was much better understood, and it was clear that UA investment was the fuel for any mobile game's engine—regardless of the IP used."[19]

On the monetization front, *Angry Birds 2* did not immediately fly high in the top-grossing charts, proving the growing pains entailed when adapting to F2P. Nonetheless, through events and updates, Liu's Stockholm team relentlessly kept fine-tuning and balancing the game until it hit the gravy sweet spot. As proven before, if games have become a service, then persistency is paramount to achieving success in this ever more crowded, volatile and competitive app space. The goldrush days were long gone. On average, 500 new games were now being released on the App Stores every week. The battle for the billions of mobile gamers' wallets was fierce. While it appeared in the top-grossing charts in its launch month, *Angry Birds 2* then fell off for an entire quarter.

Porter recognizes the pains:

> A lot of our earliest fans weren't happy that we transitioned to a free-to-play-only model, so there was a nosedive in community sentiment. *Angry Birds 2*, Rovio's biggest free-to-play game to date, initially suffered in development as the lengthy design began as a premium— or at least a mixture of models. The team did great work in pivoting much of its design to free-to-play by launch, but it took another couple years for the team to truly perfect this and turn the game into a significant revenue driver for Rovio.[20]

By introducing new mid-core monetization features in the casual game, such as the PvP Arena, Tower of Fortune, and many other proven techniques inspired by other top F2P hits, *Angry Birds 2* was able to keep improving its revenue. This extended the longevity of the title—after almost ten years, it has over 400 million downloads and over US$550 million in lifetime revenue.[21]

Meanwhile, parallel efforts were being undertaken to evolve the brand's visual style so that it was more appealing to women. It had become clear to the brand team that, overall, *Angry Birds* was still perceived as a male-centric brand. The goal was to evolve into the four quadrants darling that Hollywood giants appreciate so much.

CHAPTER SEVENTEEN

Red Bird on the Red Carpet

With David Maisel's guidance, Mikael Hed materialized the Hollywood movie dream he had long been chasing. On May 15, 2013, the worldwide distribution rights to the *Angry Birds* motion picture nested at Sony Pictures. The movie project was put in the safe hands of co-producers John Cohen (*Despicable Me*), David Maisel (stepping up from advisor into a more executive role for the occasion), and Mikael Hed himself. Jon Vitti (*The Simpsons*) took on screenplay duties. Clay Kaytis (*Cloudy with a Chance of Meatballs, Hotel Transylvania,* and *Cloudy with a Chance of Meatballs 2*) and Fergal Reilly (storyboard artist on *Spider-Man 2* and *The Iron Giant*) were selected as directors of the 3D CG-animated film.

Under advice from Maisel, Rovio Entertainment borrowed a page from the *Iron Man* Marvel playbook and took an unconventional path in Hollywood: Instead of licensing the rights in exchange for a royalty percentage on the profits, Rovio Entertainment committed to finance a $73 million movie production with its own cash as well as contribute $100 million to the Sony Pictures marketing budgets on release of the movie. In exchange, Rovio would sit among the co-producers, which would give it a share of the profits (or losses), but, more importantly, would help it retain more control over the treatment of the franchise. "People think this is about the financial upside, but it's really about controlling your own destiny,"[1] David Maisel later told Ben Fritz for the *Wall Street Journal.*

Making Movies

The year 2015 began with a change of leadership at the very top, as Mikael Hed stepped down as Rovio CEO to focus on running the Los Angeles animation studio, which was set up to hire writers, producers, animators, line producers, and other gig-based roles for the motion picture. Hed's reign as CEO had spurred a few years of unbelievable growth and expansion for the company but after a tough 2014, and with a headcount 40 times what it had been in 2009, the group was in need of a fresh direction. Hed's focus from then on would be all about the *Angry Birds* story lore, heading up Rovio Animation Inc. in Sherman Oaks, Los Angeles, a few blocks away from the Sony Pictures offices, and participating in the movie script sessions as co-producer. He was replaced as interim CEO by Pekka Rankalla, before the company's chief legal officer, Kati Levoranta, stepped up to the role at the end of 2015.

Despite Cuevas's best efforts to clean up licensing and revitalize merchandise sales through the second half of 2014, with the new lines designed to accompany the launch of *Angry Birds Go!*, *Angry Birds Stella*, and *Angry Birds Epic*, the overextension of the physical products activities by her predecessors was such that it had brought consumers to a bit of a saturation point. There was only so much *Angry Birds* merchandise they could buy over such a short period of time. The Telepods sales curve seemed to be tailing off, even after the fourth-quarter tie-in with another strong global toy brand from the catalog of partner Hasbro,

Transformers. Angry Birds Transformers had music by the iconic composer Vince DiCola, who had composed the legendary "Training Montage" score for *Rocky IV*; fanboy Ilmari Hakkola fondly remembers this as his favorite musical collaboration of his entire time at Rovio.[2] From a toy sales perspective, though, it was something of a low point.

At the end of fiscal year 2014, it was decided to give the brand a year of rest in terms of physical goods production, in anticipation of the blitz of merchandise that was expected to flood the market alongside the theatrical release of the Sony Pictures-produced movie blockbuster the following year.

As a teaser for the incoming wave, the *LEGO Angry Birds* sets were revealed at San Diego Comic-Con in the summer of 2015, the materialization of "four years of negotiation and preparation"[3] for Naz Amarchi-Cuevas. Based on the upcoming movie iterations of the characters, the Birds had feet for the first time in toy form. Still no wings, obviously.

Starting the hype for the future motion picture, the American voice cast was revealed on October 1, 2014, and featured a lot of big names, such as former *Saturday Night Live* cast Jason Sudeikis, Bill Hader, Maya Rudolph, and Kate McKinnon, *Frozen*'s Josh Gad, *Eastbound & Down*'s Danny McBride, Keegan-Michael Key, *Veep*'s Tony Hale, and even YouTube stars Ian Andrew Hecox and Anthony Padilla from the ultra-popular channel Smosh. As for the Mighty Eagle, he was incarnated by none other than Peter Dinklage, of *Game of Thrones* fame.

The first teaser footage of the movie was released on September 23. Working with Sony has its perks on the music licensing front, since the company owns both Epic and Sony Records, the labels that hold Michael Jackson's song rights in their catalog. When the first trailer for the movie came out, it revealed new-look *Angry Birds* characters with feet and talking voices, scored on the legendary 1987 song "Bad" by the late King of Pop. Sony Pictures also pulled some strings to include a balloon based on the movie look of Red Bird as part of the 2015 edition of the classic Macy's Thanksgiving Day Parade in New York City, the world's largest parade (according to Wikipedia). Glimpses of the parade are widely televised, domestically and abroad.

Whereas the *Rio* and *Star Wars* collaborations had given Rovio a taste of the Hollywood way of life back in 2012, 2016 was the year that would see the release of a blockbuster movie based on its own property. And, Red Bird got the full red-carpet treatment. Going by the motion picture industry theory that, if the Los Angeles tastemakers don't get behind something, then the other big U.S. cities like New York, Chicago or Boston won't follow, everyone did their utmost to ensure that the opening night in California would smash the competition and *The Angry Birds Movie* would come out at number one. To prepare the way, a lot of the big tentpole activities leading up to the release were aimed at the Hollywood circles themselves. Massive billboards on the famous Interstate 405 highway and other such locally strategic locations were bought and plastered with *The Angry Birds Movie* visuals.

Some of Sony's most senior individuals pored over minor creative details, which was quite a culture shock for Rovio. Steve Porter remembers one such moment. A new app called *Masquerade* was trending in the top ten on the App Store. The app allowed users to put filters over their faces. "We wanted to work with them, and it was probably made easier by Facebook recently buying them," remembers Porter. "As we started working on the partnership with the Facebook team, David Maisel did not like the creative execution at all—going as far as to demand the head of the marketing escalate the issue to Mark Zuckerberg."[4] The expectations, whether about quality, speed, or being given priority, can reach new heights in Hollywood circles.

In the months leading up to the movie's global movie premiere, Rovio rallied all its partners, old and new, so they were firing on all cylinders. The NBA was activated again with a TV segment on TNT during the playoffs. The promo starred Steve Smith as commentator introducing the movie version of Chuck as an NBA player, and, of course, Larry Bird granted us a cameo yet again. "Sony Pictures really led the effort from the U.S. offices. What we made sure we helped with from Helsinki was to reactivate those early-days partnerships. Larry Bird and also old friends at NASA showed up,"[5] Torstila outlines.

The *LEGO Angry Birds* line came out at retail sites around the world, alongside a huge new wave of licensed consumer products in pretty much every category. Special emojis were temporarily introduced into Skype, triggered by typing [red] and [pig] into the messaging field of the widespread communication software. Then, to leverage the existing fan base, the landing site *Angrify.me* enabled people around the world to add angry eyebrows to their profile pictures and upload them to their social media. It was a bit of a simplified, low-key, mass-market revisit on the *Masquerade* app experiment earlier in the year.

Two games were also designed around the movie assets and poised to release on time for the barrage of promotional activities, albeit only one made the final cut. *Angry Birds Action!* was a pinball video game developed by Tag Games. Its purpose being mostly to serve as a promotional vehicle for the movie, job done, the game was removed from the App Store just a year later. The second planned game, *Angry Birds Holiday*, featured the bird characters from the movie running vacation resort services for incoming pigs to distract them from the eggs. After the game's performance failed to impress during a soft launch in the Philippines, it was canceled without going to a global release.

Sony Pictures pitched in, too, and brought out the big guns. McDonald's Happy Meal, yet another classic achievement for a brand on a pop culture tour, offered *Angry Birds* toys in 120 markets, with multiple TV commercials to support the promotion—a deal negotiated by Sony Pictures VP of national promotions Carlo Vespe. Ziad Toubassy, VP of international promotion at Sony Pictures, also landed a sizeable co-marketing partnership with French car manufacturer Citroën, which launched four different custom television spots in 23 European markets, focusing on the tagline "Make Angry Birds happy." Besides Citroën, Jack Link's also provided media for its Peperami and BiFi brands, with a spot airing in 11 markets. French AccorHotels Novotel chain showed off movie displays in hotel lobbies that let people enter a sweepstake by taking a selfie with the standee. Danone, Nestlé, Yoplait, Dr. Oetker, Telefonica, and, quite naturally, Sony Electronics and Sony Mobile were also among the other European partners. HSBC bank also offered promotions to its customers around the globe. Last but not least, Ferrero Kinder, manufacturer of the iconic Kinder Surprise chocolate egg, was also on board on the Old Continent—such a natural brand fit you might wonder why it took so long.

Stateside, Home Depot offered kids the chance to build an *Angry Birds*-themed birdhouse. Menchie's Frozen Yogurt launched an in-store promotion in its 518 outlets and offered five collectible spoons based on the characters. There was also to be a Best of the Nest ad campaign put together for 200 furniture retailers nationwide provided by Imagine Advertising for any local stores that wanted to participate. Other companies providing package labeling and sweepstakes contests included Ziploc and PepsiCo in North America, German candy maker Trolli in Europe, and Panasonic Batteries & Torches across 48 countries in the Americas and Asia. Another Asia initiative included Jetstar Japan giving some of its Airbus A320 planes, rebranded as "Happy Jets," a special *Angry Birds* livery, with Shinobu Sakagami, a famous Japanese actor, playing the role of "Happiness" ambassador, ahead of the delayed October movie launch in Japan. There were so many other domestic and regional brand deals that it would be boring to reference them all exhaustively.

Sony Pictures also partnered with the United Nations Foundation and other organizations on the International Day of Happiness on March 20, 2016, in a joint effort to push fans to act and share for good causes, since the movie backstory of Red Bird revolves around anger management therapy and the quest for happiness. Last-minute voice-cast cameo reveals included Blake Shelton and none other than Academy Award winner Sean Penn. The film score was composed by Heitor Pereira, of *Despicable Me* and *Minions* fame. The soundtrack of the movie also included a pretty strong star-studded roster of AAA-listers, with Blake Shelton, Demi Lovato, Charli XCX, Matoma, Romeo Santos, and Steve Aoki making the cut. It's worth noting that these artists catered to different demographics and even geographies. Here again, the aim was to be as broad and wide as possible.

The Angry Birds Movie premiered in Los Angeles on May 8, 2016, then rolled out in cinemas around the globe, starting with the Philippines on May 11 and 74 other countries on May 13. It finished first in 37 territories, and second overall at the international box office behind *Captain America: Civil War*, and grossing $43 million. In its second weekend, nine additional territories were added, including China, South Korea, and the Netherlands, and grossed $55.5 million from 83 markets. Overall, the top openings for the film were recorded in China with $29.2 million, Russia with $5.7 million, and the U.K. with $3.1 million, with Germany, Mexico, and Brazil coming in just under the $3 million mark. In China, *The Angry Birds Movie* achieved the third-best opening weekend ever for an animated film, behind only *Kung Fu Panda 3* and *Stand by Me Doraemon*, according to *The Hollywood Reporter*. In North America, the film opened on May 20, 2016, grossing

$38.2 million across 3,932 theaters in its opening weekend and finishing first at the box office. It also scored the second-best debut weekend for a video game adaptation in the U.S., falling just short of *Lara Croft: Tomb Raider.*

The total value of all marketing campaigns has been estimated at $400 million by the *LA Times.* This amount factored in not only the Sony Pictures investments and Rovio's own contribution of $100 million to the marketing spend, but also the value of media obtained through the various barter deals. "*The Angry Birds Movie* may not have the ubiquity of Universal Pictures' *Minions* from last year (partners for that film generated a jaw-dropping $600 million). Still, the studio and its partners have been aggressive," said David Maisel to Ryan Faughnder of the *LA Times.* "This definitely has the marketing campaign of a major summer blockbuster, there's been no hesitation,"[6] Maisel added.

The deluge of hype around the movie launch was so vast that even in Pereira, a second-tier city of fewer than a million inhabitants in the mountains of Colombia, to which I relocated with my family in 2015, we witnessed the ubiquitous presence of the brand on our way to the local movie theater. First we got the toys at the McDonald's over lunch, then we spotted the point-of-sale rebranding of the windows of the Movistar store (the Telefonica arm in Latin America), and were surrounded by the giant posters and selfie-friendly slingshots in the theater lobby. That's not even counting the grassroot *Angry Birds*-themed birthdays that Colombian kids request from their parents on a regular basis, in fierce competition with the Disney princess and *Minions* themes, or the bootleg *Angry Birds* cakes, balloons, or popsicles I keep spotting around the country.

While the commercial blitz hit everywhere, Sony Pictures also made sure to continue Rovio's tradition of placing Red Bird in every iconic pop cultural situation imaginable, this time by crashing Cannes, the most storied and glamorous film festival in the world. On May 10, 2016, one day before the official ceremony opening, betting that all the global media and cinema moguls had already gathered in France, Sony hooked up a pre-festival commercial takeover, which might have been a first in the history of the festival, according to *Deadline*. A prominent stage was set up at the Majestic Pier for a photo call operation involving the heroes in bird costumes, as well as the international voice cast of the film: Josh Gad from the U.S. crew, local superstar Omar Sy (*Intouchables*), who voiced Red Bird in the French version, Maccio Capatonda (Red in Italy), Raya Abirached (Matilda in the Arabic version), and Timur Rodriguez (Chuck in Russia). Giant bird plushes were placed on top of the Carlton Hotel and the movie logo was drawn on nearby sandy beaches using Red Bird action figures. The movie title was legible from far away, and, closer to, fans could grab one of the hundreds of toys and claim it as their own. Since journalists were everywhere looking for something to cover, the stunt generated a whole lot of press in a multitude of languages.

In terms of total earnings, the biggest markets outside North America were China with $75.8 million, $15 million in the U.K., and Russia and Germany almost neck and neck at respectively $11.99 million and $11.97 million. In total, *The Angry Birds Movie* ended up grossing $352.3 million, $107.5 million in North America and $244.8 million overseas, making it briefly the highest-grossing video game-inspired film of all time internationally, only to be beaten a month later when *Warcraft* was released. It remains in second place at the time of writing. It is also the most successful film in Finnish movie history by revenue generated and ticket sales.

The Angry Birds Movie was released in digital HD on July 29, 2016, and on Blu-ray and DVD on August 16, 2016, with four "Hatchlings" shorts included in the package. The film topped the home video sales chart for the week ending August 21, 2016. *Deadline.com* calculated the net profit of the film to be $72 million, a cash-on-cash return of 1.32, when factoring together all expenses and revenues for the film.[7] As mentioned earlier, Rovio Entertainment was entitled to a lion's share of those profits, due to its high-risk, high-reward upfront investment in production and marketing ultimately paying off.

The back catalog of *Angry Birds* mobile games has seen an increase of 6.5 million downloads directly attributable to the movie frenzy, according to Matt Wilson.[8] This may seem like a drop in the ocean, when compared to the billions of downloads amassed by the franchise prior to the movie launch. There's no doubt that if the movie had been released earlier in the cycle of the franchise, the download impact would have been much greater. For Rovio at this stage in its growth cycle, though, there was a higher goal at play: become a permanent part of pop culture like Hello Kitty, *The Simpsons*, Mickey Mouse, *The Smurfs*, or *Pokémon*. In that respect, the movie's success has certainly helped cement this vision for the next hundred years. "I think, for Rovio, it's more important to use the movie as a vehicle to sort of elevate the brand in general across all areas—whether that's mobile games or something else," says Darren Kyman, head of retail and new business development for Rovio North America, in an interview with Chris Morris for *Fortune*. "I don't think the overall *Angry Birds* franchise is completely dependent on the movie, but it will have a huge impact. Anyone who didn't know about *Angry Birds* before, will now."[9] Torstila concurs: "We [at Rovio marcomm] supported *The Angry Birds Movie* marketing effort in multiple ways, not so much to directly generate game downloads, but to gain and maintain momentum for the brand, which had become the new challenge we had to rise up to. Whether the games helped the movie, or the movie helped the games and merchandise, at the end of the day, the brand wins."[10]

The Return of the Red Eye

With a promotional effort of this magnitude, Sony Pictures and Rovio were obviously in it for the long run and almost immediately announced that a sequel had been greenlit.

In April 2018, most of the voice cast for the second *Angry Birds* film was announced. Jason Sudeikis, Gad, Danny McBride, Maya Rudolph, Bill Hader, and Peter Dinklage were to reprise their roles from the first film. Leslie Jones joined in as well as Nicki Minaj. On its release, the teaser trailer briefly revealed that Hal, a green boomerang bird from the games and the first film, would return in the sequel, with Anthony Padilla of Smosh fame returning to voice him. The following day, producer John Cohen announced in a tweet that YouTube star Awkwafina would voice Courtney, the first named female pig in the *Angry Birds* franchise. When the film's first full trailer was released on March 27, 2019, more details about the sequel's characters and their voice roles were revealed, packed with a few additional surprises such as Rachel Bloom, Dove Cameron, and Tiffany Haddish. Both motion pictures were clearly leveraged by Rovio and Sony Pictures to associate the brand with as many stars as possible, connecting with their diverse fan bases around the world.

Heitor Pereira returned to compose the score of *The Angry Birds Movie 2*. On July 25, 2019, Kesha released her song "Best Day" for the film, and days later, Luke Combs released another song, "Let's Just Be Friends," ensuring the brand's presence in the platform music charts, too. The rest of the film's soundtrack consisted of a compilation of pop hits from the 1960s to 2000s.

The Angry Birds Movie 2 was theatrically released in Finland on August 7, 2019, and in the U.S. on August 14 in RealD 3D formats. Notably, Rovio only licensed this second outing to Sony Pictures as opposed to co-producing, thereby reducing its risk exposure, both financially and in terms of time resources and company focus. To prep up audiences, *The Angry Birds Movie* was pre-released in January of the same year on streaming platform Netflix, whose popularity in the U.S. was ever growing and which was seeing service launches across more and more territories overseas.

On the gaming front, the play this time turned to leveraging already available titles from the catalog and their existing audiences through live ops events. Steve Porter, freshly promoted to brand director after a couple of years as product marketing manager on the games catalog in between the two movies, comments that this was a conscious move: "This was the big learning lesson from the first movie. Releasing *Angry Birds Action!* had been a bit as if we were our own licensee. It made much more sense to play to our strengths and do for the sequel the same kind of cross-promotional events we had done for other brands or games within our existing ecosystem of games already available and played by millions."[11] In total, six available mobile games, including the flagship hits of the moment *Angry Birds 2*, *Angry Birds Evolution*, and *Angry Birds Dream Blast*, were all granted an update focused on the second movie contents and storylines. Some of the ad inventory inside those games was also assigned to promoting the video commercials for the film.

The marketing mix blended traditional marketing such as billboards and other out-of-home (OOH) components with more modern digital media techniques such as targeted advertising and influencer marketing, which had become all the rage. Coinciding with the buildup to the tenth anniversary celebrations of *Angry Birds* as a franchise at the end of 2019, Steve Porter concocted a campaign with his team around the theme "Bring the Anger." Teaming up with advertising agency Droga5, they created outlets for converting anger into positive energy.

They created an electric scooter powered by the user yelling into a microphone, and distributed these to over 30 creators in the U.S. They also made a "Venting Machine" and dropped it in Times Square—the currency was anger, and visitors had to punch, kick, and scream their way to get a prize from it.

The cornerstone of the campaign was enlisting over 30 YouTubers to "bring the anger" by showing their rage on camera. MrBeast did an integrated segment in his "I opened a Free Bank" video, which has garnered 121 million views to date. Marques Brownlee, Shonduras, and Team Edge were among dozens of other creators who joined the campaign, together amassing another 50 million views. All this culminated in a community goal for *Angry Birds 2* players—by collectively bringing the anger and popping millions of pigs in game, players unlocked a donation of US$100,000 to UNICEF.

Still looking for growth hacks through barter deals, Rovio also struck a partnership with popular language-learning app Duolingo, known for its daring online voice and attitude, very similar to the early days of *Angry Birds*. Steve Porter concurs: "It might have contributed to us rethinking our own tone of voice online, too. We even changed our @AngryBirds Twitter account to be simply Red tweeting as himself and being a bit of a troll."[12]

For the collaboration, both brands released a trailer on YouTube showing Red Bird and the Duo owl mascots destroying a bar because the partygoers are ignoring their app notifications. The video gathered 2 million views on the Duolingo channel and another 800,000 on the Angry Birds channel. Even Redditors liked the collaboration, with quite a few short posts surfacing and trending on the topic-centric social network. More importantly, both campaigns were integrated into the apps. Steve Porter breaks down the key details of the cross-promotion:

> Two iconic mobile apps with bird mascots that don't directly compete in terms of user motivation—this was the perfect setting for an in-app collab. We got *Angry*

> *Birds 2* integrated in Duolingo, and Duo integrated in *Angry Birds 2* as a character. We shared app ad inventory and drove traffic directly between the apps. The funnel was so sweet—we were both able to measure the impact that we had on installs, and even the retention and monetization of those particular cohorts. Even in a short time, it was a very profitable campaign delivered with minimal investment—this was definitely one of my highlights.[13]

Once again, truckloads of merchandising and toys were released simultaneously in stores around the world. The occasion saw yet another timeless pop culture product join the fore of *Angry Birds* licensees, with global confectioner Perfetti Van Melle producing legendary Chupa Chups popsicles based on birds and piggies characters.

The Angry Birds Movie 2 has grossed $41.7 million in the U.S. and Canada, and $110.1 million in other territories, for a worldwide total of $152.8 million, on a $65 million production budget. While it was not as financially successful as its predecessor, it received generally positive reviews from critics, who considered it an improvement on its predecessor. According to Rotten Tomatoes, it was the best-reviewed film adaptation of a video game on the review-aggregation website and had the highest score for an animated video game movie.

The Angry Birds Movie 2 was released on Netflix in the U.S. on August 24, 2021, further cementing the strategic partnership with the now dominant global streaming platform, in a post-COVID pandemic world which was barely coming out of quarantine.

Rovio and Netflix then collaborated more closely on an exclusive Netflix Originals series, *Angry Birds: Summer Madness*, aimed at young audiences aged between 6 and 12. While the brand is going through a wave of nostalgia among older generations, it's important to keep it relevant for future generations of children, too, keeping new fans flocking in. Rovio and Netflix used cross-promotion strategies to boost the visibility of *Angry Birds: Summer Madness*. This included promotional materials on Netflix's platform, social media campaigns, and trailers that highlighted the new series. Rovio and Netflix also integrated cross-promotional bridges between the mobile game *Angry Birds Blast!* and Netflix's *Angry Birds* content. This integration helped to bridge the gap between interactive and streaming experiences, keeping fans engaged across multiple platforms.

Throughout the span of their presence on Netflix, until the summer of 2023, the films were steady performers in the Kids category and in the Animation section, consistently charting within the top ten across dozens of countries.

When building a character-centric universe, there is only so much of the lair the games can produce. There comes a time when the bigger story must be developed, too, and that is the long-lasting value of the feature films and other linear content.

CHAPTER EIGHTEEN

A Permanent Part of Global Pop Culture

To be a permanent part of pop culture had become the verbalized common goal among Rovians pretty much since the second half of 2012, around the collaborations with NASA then Lucasfilm. "Encounters like those are life-changing because they show you that, if you dream big, it can come true, and that if you put the right people together working in the same direction, everything can come together. And to be aware of this possibility changing you forever,"[1] sums up Phil Hickey.

As I visited Helsinki again, Rovio was about to materialize its long-rumored ambitions to become a public company. Rovio Entertainment went public on September 29, 2017, through an initial public offering (IPO) on Nasdaq Helsinki (formerly Helsinki Stock Exchange). The initial price was set at €11.50 per share, with a market capitalization valued at approximately €1 billion. Rovio offered around 30 million shares in the IPO, raising about €345 million, which interestingly represented only about 20 percent of the company shareholding, leaving Kaj Hed still as sole majority owner. Rovio thus became a publicly traded company flown like a privately owned jet—gaining bigger wings through the influx of capital without compromising on velocity of flight and agile decision making in the cockpit—one of the key ingredients for Rovio's success up to that point. The performance of Rovio's stock over time has been mixed, reflecting broader market conditions.

On one journey from Pereira, Colombia to Espoo, Finland, I encountered the brand a dozen times within 15 hours. First, at the Exito supermarket, where there was a display of *Angry Birds: la película* coloring books towering near the cash register. Then, near Bogotá's airport, Burger King was having an *Angry Birds* over-the-counter promotion, offering toys with some of its meals. Other outlets in Bogotá's airport had unlicensed *Angry Birds* cakes, balloons, and handmade popsicles on sale. As I got onto the plane to Europe, a Colombian kid next to me was playing *Angry Birds Go!* on his dad's Samsung phone. *Angry Birds* was also among the games I could select to play on the seat entertainment screen, or I could just opt to watch *The Angry Birds Movie* in six different languages on that same display. On the connection flight to Helsinki, Finnish newspapers were presented to all passengers with Red Bird featured all over the front page. The article was about the IPO, encouraging Finns to take ownership in the national treasure. That sentiment was also promoted through side wrap advertising on the buses and trams I took to get to Pocket Gamer Helsinki, a mobile industry trade event where, obviously, Rovio was present in full force, showcasing its upcoming new games.

Rovio has got its marketing mojo back, finally adapting to the world of F2P mobile games, performance marketing, and user acquisition dynamics. This, and the movie bet paying off and positively contributing to the bottom line, were the two key components that helped Rovio proudly announce on February 28, 2017 that the company had returned to profitable growth.

During the following years, the brand has continued to partner with other hit entertainment franchises, such as *Trolls* or *How to Train Your Dragon* from the DreamWorks catalog, in 2020 and 2021, and later with up-and-coming sensation *Peppa Pig*. As the popularity of the beloved animated character was exploding among Generation Alpha across the U.K. (where the TV series is made) and Europe, it was in a good position to bring a new generation into the *Angry Birds* lair, much as *Angry Birds* had done the same favor for *Star Wars* a decade earlier (conversely, Rovio gave *Peppa Pig* a taste of Hollywood-level marketing, much as Fox had done for Rovio also ten years previously). *Angry Birds x Peppa Pig: The Big Adventure* was announced in 2021, with various contents and products related to it rolling out throughout the year in mobile games, merchandise, and promotional events. Rovio incorporated *Peppa Pig*-themed levels into several of its *Angry Birds* games. These levels featured *Peppa Pig* characters and environments, blending the gameplay mechanics of *Angry Birds* with themes from the *Peppa Pig* universe. The collaboration extended to merchandise, including toys and clothing that featured both *Angry Birds* and *Peppa Pig* characters.

The AngryVerse

Rovio also remained true to its commitment to keep on delivering a diverse slate of entertainment touch points across multiple emerging platforms and new technologies. In 2019, *Angry Birds: Isle of Pigs* slingshot the game into augmented reality (AR), leveraging the Apple ARKit to let iPhone and iPad users shoot birds at pigs in 3D within their own real-world environment. The 3D all-around gameplay style was then ported to virtual reality (VR), with *Isle of Pigs* seeing a release that same year on Oculus Rift, HTC VIVE, and PlayStation VR.

More noteworthy, *Angry Birds* became part of two of the most successful video game phenomena of the current generation: *Minecraft* and *Roblox*.

Released in 2011 by Mojang Studios, *Minecraft* has sold over 300 million paid copies across various platforms (it holds the Guinness World Record for the bestselling game of all time), including PCs, consoles, and mobile devices. *Minecraft*'s popularity is evident from its massive player-base, which has exceeded 200 million active users worldwide. The game introduced unique sandbox gameplay that allows players to mine, build, and explore vast, blocky worlds. Its simplicity and creativity have led to a robust and passionate community that creates and shares custom content, such as mods and maps. The game's influence extends beyond its original boundaries, inspiring a range of merchandise, spinoffs, references in TV shows and movies, and even a dedicated convention, MineCon. *Minecraft* is so culturally relevant for younger consumers that it is constantly ranked within the top-20 most searched terms across the whole of YouTube, both in the U.S. and in the global aggregate data category, and this for the last ten years in a row! The official *Minecraft* channel on YouTube itself has garnered 25 million subscribers, not to mention the thousands upon thousands of so-called "Let's Play" channels dedicated 100 percent to streaming this singular game. It was acquired by Microsoft in 2014 for US$2.5 billion.

The *Minecraft Angry Birds* mashup was announced on April 23, 2020, with the crossover content dropping from late 2020 into early 2021 on various platforms where *Minecraft* is played, including Xbox, PlayStation, Nintendo Switch, Windows 10, and Mobile. The collaboration featured a special *Angry Birds* skin pack, a texture pack, and *Angry Birds*-themed maps and adventure scenarios, incorporating structures and challenges inspired by the *Angry Birds* lair. Special minigames were developed to reflect the gameplay mechanics of *Angry Birds*, allowing players to launch projectiles and destroy structures in a *Minecraft* setting.

Angry Birds and *Minecraft* used their respective massively followed social media channels to promote the collaboration, circulating teaser trailers, screenshots, and behind-the-scenes content to generate excitement among fans. The advantages of *Minecraft* being a Microsoft property led to the *Minecraft Angry Birds* mashup being promoted across various other assets owned by Microsoft. This included promotions on the official *Minecraft* website, Xbox Live, and the Microsoft Store for Windows PCs.

Shortly after, *Angry Birds* also popped up into the ultra-dominant gaming platform among younger consumers, *Roblox*. *Roblox* enables users to easily create and design their own game experiences leveraging physics, animations, and mechanics that preexist and are already built into the Avatar system. It's the closest thing to the concept experts like to call the Metaverse, along with *Fortnite* ever since the launch of its UEFN (Unreal Engine for Fortnite) content-creation tool, and maybe *Avakin Life* or *ZEPETO* in Asia. *Roblox* boasts 70 million daily active users and a staggering 196 million monthly active users.

On December 13, 2021, the official Red Twitter account tweeted a picture of Red Bird made out of cardboard boxes in *Roblox* style, standing in the Rovio offices lobby in Espoo, Finland. The caption read: "This is a teaser." The same account tweeted an hour later: "How do u log in to roblox?" On December 16, a more official teaser trailer was revealed across social media, and the official roleplaying experience *Angry Birds: Bird Island* came out of closed beta to become available worldwide.

Both *Minecraft* and *Roblox* are helping to feed younger fans into the brand, true to four-quadrant brand thinking. Don't forget that, in mobile games, for Rovio as well as for most F2P mobile developers and publishers, the tendency is to not have age-gating at the intro in order to avoid friction and churn, but this means they could not address children under 13 years old due to COPPA (Children's Online Privacy Protection Act) and GDPR (General Data Protection Regulation) laws in the U.S. and European Union. *Minecraft* and *Roblox* are great venues to entertain these demographics.

Staying Angry

Proving the evergreen—oops, sorry, ever-red—appeal of the franchise, the iconic brand also got cherry-picked by one of the most subscribed and viewed YouTube channels of the creator economy, Dude Perfect, for an organic video reproducing the slingshot mechanic seen in the game. The video, titled "Angry Birds in Real Life" and released in 2023, has, at the time of writing in 2024, already garnered 9 million views. My trained eye can observe that the video wasn't sponsored by Rovio: Rather than using official *Angry Birds* merch, the dudes used all kinds of bird toys and balloons (no piggies!), changed the shape of the slingshot, and went out of their way to approximate the official *Angry Birds* lettering on the transitional screens, without it actually being the same font. Someone was paying attention not to be sued for copyright infringement here. Were it a paid brand deal, things would have gone the other way: precise respect for the branding elements of the sponsor, as per the brief on signature of the deal.

As influencer marketing has grown into one of the hot trends of the last ten years, brands regularly splash six-digit budgets on paid collaborations and sponsored videos. Yet *Angry Birds* just happens to score one of the biggest possible creators for free! The reason is brand's continuing power as a keyword in online searches. As I had a chance to witness first-hand when briefly serving as a consultant for one of MrBeast's companies, all top YouTubers use sophisticated A/B testing techniques on key funnel elements such as the title and the thumbnail of the video. Their focus is above all else on "retention" across the video, making sure people not only click but keep watching until the end, as these are the key factors for the algorithm to accelerate the appearance of the video across more people's front pages. Add growth velocity into the mix and you've got yourself a so-called "trending" video. Sustain this over a few days or weeks, and you achieve the holy grail of "viral" status. Whereas viral happens once every blue moon, "trending" is a feat most top YouTubers with high-frequency posts, high engagement, and high subscriber bases can hit consistently ... *if* they propose content people actually want to watch. You can assume Dude Perfect dropped this video with that title, not just out of love for the game but mainly because its data showed it would perform well in terms of number of views and correlated advertising revenue. It's the good old difference between a push-product and a pull-product: The push-product must be sold to people; the pull-product is already in demand and attracts people. The commercial relationship among partners shifts depending on which you are. To this day, *Angry Birds* is still pretty much a pull-product— a flavor you better have in store; a wave to ride.

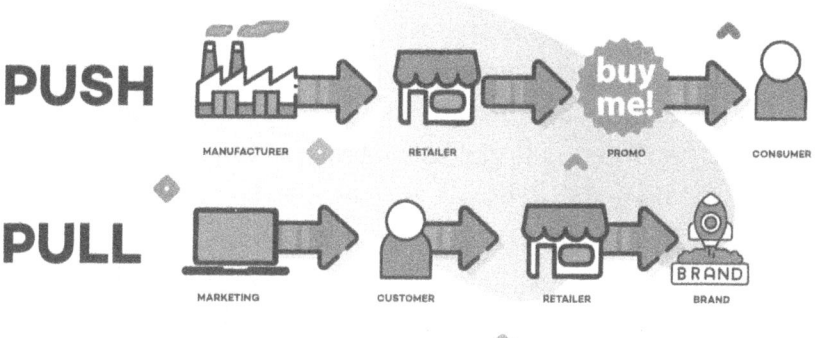

Push and Pull Products

For fans of the original series, 15 years ago, there is even a wave of nostalgia around the brand. YouTube is the theater for a "title-jacking" trend around the Bad Piggies theme song by Ilmari Hakkola from ten years before. One could think the resurgence was fire-started by the release of F2P mobile game *Bad Piggies 2* in 2021, but in fact predates it by around a year. It seems the origin of the whole frenzy came from a post on *iFunny.co* in which the track is played to footage of a man with a Mozart hairdo playing frantically on a piano on fire, captioned "Rovio: it's just a fun little game about pigs. Ilmari Hakkola." Soon after, the YouTube channel Sheet Music Boss released an Impossible Piano Remix of the song, which gathered 3.9 million views in musical connoisseur circles. It snowballed from there and took on a life of its own between 2022 and 2024, achieving proper viral status. Basically, the trend is all about dropping the fast-paced piano theme of Hakkola over mis-matched footage, then titling your video "[INSERT TITLE] only it's the Bad Piggies Theme Song." For example, "It's the end of the world, only it's the Bad Piggies theme song." Hundreds of such user-generated videos have been made, some of them gathering millions of views on their own. Then there's the a cappella version from 2023 sitting at 1.2 million views. There is even a symphonic orchestra performing it on stage in a video that has been viewed 2.4 million times since 2022. Ilmari noticed quite a steady spike on plays of the song on streaming platforms, with 11 million through Spotify alone, and another 9 million across the different publica-tions on YouTube. Salla Hakkola admits with a laugh: "After the tracks are done and released, it's not in our hands how people receive it. I love Ilmari's song because it bears so much of his personality, and it fits the game better than my canceled theme for it. A meme was dedicated to my brother because of that, and it just shows how much other people love it too!"[2] Her own and her brother's persistence with the top management a decade ear-lier was actually spot on: Invest more in music and it will reap rewards for the company and the brand, because music has its own life, possibly for decades after its first release.

Angry Birds games had triggered a staggering aggregate of 5 billion downloads, as of 2023. According to a survey conducted by Sony Pictures at the end of 2013, right before it inked the motion picture deal, 90 percent of Americans were familiar with the *Angry Birds* brand. What's more, 93 percent of the urban population of China had at least heard of *Angry Birds*. The craziest stat comes from South Korea, though, where, out of 65 million inhabitants, 60 million have played the game at least once. "A fan once tweeted us a picture of a local kid in his *Angry Birds* T-shirt in the rain forest of Myanmar,"[3] laughs Robin Squire. When I heard that, I joked to her that *Angry Birds* was everywhere except in North Korea. It's a line I often use to (dark) humorously say that something is truly global. North Korea is such a closed dictatorship that nothing passes the border without approval from supreme leader Kim Jong Un. Absolutely nothing. Well, according to the *Washington Post*, as of November of 2013, a pirated copy of *Angry Birds Rio*, translated into Korean, came preloaded on the state-approved tablet, the Android-based Samjiyon, released by the North Korean Computer Center that year.[4] I stand corrected.

On April 17, 2023, Tokyo-headquartered Sega Sammy Holdings recognized the value of Rovio at US$776 million, acquiring the company, its teams, and assets during a tough year of consolidation in the video games industry. It beat several competitive offers for the company, in a bidding war that started through an initial hostile takeover raid by Tel Aviv District-based Playtika, initially rejected due to the acquisition of fellow Finnish companies Reworks (*Redecor*) and Seriously (*Best Fiends*) going sour in terms of culture-fit and integration. Rovio went shopping for other bidders, and the board of directors ended up accepting Sega's friendly bid, at a 19 percent increase valuation per share. In hindsight, Kaj Hed keeping a decisive majority stake proved to be a great defensive tool when navigating this situation.

Sega Sammy president and group CEO Haruki Satomi said of the deal:

> Among the rapidly growing global gaming market, the mobile gaming market has especially high potential, and it has been Sega's long-term goal to accelerate

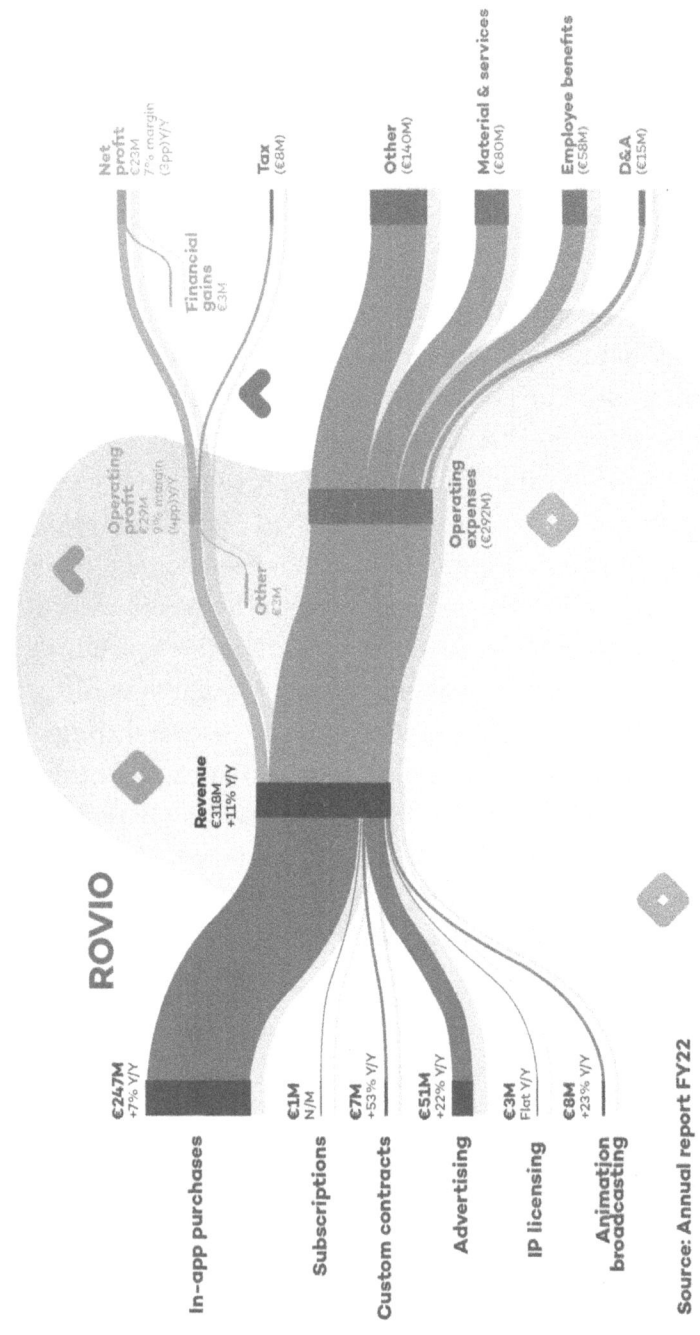

ROVIO

Revenue
€318M
+11% Y/Y

In-app purchases
€247M
+7% Y/Y

Subscriptions
€1M
N/M

Custom contracts
€7M
+53% Y/Y

Advertising
€51M
+22% Y/Y

IP licensing
€3M
Flat Y/Y

Animation broadcasting
€8M
+23% Y/Y

Operating profit
€29M
9% margin
(4pp)Y/Y

Operating expenses
(€292M)

Net profit
€23M
7% margin
(3pp)Y/Y

Financial gains
€3M

Tax
(€8M)

Other
€3M

Other
(€140M)

Material & services
(€80M)

Employee benefits
(€58M)

D&A
(€15M)

Rovio Diversification Financials

Source: Annual report FY22

its expansion in this field. I feel blessed to be able to announce such a transaction with Rovio, a company that owns *Angry Birds*, which is loved across the world, and home to many skilled employees that support the company's industry-leading mobile game development and operating capabilities.[5]

"Historically, as represented by the *Sonic the Hedgehog* series, Sega has released countless video game titles to various gaming platforms," continued Satomi. "I am confident that, through a combination of both companies' brands, characters, fanbase, as well as corporate culture and functionality, there will be significant synergies created going forward."[6] Rovio CEO Alexandre Pelletier-Normand added: "I grew up playing *Sonic the Hedgehog*, captivated by its state-of-the-art design. Later, when I played *Angry Birds* for the first time, I knew that gaming had evolved into a true mainstream phenomenon, with the power to shape modern culture. Joining Rovio has been an honor and I am proud to have seen *Angry Birds* continue to grow, as we released new games, series and films."

Shortly after the acquisition, there was a taste of things to come, with a mega crossover among all games and characters from both the *Angry Birds* universe and the *Sonic* lair, Sega's own crown jewel, during March 2024. Sonic and Red must team up to defeat Dr. Eggman, his Badniks, and the pigs across both universes, in *Angry Birds 2, Angry Birds Dream Blast, Angry Birds Friends, Sonic Forces*, and *Sonic Dash*. Not limiting collabs to the Sega catalog, *Angry Birds* also teamed up with *My Talking Tom* in December 2024. Developed and published by Outfit7 out of Slovenia, the *My Talking Tom* franchise is all about petting your cartoonish cat through voice commands. *Talking Tom* has grown into the most downloaded mobile game series of all times, with 9 billion installs to date. As with *Sonic*, the crossover went both ways. In *My Talking*

Tom 2, players found two *Angry Birds*-themed mini-games: a fast-paced whack-a-mole challenge and a fun slingshot game reminiscent of the classic *Angry Birds* game mechanics. Meanwhile, a chili-themed *Talking Tom* event dropped in *Angry Birds 2*. Rovio released two animated episodes where the birds and Tom join forces against the piggies in Red's dreams. Blame it on the piggies. Turns out cats and birds can get along just fine ... when they're among download billionaires. Jernej Česen, senior VP of distribution and business intelligence at Outfit7, said in the press release: "Bringing *Angry Birds* into *My Talking Tom 2* is more than just a fun crossover—it's an opportunity to celebrate two pioneering franchises that have defined mobile gaming for over a decade."[7]

On June 6, 2024, through press releases and Instagram posts, Rovio Entertainment, Sega, and Namit Malhotra's Mumbai-based production company Prime Focus Studios announced that they were starting production on *The Angry Birds Movie 3*, just as *Angry Birds* was celebrating its fifteenth anniversary. As I doomscroll my Instagram feed, procrastinating just a little bit before concluding our story, I see Rovio has manufactured limited-edition multicolored rugs that would look pretty neat on my bathroom floor.

Like *Mario*, *Sonic*, or *Pokémon* before it, *Angry Birds* is now a part of the video game pantheon. Love it or hate it, it's undisputable that *Angry Birds* has become iconic in its own right, and although there are sure to be ups and downs along its path, the brand is here to stay.

Usually, to assess the potential of such a rising star, you'd say, "The sky's the limit." As proven by its launch stunt from space, sometimes you can reach beyond that point. The amount of time and money it took for Rovio to push its brand to such astronomical heights is nonetheless as low as it can get.

When you don't have a rocket or even wings, use slingshots instead.

Endnotes

Chapter One

1 Tom Cheshire, "In depth: How Rovio made *Angry Birds* a winner (and what's next)," *wired.co.uk*, March 7, 2011.
2 Ibid.
3 Ibid.
4 Jaakko Iisalo, Skype conversation with author, January 17, 2014.
5 Ibid.
6 Cheshire, "In depth."
7 Ibid.
8 http://www.box2d.org
9 Cheshire, "In depth."
10 Ibid.
11 Matthew Wilson, conversation with author, Espoo, December 11, 2013.
12 Cheshire, "In depth."
13 David Trottier, *The Screenwriting Bible*, 7th ed., Silman-James Press, 2019.

Chapter Two

1 Jaakko Iisalo, Skype conversation with author, January 17, 2014.
2 Don Daglow, speaking at GDC Europe 2012, as reported by Matt Martin for *GamesIndustry.biz*, August 2012, http://www.gamesindustry.biz/articles/2012-08-13-what-european-developers-need-to-know-about-american-online-gamers
3 Ibid.
4 Jaakko Iisalo, Skype conversation with author, January 17, 2014.
5 Mark Griffiths, professor of psychology heading the International Gaming Research at Nottingham Trent University, talking to WIRED.
6 Ari Pulkkinen quoted on the Rovio blog.
7 Ibid.

Chapter Three

1 A so-called "featuring" is a premium real-estate spot located within both iTunes and the App Store where Apple gives exposure to apps that it finds noteworthy, for a limited period, at its sole editorial discretion. Given that millions of users check the App Store daily straight from the device that they use to download, install, and use an app, the spike in sales that it generates is notoriously huge.

2 Matthew Wilson, speaking at Casual Connect 2012 in Kiev, Ukraine, http://www.youtube.com/watch?v=wz-G3_2Aidw

3 Ibid.

4 Matthew Wilson, conversation with author, Espoo, December 11, 2013.

5 Wilson, speaking at Casual Connect 2012.

6 Wilson, conversation with author, Espoo, December 11, 2013.

7 Wilson, speaking at Casual Connect.

8 Paraphrasing W. Chan Kim and Renée Mauborgne, *Blue Ocean Strategy*, Harvard Review Business Press, 2005/2015.

9 Georges Wolinski, "L'humour est le plus court chemin d'un homme à un autre."

10 Lauri Konttori, Skype conversation with author, January 29, 2014.

11 Wilson, speaking at Casual Connect 2012.

12 Lauri Konttori, Skype conversation with author, January 29, 2014.

13 Term coined by anthropologist Jyri Engeström.

14 Hugh McLeod, *Gapingvoid.so*, http://gapingvoid.com/so/

15 Wilson, conversation with author, Espoo, December 11, 2013.

16 Jaakko Iisalo, Skype conversation with author, January 17, 2014.

17 Ibid.

18 Wilson, conversation with author, Espoo, December 12, 2013.

Chapter Four

1 Raph Koster, *The Laws of Online World Design*, 1997, https://www.raphkoster.com/games/laws-of-online-world-design/the-laws-of-online-world-design/

2 Jaakko Iisalo, Skype conversation with author, January 17, 2014.

3 Lauri Konttori, Skype conversation with author, January 29, 2014.

4 Miguel Francisco, Google Meet call with author, July 30, 2024.

5 USP stands for "unique sales proposition" and is a very routine acronym in advertising jargon.

6 Peter Vesterbacka, Skype conversation with author, February 7, 2014.

7 Peter Vesterbacka, conversation with author, Espoo, December 11, 2013.

8 Matthew Wilson, conversation with author, Espoo, December 11, 2013.

9 Ibid.

10 Ibid.

11 Ibid.

12 Ibid.

13 Ibid.

Chapter Five

1 Ari Pulkkinen quoted on the Rovio blog.

2 Matthew Wilson, conversation with author, Espoo, December 11, 2013.

3 Jaakko Iisalo, Skype conversation with author, January 17, 2014.

4 Ibid.

5 Mikael Hed in Marc Graser, "*Angry Birds* Flies with Hollywood," *Variety*, August 24, 2010, http://variety.com/2010/biz/news/angry-birds-flies-with-hollywood-1118023224/

6 Wilson, conversation with author, Espoo, December 11, 2013.

7 Ayzenberg Group, "[a]insight," Mobile Gaming White Paper, February 2011.

8 Wilson, conversation with author, Espoo, December 11, 2013.

9 Saara Bergström, conversation with author, Espoo, December 12, 2013. Saara would join Rovio in summer 2011 and was still working for Nokia at this point.

10 Ibid.

11 Mark Earls, *The Hidden Truth about Who We Are*, December 30, 2007, http://herd.typepad.com/herd_the_hidden_truth_abo/2007/12/on-the-seventh.html

12 Philip Hickey, Google Meet call with author, August 8, 2024.

13 Ibid.

14 Anja Pärson, interview with Kristoffer Bergström, *Aftonbladet*, February 19, 2010, http://www.aftonbladet.se/sportbladet/vinter-sport/os2010/article12176250.ab

15 Anna Kendrick, *TIME*, "2011 TIME 100," April 21, 2011.

Chapter Six

1 Matthew Wilson, conversation with author, Espoo, December 11, 2013.

2 Ibid.

3 Ibid.

4 Ibid.

5 David Helgason, interview with Matthew Handrahan for *Games-Industry.biz*, August 15, 2011.

Chapter Seven

1 Matthew Wilson, speaking at Casual Connect 2012 in Kiev, Ukraine.

2 Wilson, conversation with author, Espoo, December 11, 2013.

3 Ibid.

4 Lauri Konttori, Skype conversation with author, January 29, 2014.

5 Marja Konttinen, Skype conversation with author, January 20, of 2014.

6 Ibid.

7 Ibid.

8 Ibid.

9 Wilson, conversation with author, Espoo, December 11, 2013.

10 Ibid.

Chapter Eight

1 Andrew Stalbow speaking at MIPCOM conference in November 2012. Moderation by Kate Bulkley.

2 Andrew Stalbow, in Danny Graydon, *Angry Birds: Hatching a Universe*, Insight Editions, 2013.

3 Peter Vesterbacka, conversation with author through Skype, February 2014.

4 Peter Vesterbacka, conversation with author, Espoo, December 11, 2013.

5 Lauri Konttori, Skype conversation with author, January 29, 2014.

6 Ibid.

7 Pascal Clarysse, "From E.T. to Star Wars," *EDGE*, September 23, 2008.

8 Vesterbacka, conversation with author, Espoo, December 11, 2013.

9 Pamela McClintock, *The Hollywood Reporter*, February 1, 2011.

10 Matthew Wilson, conversation with author, Espoo, December 11, 2013.

11 Vesterbacka, conversation with author, Espoo, December 11, 2013.

12 Andrew Hampp, "Family films like *Rio, Hop* and *Rango* rescue Hollywood ticket sales," *AdAge*, April 27, 2011, http://adage.com/article/media/rio-hop-rescue-hollywood-ticket-sales/227226/

13 Dorothy Pomerantz, "Rio Plus *Angry Birds* Equals a Hit," *Forbes*, April 14, 2014, http://www.forbes.com/sites/dorothypomerantz/2011/04/14/rio-plus-angry-birds-equals-a-hit/

14 Ibid.

15 Vesterbacka, conversation with author, Espoo, December 11, 2013.

16 Andrew Stalbow speaking at Web 2.0 Summit in April 2012.

17 Andrew Stalbow speaking at MIPCOM conference in November 2012. Moderation by Kate Bulkley.

18 Marja Konttinen, Skype conversation with author, January 20, 2014.

19 Vesterbacka, conversation with author, Espoo, December 11, 2013.

20 Matthew Wilson, conversation with author, Espoo, December 11th, 2013.

Chapter Nine

1 Matthew Wilson, conversation with author, Espoo, December 11, 2013.

2 Ibid.

3 David Maisel speaking at *Variety*'s Venture Capital & New Media Summit in July 2011, http://variety.com/2011/digital/news/maisel-talks-angry-birds-marvel-at-summit-1118039627/

4 Rovio press release, June 27, 2011.

5   Wilson, conversation with author, Espoo, December 11, 2013.

6   Ilmari Hakkola, Google Meet interview with author, July 31, 2024.

7   Salla Hakkola, Google Meet interview with author, July 31, 2024.

8   Ilmari Hakkola, Google Meet interview with author, July 31, 2024.

9   Ibid.

10 Marja Konttinen, Skype conversation with author, January 20, 2014.

11 Salla Hakkola, Google Meet interview with author, July 31, 2024.

12 Ilmari Hakkola, Google Meet interview with author, July 31, 2024.

13 Wilson, conversation with author, Espoo, December 11, 2013.

14 Peter Vesterbacka, speaking to Stuart Dredge, *The Guardian*, March 1, 2012.

15 Peter Vesterbacka, speaking at a panel during SXSW 2011, reported by Anthony Ha, *Venture Beat*, March 13, 2011.

16 Peter Vesterbacka, *TIME* interview, March 19, 2012.

17 The origin of the statement, focusing on the China market alone, appears first in Nicole Perlroth's "Audacious Birds" article for *Forbes* on June 29, 2011. The statement was reiterated during an interview with *Business Insider* at the Ignite West conference on March 22, 2012.

18 Vesterbacka, Skype conversation with author, February 7, 2014.

19 Philip Hickey, Skype conversation with author, January 21, 2014.

20 Ville Heijari, interviewed by *the Financial Times*, December 16, 2011.

21 According to estimates compiled by analytic firm Flurry.

22 Andrew Stalbow, interviewed by *TechCrunch*, September 12, 2011, http://techcrunch.com/2011/09/12/angry-birds-the-brand-rovio-sells-1m-t-shirts-and-1m-plush-toys-per-month/

23 Benedict Evans, mobile analyst at Enders Analysis, speaking to *the Financial Times*, December 16, 2011, http://www.ft.com/intl/cms/s/2/37c3d96e-280c-11e1-a4c4-00144feabdco.html

Chapter Ten

1   Matthew Wilson, conversation with author, Espoo, December 11, 2013.

2   Tianyi Pan, Skype conversation with author on January 21, 2014.

3   Tianyi Pan quoting Peter Vesterbacka's words in a Skype conversation with author in January, 2014.

4   Paul Chen, Skype conversation with author, January 14, 2014.

5 Peter Vesterbacka, Skype conversation with author on January 23, 2014.

6 Tianyi Pan, Skype conversation with author on January 21, 2014.

7 Ibid.

8 Melanie Lee and Samuel Shen, "Apple Pays $60 to Settle China," *Reuters*, July 2, 2012, http://www.reuters.com/article/2012/07/02/us-apple-china-idUSBRE86104320120702

9 Peter Vesterbacka, Skype conversation with author on January 23, 2014.

Chapter Eleven

1 Bob Jacobs, phone conversation with author, January 31, 2014.

2 Ibid.

3 Ibid.

4 Marja Konttinen, Skype conversation with author, January 20, 2014.

5 Ibid.

6 Ibid.

7 Ibid.

8 Ibid.

9 Lauri Konttori, Skype conversation with author, January 29, 2014.

10 Jaakko Iisalo, Skype conversation with author, January 17, 2014.

11 Bob Jacobs, phone conversation with author, January 31, 2014.

12 Marja Konttinen, Skype conversation with author, January 20, 2014.

13 Philip Hickey, email correspondence with author, April 17, 2014.

14 Marja Konttinen, Skype conversation with author, January 20, 2014.

15 Tianyi Pan, Skype conversation with author on January 21, 2014.

16 Marja Konttinen, Skype conversation with author, January 20, 2014.

17 Phil Larsen talking to *Joystiq*, February 8, 2012, https://www.engadget.com/2012-02-08-fruit-ninja-kinect-sells-a-half-million-copies-jetpack-joyride.html

18 Natalia Luckyanova talking to *Gamasutra*, January 23, 2012, https://www.gamedeveloper.com/business/-em-temple-run-em-s-switch-to-free-more-than-quadrupled-its-revenue

19 Marja Konttinen, Skype conversation with author, January 20, 2014.

20 Ibid.

21 Excerpts from Don Pettit's email to Marja Konttinen, March 2012.

22 Konttinen, Skype conversation with author, January 20, 2014.

23 Ibid.

24 Ibid.

25 Philip Hickey, email correspondence with author, April 17, 2014.

26 Ibid.

27 Ibid.

28 Ibid.

29 Dean Takahashi, *VentureBeat*, March 26, 2012.

30 Hickey, email correspondence with author, April 17, 2014.

31 Ibid.

32 Shigeru Miyamoto quoted by Nathan Brown in "Miyamoto heaps praise on *Angry Birds*," *EDGE*, April 12, 2012, https://web.archive.org/web/20120517210523/http://www.edge-online.com/news/miyamoto-heaps-praise-angry-birds?page=show

33 Jaakko Iisalo, Skype conversation with author, January 17, 2014.

34 Peter Vesterbacka, conversation with author, Espoo, December 11, 2013.

35 Ibid.

36 Konttinen, Skype conversation with author, January 20, 2014.

37 Ibid.

38 Bob Jacobs, FCW, "NASA helps launch *Angry Birds Space* game," March 13, 2012, https://web.archive.org/web/20120315211255/http://fcw.com/articles/2012/03/13/nasa-angry-birds.aspx

39 Jacobs, phone conversation with author, January 31, 2014.

40 Ibid.

41 Ibid.

42 Konttinen, Skype conversation with author, January 20, 2014.

43 Ibid.

44 Ilmari Hakkola, Google Meet call with author, July 31, 2024.

45 Slash, "Behind the scene: Slash covers the *Angry Birds Space* tune," YouTube.

46 Ibid.

47 Bob Jacobs, correspondence with author, January 30, 2014.

48 Kai Torstila, Google Meet interview with author, August 14, 2024.

Chapter Twelve

1 Lauri Konttori, Skype conversation with author, January 29, 2014.
2 Marja Konttinen, Skype conversation with author, January 20, 2014.
3 Juhana Rossi and Sven Grundberg, "*Angry Birds* maker Rovio aims for the next level," *The Wall Street Journal*, May 6, 2014.
4 Lauri Konttori, Skype conversation with author, January 29, 2014.
5 Konsta Klemetti, conversation with author, Espoo, December 12, 2013.
6 Salla Hakkola, Google Meet interview with author on July 31, 2024.
7 Ilmari Hakkola, Google Meet interview with author on July 31, 2024.
8 Saara Bergström, secondhand, quoting email to author, Espoo, December 12, 2013.

Chapter Thirteen

1 Philip Hickey, Skype conversation with author, January 21, 2014.
2 Jaakko Iisalo, Skype conversation with author, January 17, 2014.
3 Danny Graydon, *Angry Birds: Hatching a Universe*, Insight Editions, 2013.
4 Salla Hakkola, Google Meet interview with author on July 31, 2024.
5 Naz Cuevas, conversation with author, Espoo, December 12, 2013.
6 Philip Hickey, Skype conversation with author, January 21, 2014.
7 Ibid.
8 Paul Southern, vice president of licensing and consumer products marketing at Lucasfilm, speaking to JJ McCorvey for *FastCompany*, October 5, 2012.
9 Philip Hickey, Skype conversation with author, January 21, 2014.
10 Paul Southern, vice president of licensing and consumer products marketing at Lucasfilm, speaking to JJ McCorvey for *FastCompany*, October 5, 2012, http://www.fastcompany.com/3001942/rovio-teases-nov-8-launch-of-angry-birds-star-wars-toys-to-debut-monday
11 Philip Hickey, Skype conversation with author, January 21, 2014.

12 Miguel Francisco, Google Meet interview with author on July 30, 2024.
13 Naz Cuevas, conversation with author, Espoo, December 12, 2013.
14 Philip Hickey, Skype conversation with author, January 21, 2014.
15 Ibid.
16 "*Angry Birds Star Wars 2*: Behind-the-scenes with Ian McDiarmid," RovioMobile channel, YouTube.
17 Ibid.
18 Philip Hickey, Google Meet interview with author on August 8, 2024.
19 https://x.com/angrybirds/status/380007479901294592?s=46&t= KM9buDu2I9-wT4IZnhoIYQ
20 Philip Hickey, Google Meet interview with author on August 8, 2024.
21 Kai Torstila, Google Meet interview with author on August 16, 2024
22 McCarthy, E. Jerome, *Basic Marketing*, Irwin/McGraw-Hill imprint, 1960.
23 David Amerland, *Forbes*, November 13, 2013.
24 Kimberly Kadlec, Interview with *AdAge*, July 6, 2012.
25 David Amerland, *Forbes*, November 13, 2013.
26 Konsta Klemetti, conversation with author, Espoo, December 12, 2013.

Chapter Fourteen

1 Peter Vesterbacka, Skype conversation with author, February 7, 2014.
2 B.R.I.C.S. stands for Brazil, Russia, India, China, and South Africa.
3 Peter Vesterbacka, Skype conversation with author, February 7, 2014.
4 Peter Vesterbacka shared the words of President Dmitry Medvedev speaking at SPIEF in July 2011 in a Skype conversation with author, January 23, 2014.
5 Peter Vesterbacka, Skype conversation with author, February 7, 2014.
6 Ibid.
7 Ibid.
8 Ibid.
9 Kai Torstila, Skype conversation with author, February 7, 2014.

10 Ibid.
11 Peter Vesterbacka, Skype conversation with author, February 7, 2014.
12 Kai Torstila, Skype conversation with author, February 7, 2014.

Chapter Fifteen

1 Lauri Konttori, Skype conversation with author, January 29, 2014.
2 Nick Dorra conversation with author, Espoo, December 11, 2013.
3 Ibid.
4 Ibid.
5 Ibid.
6 Marc Graser, *Variety*, "How Rovio just played Hollywood with *Angry Birds*," March 11, 2013, http://variety.com/2013/digital/games/how-rovio-just-played-hollywood-with-angry-birds-1200007011/
7 Ibid.
8 Andrew Stalbow speaking to National Public Radio, March 15, 2013, http://www.npr.org/2013/03/15/174331663/angry-birds-tv-coming-to-a-mobile-screen-near-you
9 Peter Vesterbacka, conversation with author in Espoo, December 11, 2013.
10 Nick Dorra, conversation with author, Espoo, December 11, 2013.
11 Green Day, "Good Riddance," lyrics.
12 Salla Hakkola, Google Meet interview with author, July 31, 2024.

Chapter Sixteen

1 James Ball, "Angry Birds and 'leaky' phone apps targeted by NSA and GCHQ for user data," *The Guardian*, January 28, 2004, https://www.theguardian.com/world/2014/jan/27/nsa-gchq-smartphone-app-angry-birds-personal-data
2 Naz Cuevas, conversation with author, Espoo, December 12, 2013.
3 Ibid.
4 Ibid.
5 Naz Cuevas, Skype conversation with author, February 4, 2014.
6 Ibid.

7 Ibid.

8 Naz Cuevas, conversation with author, Espoo, December 12, 2013.

9 Naz Cuevas, Skype conversation with author, February 4, 2014.

10 Kai Torstila, Google Meet interview with author, August 16, 2024.

11 Ibid.

12 Ibid.

13 Ibid.

14 Ibid.

15 Ibid.

16 Ville Heijari, August 12, 2020, Rovio blog.

17 Matthew Wilson, conversation with author, Espoo, December 11, 2013.

18 Steve Porter, Google Meet interview with author on August 21, 2024.

19 Ibid.

20 Ibid.

21 Source: SensorTower.

Chapter Seventeen

1 Ben Fritz, "*Angry Birds* film is a gamble for Rovio entertainment," *The Wall Street Journal*, May 15, 2016, https://www.wsj.com/articles/angry-birds-film-is-a-gamble-for-rovio-entertainment-1463343198

2 Ilmari Hakkola, Google Meet interview with author on July 31, 2024.

3 Vesterbacka, SMS text message to author, July 3, 2015.

4 Steve Porter, Google Meet interview with author, August 21, 2024.

5 Kai Torstila, Google Meet interview with author, August 16, 2024.

6 Ryan Faughnder, *LA Times*, May 17, 2016.

7 Mike Fleming Jr, *Deadline*, March 21, 2017, http://deadline.com/2017/03/the-angry-birds-movie-box-office-profit-2016-1202047527/

8 Matt Wilson, conversation with author at PocketGamer Helsinki, September 2017.

9 Chris Morris, *Fortune*, May 20, 2016.

10 Kai Torstila, Google Meet interview with author on August 16, 2024.

11 Steve Porter, Google Meet interview with author on August 21, 2024.

12 Steve Porter, Google Meet interview with author, August 21, 2024.

13 Ibid.

Chapter Eighteen

1   Philip Hickey, Google Meet interview with author, August 8, 2024.

2   Salla Hakkola, Google Meet interview with author, July 31, 2024.

3   Robin Squire, conversation with author, Espoo, December 13, 2013.

4   Andrea Peterson, "It seems like North Korea pirated *Angry Birds*," *The Washington Post*, November 6, 2013, http://www.washingtonpost. com/blogs/the-switch/wp/2013/11/06/it-seems-like-north-korea-pirated-angry-birds/

5   Haruki Satomi, press release, April 17 2024.

6   Ibid.

7   Jernej Česen, press release November 6 2024.

Abbreviations Glossary

IAP: In-App Purchase, also known as microtransactions. Purchases of digital goods in games and apps on mobile.

HP: Hewlett-Packard.

CEO: Chief Executive Officer.

COO: Chief Operating Officer.

CMO: Chief Marketing Officer.

EMT: Executive Management Team.

LAN: Local Area Network.

GDC: Game Developer Conference.

A/B Testing: Comparison data test between option A and option B.

UA: User Acquisition.

PR: Public Relations, or Press Relations.

USP: Unique Selling Points. The specific attributes of a product that make it unique for the consumers.

OS: Operating System.

iOS: The Apple Operating System on iPhones, iPads and other iDevices.

POS: Point of Sale. Might refer to a store, a shop, a restaurant or other sales outlets depending on the business category being considered.

UN: United Nations.

COPPA: Children's Online Privacy Protection Act. Set of American laws to protect children online.

GDPR: General Data Protection Regulation. Set of European Union laws to protect children online.

NBA: National Basketball League in the U.S.

NFL: National Football League in the U.S.

NHL: National Hockey League in the U.S.

SXSW: South by Southwest Festival.

IP: Intellectual Property.

KPI: Key Performance Indicator.

SDK: Software Development Kit.

AAA: Top quality label.

EA: Electronic Arts.

NDA: Non-Disclosure Agreement.

EBIT: Earnings before interest and taxes.

VP: Vice-President.

BRICS: Brazil Russia India China South Africa.

IMDB: International Movie Database.

EDM: Electronic Dance Music.

NIL: Name, Image, and Likeness. Refers to the assets being licensed when agreeing with a celebrity.

IPO: Initial Public Offering. Refers to the first time a company lists on the stock exchange.

R&D: Research and Development.

F2P: Free-to-Play.

PvP: Player versus Player.

RPG: Role-Playing Game.

CG: Computer Generated.

CGI: Computer Generated Imagery.

WWE: World Wrestling Entertainment.

VR: Virtual Reality.

AR: Augmented Reality.

UEFN: Unreal Engine in Fortnite, program run by Epic Games.

Timeline

2003

▶ Niklas Hed, Jarno Väkeväinen, and Kim Dikert participate together in a Students, Competition, Assembly Demo Party

▶ Meet Peter Vesterbacka from HP in the jury

▶ Founding of Relude Studio

2004–2009

▶ Relude changes name to Rovio

▶ Kaj Hed invests €1 million for majority ownership

▶ 51 games published as work-for-hire contracts for various publishers

2009

▶ Almost bankrupted. 2/3 of team laid off

▶ Release of *Angry Birds* on Apple App Store

▶ Original cinematic trailer release

2010

▶ First featuring by Apple

▶ Updates add new levels to the title

▶ Peter Vesterbacka joins full-time

▶ Release on Android

The Slingshot Formula

- ▶ Release of *Angry Birds Halloween*
- ▶ T-shirts licensing deal with Fifth Sun
- ▶ Plush toys line self-launch

2011

- ▶ *Angry Birds Rio* collaboration with Fox
- ▶ Plush toys licensing deal with Commonwealth Toys
- ▶ *Angry Birds Rio* hint featured in Super Bowl commercial of *Rio*
- ▶ *Angry Birds Halloween* becomes *Angry Birds Seasons*
- ▶ *Angry Birds Friends* on Facebook
- ▶ China distribution deal with iDreamSky
- ▶ Animation series debut on YouTube
- ▶ Massive team growth
- ▶ Acquisition of Studio Kombo

2012

- ▶ *Angry Birds Space* release at #1
- ▶ *Angry Birds Star Wars* release at #1
- ▶ *Bad Piggies* release at #1
- ▶ ISS launch collaboration with NASA
- ▶ Slash Bird

2013

- ▶ *Angry Birds Star Wars II* release at #1
- ▶ Telepods toys with Hasbro
- ▶ *Toons* TV debut
- ▶ *Angry Birds* drinks outsell Coca-Cola in Russia and Finland

▶ Launch of *Angry Birds Stella* and *Angry Birds Go!* as free-to-play

▶ Inks movie rights deal with Sony Pictures

2014

▶ Hockey Bird becomes mascot of NHL

▶ Official partnership with NBA

▶ Release of *Angry Birds Epic* and *Angry Birds Transformers*

▶ Presidential Easter Egg Roll invite by President Barack Obama

2015

▶ Global licensing deal with *Striker Entertainment*

▶ Licensing deal with Global Eagle (now Anuvu), making *Angry Birds World Tour* playable in airplanes around the world

▶ Release of *Angry Birds 2* as free-to-play

▶ Shakira Bird

▶ Licensing deal with Sanrio in Japan

▶ Macy's Thanksgiving Parade

2016

▶ *The Angry Birds Movie*, theatrical release

▶ LEGO Angry Birds sets

▶ McDonald's Happy Meals

▶ Kinder partnership

2017

▶ Official partnership with NFL

▶ Everton FC shirt-sleeve sponsor

- ▶ *Angry Birds Evolution* release
- ▶ Rovio IPO

2018

- ▶ Chicago Bulls partnership
- ▶ *Angry Birds Dream Blast* release

2019

- ▶ *Angry Birds The Movie 2*, theatrical release
- ▶ Chupa Chups *Angry Birds* popsicles
- ▶ *Angry Birds The Movie* Netflix release
- ▶ "Bring the Anger" 10th anniversary campaign
- ▶ *Angry Birds: Isle of Pigs* on AR and VR
- ▶ *Angry Birds* x Duolingo cross-over

2020

- ▶ *Angry Birds* attraction playable at Topgolf venues
- ▶ *Angry Birds* x *Minecraft* mash-up

2021

- ▶ *Angry Birds The Movie 2* Netflix release
- ▶ *Angry Birds* x *Peppa Pig*
- ▶ *Bad Piggies 2* release
- ▶ *Angry Birds Reloaded* on Apple Arcade

2022

- ▶ *Angry Birds: Bird Island* in Roblox
- ▶ Netflix Originals *Angry Birds: Summer Madness*

2023

▶ Acquisition by Sega

2024

▶ *Angry Birds* x *Sonic* cross-over

▶ *Angry Birds* x *My Talking Tom* cross-over

▶ *Angry Birds The Movie 3* begins production

▶ 15th anniversary

Acknowledgments

Special thanks to Peter Vesterbacka, Niklas Hed, Paul Chen, Jaakko Iisalo, Coach Phil Hickey, Marja Konttinen, Matt Wilson, Naz Amarchi Cuevas, Lauri Konttori, Miguel Francisco, Ilmari Hakkola, Salla Hakkola, Sanna Lukander, Saara Bergström, Kai Torstila, Steve Porter, Fernando Vasconez, Konsta Klemetti, Tianyi Pan, Nick Dorra, Bob Jacobs and Robin Squire.

Would you like your people to read this book?